T0062712

Outwitting
the Devil

The Original Unedited Complete Text
Including Content Never Before Published

Outwitting *the* Devil

◆

Napoleon Hill

AN OFFICIAL PUBLICATION OF
THE NAPOLEON HILL FOUNDATION

© Copyright 2020–Napoleon Hill Foundation

All rights reserved. This book is protected by the copyright laws of the United States of America. No part of this publication may be reproduced, stored in or introduced into a retrieval system, or transmitted, in any form or by any means (electronic, mechanical, photocopying, recording or otherwise), without the prior written permission of the publisher. For permissions requests, contact the publisher, addressed "Attention: Permissions Coordinator," at the address below.

Published and distributed by:
SOUND WISDOM
P.O. Box 310
Shippensburg, PA 17257-0310
717-530-2122

info@soundwisdom.com
www.soundwisdom.com

While efforts have been made to verify information contained in this publication, neither the author nor the publisher assumes any responsibility for errors, inaccuracies, or omissions. While this publication is chock-full of useful, practical information, it is not intended to be legal or accounting advice. All readers are advised to seek competent lawyers and accountants to follow laws and regulations that may apply to specific situations. The reader of this publication assumes responsibility for the use of the information. The author and publisher assume no responsibility or liability whatsoever on the behalf of the reader of this publication.

The scanning, uploading and distribution of this publication via the Internet or via any other means without the permission of the publisher is illegal and punishable by law. Please purchase only authorized editions and do not participate in or encourage piracy of copyrightable materials.

Cover/jacket design by Eileen Rockwell
Interior design by Terry Clifton

ISBN 13 HC: 978-1-64095-181-5
ISBN 13 TP:978-1-64095-222-5
ISBN 13 eBook: 978-1-64095-182-2
Library of Congress Control Number: 2020938348

For Worldwide Distribution, Printed in the U.S.A.
8 9 10 / 25 24 23

Dedicated to all people who have the courage to acquire knowledge and accept facts which may not harmonize with their own personal beliefs, with the hope that this volume may open to them new paths to truth which could bring harmony out of chaos in this age of frustration and fear.

—THE AUTHOR

Into this Universe, and Why not knowing
Nor Whence, like Water willy-nilly flowing;
And out of it, as Wind along the waste,
I know not Whither, willy-nilly blowing.

Myself when young did eagerly frequent
Doctor and Saint, and heard great argument
About it and about: but evermore
Came out by the same door where in I went.

—OMAR KHAYYAM

CONTENTS

> Brief story of the author's background describing the dramatic events which led up to the astounding interview with the Devil, after having broken the Devil's code and forcing from him a confession of the methods by which he takes control over human beings.

> A description of the author's system for acquiring information through ESP (extra sensory perception). An alleged interview with Thomas A. Edison after he had been dead for two years.

> Outlining the dramatic events which led to the famous interview which took place during a Master Mind meeting between the author and his wife, and a detailed description of the Devil, who he is, where he dwells and how he operates.

> The astonishing analysis of the principle through which the Devil claims to control 98% of the people of the world, including most of the clergy of all denominations. An entirely new version of the nature of the Devil.

> A newly discovered law of nature revealed to the author during his interview with the Devil, believed by some to be of more importance to mankind than Newton's discovery of the law of gravitation, because it explains the major causes of all failures and all misery, and indicated how one may become independent and self-determining.

OUTWITTING THE DEVIL

This is the strange story of how the Devil's code was broken and he was forced to confess all of the methods by which he takes possession of the minds of people, with a clear description of where the Devil dwells.

Here is a story which has never been told before, and it is one which may well lead you to a better understanding of your religion and what you may expect after this life. Read it with an open mind, and it may aid you in mastering all of your fears, doubts and suspicions regarding the next life.

This book was written by Napoleon Hill in the year 1938, five years after he left the service of Franklin D. Roosevelt, while the dramatic circumstances which occurred during the Roosevelt era were still fresh in his mind, just following the release of *Think and Grow Rich* which became a best-seller throughout this and all other civilized nations. If you fear or resent truths which may not agree with your own beliefs, you had better not read this volume.

—THE AUTHOR

PUBLISHER'S INTRODUCTION

◆

This strange document is a combination of fact, fiction and allegory, so woven together that each has been clearly marked for what it is.

The story is no stranger than the man who wrote it! Briefly, this is his history. He was born in the mountains of Southwest Virginia. He came into the world cursed by poverty of the most pronounced type. He came from a long line of ancestors who had been contented to remain "poor but honest," illiterate and ignorant of the nature of the men and the world beyond the confines of their own mountain section.

Before he was forty years of age, he had undergone more failures than almost any man now living, and had made and lost or given away half a dozen fortunes, and had dipped his hands into almost every conceivable type of human endeavor, from day labor to the management of large corporations.

He was the general manager of a large coal company while he was in his teens and the head of three educational institutions before he was thirty. He started a national magazine (*The Golden Rule*) without a penny and made it pay dividends the first year, and walked off and left it to his associates by the end of the second year. He drifted in and out of the practice of law, and changed his occupation so often that his friends generally looked up on him as being a failure, little realizing that there was a definite central motive back of every move he made, that motive being his determination to learn first hand *why most people go through life miserable and end as failures*!

Before he was out of his teens, he had the good fortune to meet and to attract the attention of Andrew Carnegie, who planted in his mind an idea which changed his entire life and gave him the privilege of changing the lives of many thousands of others. The idea which Mr. Carnegie gave him was organized into a philosophy of individual achievement with a following throughout the world. It was organized from careful study, over a period of more than twenty years, of the lives of more than five hundred of the most prominent business and industrial leaders of America, including Mr. Carnegie, Thomas A. Edison, John Wanamaker, Frank A. Vanderlip, Henry Ford and others of their type.

The philosophy, in its original form, consisted of seventeen principles, through some combination of which all success is attained. The embarrassing feature of the philosophy was the fact the author himself could not make it work successfully except on rare occasions. It was his insatiable thirst for knowledge and his determination to learn what was missing in his philosophy that led him to the strange interview with the Devil described in his book.

When chided by a friend for seeking information from the Devil instead of the other source, the author replied that he had unsuccessfully sought aid from the other side so often that he was left no alternative but to go to the Devil or quit searching and accept from life whatever it forced upon him.

No matter what you may think of the author of this strange story, or of his interview with the Devil, you must admit that anyone who can make life yield to him all that he asks of it, as the author has done, is worthy of careful study no matter from whom he learned his secret of successful living.

The man whose story you are about to read has mastered poverty. He has given himself mental, spiritual and physical freedom to live where he chooses and as he chooses. He has mastered fear in all its forms. His books are bestsellers in this and other countries. He is old enough to have learned much from the follies of youth, young enough to have before him time in which to make you and many others better for his having passed this way.

Here then is a record of human achievement that is rich with possibilities for all who have not made life yield to them what they asked of it. Enough of the history of the author's early life has been included to provide a definite understanding of the secret by which he forced the Devil to enter into this unusual interview. Approximately thirty years of struggle went into this uncovering of the natural law through which the author outwitted the Devil and forced that unsavory person into a confession disclosing the methods by which he gains control of the minds of human beings.

It is not likely that many readers of this book would have either the time or the inclination to search, for thirty years, for the road that leads to self-determination and happiness, even if they were willing to pay the price for whatever they want of life. Therefore the strange story you are about to read gives you the privilege of examining and testing, if you wish, one of nature's laws through which at least two people have made their lives to order.

In examining this story, it will be more beneficial if you test the principles described by the author instead of placing the author or his dramatic story on trial.

The author is not on trial in this book, but the public schools, the churches, and the organized forces of what the world calls "civilization" are on trial.

The frankness with which the author has told the story relieves him from all suspicion that he is seeking the approbation of those who read the book. He must have known full well, as he wrote, that his interview with the Devil would bring down on his head an avalanche of disapproval and hatred from those who are not yet ready to meet the Devil face to face; yet he did not pull his punches nor pander to the fears and limitations of mankind anywhere in his story.

The central theme of the book plainly describes a newly discovered natural law, believed to offer so many benefits to human beings that it will rank favorably with Newton's discovery of the law of gravity. This feature of the book alone is sufficient to entitle it to unbiased examination by all who are honestly and earnestly searching for ways and means of making life pay dividends in happiness. The book was not written until it was lived, and its contents came from the very crucible of life's melting pot of daily experience.

Last, but by no means least, anyone who makes even a mild pretense of thinking, and devotes thirty years to the study of a single subject, is bound to make highly informative discoveries concerning that subject.

The fact that Napoleon Hill's previous works on the subject of self-determination have been generously endorsed by leading thinkers all over the world is enough to caution all readers of this unusual book to read it with an open mind.

It is both impressive and significant that the books written by the author have been published and widely distributed in almost every country of the world without the aid of business management or promotion capital.

His books have become bes-tsellers because of the word-of-mouth advertising they have received from those who have benefitted by them.

Think and Grow Rich, his most popular single volume, was published in 1937. It became a best-seller from the start, and it has remained in this category ever since. This book came to the attention of Mahatma Gandhi of India, and it was through his influence that the book was published and widely distributed throughout India.

A little later it was translated into the Portuguese language and widely distributed throughout Brazil and other southern countries. Subsequently, because of the popularity of *Think and Grow Rich,* all of the author's books were published and widely distributed in the Portuguese language.

Other books by the author are *How to Sell Your Way Through Life, Master-Key to Riches, How to Raise Your Own Salary, The Law of Success* (in eight volumes), and *The Science of Personal Achievement,* a home study training course in seventeen lessons, covering twenty years of research in connection with the experiences of more than five hundred of America's most distinguished business and professional men and women.

Napoleon Hill is said, by those who know most about his service to others, to have helped to make more people successful than has any other living person. And the recipients of his benefactions are both men and women, representing practically every business, profession and calling in this and other countries.

Here is an established fact which should condition the minds of the readers of this book to pay high respect to the author although they may not accept or agree with his conclusions.

The author's interview with the Devil does not place him in agreement with all that the Devil has stated. But there is no escape from the conclusion that this interview is both controversial and thought-provoking.

Before presenting the interview, the author has chosen to describe some very interesting phases of his experiences which led him to discover that there are invisible forces at work in the lives of the people which are far more important than the obvious forces with which everyone is familiar.

It is the author's belief that the main benefit of this book consists of the possibility that many of its readers may grasp the importance and the potential powers of their own minds.

And by so doing, they may reach satisfactory conclusions as to the purpose of life as well as how to make life pay off on their own terms.

—THE PUBLISHER

CHAPTER ONE

MY FIRST MEETING WITH ANDREW CARNEGIE

Its Effect in Shaping My Life

For more than a quarter of a century, my major purpose has been that of isolating and organizing into a philosophy of achievement the cause of both failure and success, with the object of being helpful to others who have neither the inclination nor the opportunity to engage in this form of research.

My labor began in 1908, as the result of an interview which I had with the late Andrew Carnegie.

I frankly told Mr. Carnegie that I wished to enter law school, and that I had conceived the idea of paying my way through school by interviewing successful men and women, finding out how they came by their success, and writing stories of my discoveries for magazines.

At the end of our first visit, Mr. Carnegie asked whether or not I possessed enough courage to carry out a suggestion he wished to offer me. I replied that courage was about all I did have, and that I was prepared to do my best to carry out any suggestion he cared to offer.

He then said, "Your idea of writing stories about men and women who are successful is commendable, as far as it goes, and I have no intention of trying to discourage you from carrying out your purpose, but I must tell you that if you wish to be of enduring service, not only to those now living, but to posterity as well, you can do so if you will take the time to organize all of the causes of failure as well as all of the causes of success.

"There are millions of people in the world who have not the slightest conception of the causes of success and failure. They are willing to be taught, but there are no teachers. The schools and colleges teach practically everything except the principles of individual achievement. They require young men and women to spend from four to eight years delving into academic unreality and acquiring abstract knowledge, but do not teach them what to do with this knowledge after they get it.

"The world is in need of a practical, understandable philosophy of achievement, organized from the factual knowledge gained from the experience of men and women in the great university of life. In the entire field of philosophy I find nothing which even remotely resembles the sort of philosophy which I have in mind.

"If this worldwide need of which I speak appeals to you, may it not be possible that the organization of such a philosophy would offer you greater honors than any you might win as a lawyer? We have enough lawyers now, but we have few philosophers who are capable of teaching men and women the art of living.

"It seems to me that here is an opportunity which should challenge an ambitious young man of your type; but ambition alone is not enough for this task which I have suggested. The one who undertakes it must have courage and tenacity.

"The job will require at least twenty years of continuous effort, during which the one who undertakes it will have to earn his living from some other source, because this sort of research is never profitable at the outset, and generally those who have contributed to civilization through work of this nature have had to wait a hundred years or so after their own funerals to receive recognition for their labor.

"If you undertake this job you should interview not only the few who have succeeded, but the many who have failed. As inconsistent as it may seem, you will learn more about how to succeed from the failures than you will from the so-called successes. They will teach you what not to do.

"You should carefully analyze many thousands of people who have been classed as 'failures,' and I mean by the term 'failures' men and women who come to the closing chapter of life disappointed because they did not attain the goal which they had set their hearts upon achieving.

"Along toward the end of your labor, if you carry it through successfully, you will make a discovery which may be a great surprise to you. *You will discover that the cause of success is not something separate and apart from the men; it is a force so intangible in nature that the majority of men never recognize it—a force which might be properly called the 'other self.'*

"Noteworthy is the fact that this 'other self' seldom exerts its influence or makes itself known excepting at times of unusual emergency, when men are forced, through adversity and temporary defeat, to change their habits and to think their way out of difficulty.

"My experience has taught me that a man is never quite so near success as when that which he calls 'failure' has overtaken him, for it is on occasions of this sort that he is forced to think. If he thinks accurately, and with persistence, he discovers that so-called failure usually is nothing more than a signal to re-arm himself with a new plan or purpose. Most real failures are due to limitations which men set up in their own minds. If they had the courage to go one step further they would discover their error."

Mr. Carnegie's speech reshaped my entire life and planted in my mind a burning purpose which has driven me ceaselessly for half a century, and this despite the fact that I had but a vague idea as to what he meant by the term "other self."

During my labor of research into the causes of failure and success, I have had the privilege of analyzing more than 25,000 men and women who were rated as "failures," and over 500 who were classed as "successful." Many years ago I caught my first glimpse of that "other self" which Mr. Carnegie had mentioned. The discovery came, as he said it would, as the result of two major turning points of my life, which constituted emergencies that forced me to think my way out of difficulties such as I had never before experienced.

I wish it were possible to describe this discovery without the use of the personal pronoun, but this is impossible because it came through personal experiences from which it cannot be separated. To give you the complete picture, I shall have to go back to the first of these two major turning points and bring you up to the discovery step by step.

The research necessary for the accumulation of the data from which the seventeen principles of achievement and the thirty major causes of failure were organized required four years of labor, so we shall start now at the beginning of the two major turning points of my life which introduced me to my "other self."

I had reached the false conclusion that my task of organizing a complete philosophy of personal achievement had been completed. Far from having been completed, my work had merely begun. I had erected the skeleton of a philosophy by organizing the seventeen principles of achievement and the thirty major causes of failure, but that skeleton had to be covered with the flesh of application and experience. Moreover, it had to be given a soul through which it might inspire men and women to meet obstacles without going down under them.

The "soul," which had yet to be added, as I discovered later, became available only after my "other self" made its appearance, through the two major turning points of my life.

I AM DRIVEN BY DISCONTENT

Resolving to turn my attention, and whatever talents I might possess, into monetary returns through business and professional channels, I decided to go into the profession of advertising, and I became the Advertising Manager of the LaSalle Extension University of Chicago. Everything went along beautifully for one year, at the end of which I was seized by violent dislike for my job and resigned.

I then entered the chain store business, with the former president of the LaSalle Extension University, and became the President of the Betsy Ross Candy Company. Unfortunate—or what seemed to me at the time to be unfortunate—disagreements with business associates disengaged me from that undertaking.

The lure of advertising still was in my blood, and I tried again to give expression to it by organizing a School of Advertising and Salesmanship, as a part of Bryant & Stratton Business College.

The enterprise was sailing smoothly and we were making money rapidly when the United States entered World War I. In response to an inner urge which no words can describe, I walked away from the school and entered the service of the United States government, under President Woodrow Wilson's personal direction, leaving a perfectly sound business to disintegrate.

On Armistice Day, 1918, I began the publication of *The Golden Rule Magazine*. Despite the fact that I did not have a penny of capital, the magazine grew rapidly and soon gained a nationwide circulation of nearly half a million, ending its first year's business with a profit of $3,156.

Some years later I learned, from an experienced publisher, that no man experienced in the publication and distribution of national magazines would think of starting such a magazine with less than half a million dollars of capital.

The Golden Rule Magazine and I were destined to part company. The more we succeeded the more discontented I became, until finally, due to an accumulation of petty annoyances caused by business associates, I made them a present of the magazine and stepped out. Through that move perhaps I tossed a small fortune over my shoulder.

Next I organized a training school for salesmen. My first assignment was an order to train a sales army of 3,000 people for a chain store company, for which I received $10 for each salesman who went through my classes. Within six months my work had netted me a little over $30,000. Success, as far as money was concerned, was crowning my efforts with abundance. Again I became "fidgety" inside. I was not happy. It became more obvious every day that no amount of money would ever make me happy.

Without the slightest reasonable excuse for my actions, I stepped out and gave up a business from which I might easily have earned more than the President of the United States receives as his salary. My friends and business associates thought that I was crazy, and they were not backward about saying so.

Frankly, I was inclined to agree with them, but there seemed nothing I could do about it. I was seeking happiness and I had not found it. At least that is the only explanation I could offer for my unusual actions. What man knows himself?

That was during the late fall of 1923. I found myself stranded in Columbus, Ohio, without funds and worse still, without a plan by which to work my way out of my difficulty. It was the first time in my life that I had actually been stranded because of lack of funds.

Many times previously I had found money to be rather shy, but never before had I failed to get what I need for my personal conveniences. The experience stunned me. I seemed totally at sea as to what I could or should do.

I thought of a dozen plans by which I might solve my problem, but dismissed them all as being either impractical or impossible of achievement. I felt like one who was lost in a jungle without a compass. Every attempt I made to work my way out brought me back to the original starting point.

For nearly two months I suffered with the worst of all human ailments—indecision. I knew what were the seventeen principles of achievement, but what I did not know was how to apply them! Without knowing it, I was facing one of those emergencies of life through which, Mr. Carnegie had told me, men sometimes discover their "other selves."

My distress was so great that it never occurred to me to sit down and analyze its cause and seek its cure.

DEFEAT IS CONVERTED INTO VICTORY

One afternoon I reached a decision through which I found the way out of my difficulty. I had a feeling that I wanted to get out into the "open spaces" of the country, where I could get a breath of fresh air and think!

I began to walk and had gone seven or eight miles when I felt myself brought suddenly to a standstill. For several minutes I stood there as if I had been glued to my tracks. Everything around me went dark. I could hear the sound of some form of energy which was vibrating at a very high rate, similar to the sound one may hear when near an electric generator when electric energy is being condensed.

Then my nerves became quiet, my muscles relaxed, and a great calmness came over me. The atmosphere began to clear, and as it did so, I received a command from within which came in the form of a thought, as near as I can describe it.

The command was so clear and distinct that I could not misunderstand it. In substance it said, "The time has come for you to complete the philosophy of achievement which you began at Carnegie's suggestion. Go back home at once and begin transferring the data you have gathered from your own mind to written manuscripts." My "other self" had awakened.

For a few minutes I was frightened. The experience was unlike any I had ever undergone before. I turned and walked rapidly until I reached home. As I approached the house, I saw my three little boys looking out of a window of our house at our neighbor's children, who were dressing a Christmas tree in the house next door.

Then I recalled that it was Christmas Eve. Moreover, I recalled, with a feeling of deep distress such as I had never known before, that there would be no Christmas tree at our house. The look of disappointment on the faces of my children reminded me painfully of that fact.

WHAT THE END OF "THE RAINBOW" DISCLOSED.

I went into the house, sat down at my typewriter and began at once to reduce to writing the discoveries I had made concerning the causes of success and failure. As I placed the first sheet of paper in the typewriter, I was interrupted by that same strange feeling which had come over me out in the country a few hours before, and this thought flashed into my mind:

"Your mission in life is to complete the world's first philosophy of individual achievement. You have been trying in vain to escape your task, each effort having brought you failure. You are seeking happiness. Learn this lesson, once and forever, that you will find happiness only by helping others find it! You have been a stubborn student. You had to be cured of your stubbornness through disappointment. Within a few years from now, the whole world will start through an experience which will place millions of people in need of the philosophy which you have been directed to complete. Your big opportunity to find happiness by rendering useful scrvice will have come. Go to work, and do not stop until you have completed and published the manuscripts which you have begun." I was conscious of having arrived, at last, at the end of life's rainbow, and I was happy!

DOUBT MAKES ITS APPEARANCE

The "spell," if the experience may be so called, passed away. I began to write. Shortly thereafter, my "reason" suggested to me that I was embarking upon a fool's missions. The idea of a man who was down and almost out, presuming to write a philosophy of personal achievement seemed so ludicrous that I laughed hilariously, perhaps scornfully.

I squirmed in my chair, ran my fingers through my hair, and tried to create an alibi that would justify me in my own mind in taking the sheet of paper out of my typewriter before I had really begun to write, but the urge to continue was stronger than the desire to quit. I became reconciled to my task and went ahead.

Looking backward now, in the light of all that has happened, I can see that those six minor experiences of adversity through which I had passed were among the most fortunate and profitable of all of my experiences. They were blessings in disguise because they forced me to continue a work which finally brought me an opportunity to make myself more useful to the world than I might have been had I succeeded in any previous plan or purpose.

MY WORK COMPLETED, I TURN AGAIN TO BUSINESS

For almost three months I worked on those manuscripts, completing them during the early part of 1924. As soon as they had been completed, I felt myself again being lured by the desire to get back into the great American game of business.

Succumbing to the lure, I purchased the Metropolitan Business College in Cleveland, Ohio, and began to lay plans for increasing its capacity. By the end of 1924, we had developed and expanded, by adding new courses, until we were doing business nearly double the best previous record the school had ever known.

Again the germ of discontentment began to make itself felt in my blood. Again I knew that I could not find happiness in that sort of endeavor. I turned the business over to my associates and went on the lecture platform, lecturing on the philosophy of achievement, to the organization of which I had devoted so many of my previous years.

I MEET MY GREATEST TRAGEDY

ITS FAR-FLUNG EFFECT!

One night I was booked to lecture in Canton, Ohio. Fate, or whatever it is that seems sometimes to shape the destiny of men, no matter how hard they may try to battle against it, again stepped into the picture and brought me face to face with a painful experience.

In my Canton audience sat Don R. Mellett, publisher of the Canton Daily News. Mr. Mellett became so thoroughly interested in the philosophy of individual achievement on which I lectured that night, that he invited me to come to see him the following day.

That visit resulted in a partnership agreement which was to have taken place on the first of the following January, when Mr. Mellett planned to resign as publisher of the Daily News, to take charge of the business and publishing responsibilities incidental to the distribution of the philosophy on which I had been working.

About the middle of July, 1926, Mr. Mellett was murdered by Pat McDermott, an underworld character, and a Canton, Ohio, policeman, both of whom were sentenced to life imprisonment. He was murdered because he was exposing in his newspaper a hook-up between the bootleggers and certain members of the Canton police force. The crime was one of the most shocking that the Prohibition era produced.

CHANCE(?) SAVES MY LIFE

The morning after Mr. Mellett's death, I was called on the telephone and put on notice, by some unknown person, that I had one hour in which to get out of Canton; that I could go voluntarily within the hour, but if I waited longer, I probably would go in a pine box. My business association with Mr. Mellett had apparently been misunderstood. His murderers evidently believed I was connected with the exposé he was making in his newspapers.

I did not wait for the one-hour time limit to expire, but immediately got into my automobile and drove down to the home of relatives in the mountains of West Virginia, where I remained until the murderers had been placed in jail, some six months later.

FOR THE FIRST TIME I KNOW
THE PAIN OF FEAR

That experience came well within the category described by Mr. Carnegie as an "emergency" which forces men to think. For the first time in my life I knew the pain of constant fear. My experience of a few years before, in Columbus, had filled my mind with doubt and temporary indecision, but this one had filled it with fear which I seemed unable to remove. During the time that I was in hiding, I seldom left the house at night, and when I did step out, I kept my hand on an automatic pistol in my coat pocket, with the safety catch unlatched for immediate action. If a strange automobile stopped in front of the house where I was hiding, I went into the basement and carefully scrutinized its occupants through the basement windows.

MY "GARDEN OF GETHSEMANE" APPEARS

After some months of this sort of experience, my nerves began to "crack." My courage had completely left me. The ambition which had heartened me during the long years of labor in my search for the causes of failure and success also had departed.

Slowly, step by step, I felt myself slipping into a state of lethargy from which I was afraid I should never be able to emerge. The feeling must have been closely akin to that experienced by one who suddenly steps into quicksand and realizes that every effort to extricate himself carries him just so much deeper. Fear is a self-generating morass.

If the seed of insanity had been in my make-up, surely it would have germinated during those six months of living death. Foolish indecision, irresolute dreams, doubt and fear were my mind's concern, day and night.

The "emergency" I faced was disastrous in two ways. First, the very nature of it kept me in a constant state of indecision and fear. Secondly, the forced concealment kept me in idleness, with its attendant heaviness of time, which I naturally devoted to worry.

My reasoning faculty had almost been paralyzed. I realized that I had to work myself out of this state of mind. But how? The resourcefulness which had helped me to meet all previous emergencies seemed to have completely taken wing, leaving me helpless.

SELF-DERISION GRIPS ME

Out of my difficulties, which were burdensome enough up to this point, grew another which seemed more painful than all the others combined. It was the realization that I had spent the better portion of my past years in chasing a rainbow, searching hither and yon for the causes of success, and finding myself now more helpless than any of the 25,000 people whom I had judged as being "failures."

This thought was almost maddening. Moreover, it was extremely humiliating, because I had been lecturing all over the country, in schools and colleges and before business organizations, presuming to tell other people how to apply the seventeen principles of success, while here I was, unable to apply them myself. I was sure that I never could again face the world with a feeling of confidence.

Every time I looked at myself in a mirror, I noticed an expression of self-contempt on my face, and not infrequently I did say things to the man in the mirror which are not printable. I had begun to place myself in the category of charlatans who offer others a remedy for failure which they themselves cannot successfully apply.

IN THE CLUTCHES OF FEAR

The criminals who had murdered Mr. Mellett had been tried and sent to the penitentiary for life; therefore, it was perfectly safe, as far as they were concerned, for me to come out of hiding and again take up my work. I could not come out, however, because now I faced circumstances more frightful than the criminals who had sent me into hiding.

The experience had destroyed whatever initiative I had possessed. I felt myself in the clutches of some depressing influence which seemed like a nightmare. I was alive; I could move around, but I could not think of a single move by which I might continue to seek the goal which I had, at Mr. Carnegie's suggestion, set for myself. I was rapidly becoming indifferent, not only toward myself, but worse still, I was becoming grouchy and irritable toward those who had given me shelter during my emergency.

I faced the greatest emergency of my life. Unless you have gone through a similar experience, you cannot possibly know how I felt. Such experiences cannot be described. To be understood, they must be felt.

THE MOST DRAMATIC MOMENT OF MY LIFE APPEARS

The turn in my affairs came suddenly, in the fall of 1927—more than a year after the Canton incident. I left the house one night and walked up to the public school building, on top of a hill above the town.

I had reached a decision to fight the matter out with myself before that night ended.

I began to walk around the building, trying to force my befuddled brain to think clearly. I must have made several hundred trips around the building before anything which even remotely resembled organized thought began to take place in my mind. As I walked, I repeated over and over to myself, "There is a way out and I am going to find it before I go back to the house." I must have repeated that sentence a thousand times. Moreover, I meant exactly what I was saying. I was thoroughly disgusted with myself, but I entertained a hope of salvation.

BLESSED ARE "IDEAS"

Then, like a flash of lightning out of a clear sky, an idea burst into my mind with such force that the impulse drove my blood up and down my veins with a feeling something like that which one experiences when under the spell of music. The thought which flashed into my mind was this:

"This is your testing time. You have been reduced to poverty and humiliated in order that you might be forced to discover your 'other self.'"

For the first time in years, I recalled what Mr. Carnegie had said about this "other self." I recalled now that he said I would discover it along toward the end of my labor of research into the causes of failure and success, and that the discovery usually came as the result of an emergency, when men are forced to change their habits and to think their way out of difficulty.

I continued to walk around the schoolhouse, but now I was walking on air. Subconsciously, I seemed to know that I was about to be released from the self-made prison into which I had cast myself.

Without doubt, this was the happiest moment of my life. I realized that this great emergency had brought me an opportunity, not merely to discover my "other self," but to test the soundness of the philosophy of achievement which I had been teaching others as being workable. Soon I would know whether it would work or not. I made up my mind that if it did not work, I would burn the manuscripts I had written and never again be guilty of telling other people that they were the "Masters of their fate, the Captains of their souls."

A HAPPY THOUGHT OCCURS TO ME

The full moon was just rising over the mountain top. I had never seen it shine so brightly before. As I stood gazing at it, another thought flashed into my mind. It was this:

"You have been telling other people how to master fear and how to surmount the difficulties which arise out of the emergencies of life. From now on, you can speak with authority because you are about to rise above your own difficulties with courage and purpose, resolute and unafraid."

With that thought came a change in the chemistry of my being which lifted me into a state of exaltation such as I had never before known. My brain began to clear itself of the state of lethargy into which it had lapsed. My faculty of reason began to work once more.

For a brief moment at least, I was happy to have had the privilege of going through those long months of torment, because the experience had culminated in an opportunity for me to test the soundness of the principles of achievement which I had so laboriously wrested from my research.

When this thought came to me, I stopped still, drew my feet closely together, saluted (I did not know what or whom) and stood rigidly at attention for several minutes.

This seemed, at first, like a foolish thing to do, but while I was standing there, another thought came through in the form of an "order" that was as brief and snappy as any ever given by a military commander to a subordinate.

The order said, "Tomorrow get into your automobile and drive to Philadelphia, where you will receive aid in publishing your philosophy of achievement."

There was no further explanation and no modification of the order. As soon as I received it, I walked back to the house, went to bed, and slept with peace of mind such as I had not known for over a year.

When I awoke the following morning, I got out of bed and immediately began to pack my clothes and to make ready for the trip to Philadelphia. My reason told me that I was embarking upon a fool's mission. Whom did I know in Philadelphia to whom I might apply for financial aid in publishing eight volumes of books, at a cost of $25,000?

Instantly, the answer to that question flashed into my mind, as plainly as if it had been uttered in audible words: "You are following orders now, instead of asking questions. Your 'other self' will be in charge during this trip."

There was another condition which seemed to make my preparation to go to Philadelphia absurd. I had no money! This thought had barely occurred to me when my 'other self' exploded it by giving another sharp order, saying, "Ask your brother-in-law for fifty dollars and he will lend it to you."

The order seemed definite and final. Without further hesitation, I followed instructions. When I asked my brother-in-law for the money, he said, "Why certainly you can have fifty dollars, but if you are going to be gone very long, you had better take a hundred dollars." I thanked him and said I thought fifty dollars would be enough. I knew it was not enough, but that was the amount my 'other self' had commanded me to ask for and that is the amount I secured.

I was greatly relieved when I found that my brother-in-law was not going to ask me why I was going to Philadelphia. If he had known all that had taken place in my mind during the previous night, he perhaps would have thought I should go to a psychopathic hospital for treatment instead of going to Philadelphia on a wild goose chase.

MY "OTHER SELF" TAKES COMMAND

I left with my head telling me I was a fool and my 'other self' commanding me to ignore the challenge and carry out my instructions.

I drove all night, arriving in Philadelphia early the next morning. My first thought was to look up a modestly priced boarding house where I could rent a room for about one dollar a day.

Here again, my 'other self' took charge and gave the command to register at the most exclusive hotel in the city. With a little more than forty dollars of my remaining capital in my pocket, it seemed like financial suicide when I marched up to the desk and asked for a room; or rather I should say, I started to ask for a room when my newly discovered 'other self' gave the order to ask for a suite of rooms, the cost of which would about consume my remaining capital in two days. I obeyed.

OUTWITTING MY INFERIORITY COMPLEX

The bellboy picked up my bags, handed me my check for my automobile and bowed me toward the elevator as if I were the Prince of Wales. It was the first time in more than a year that any human being had shown me such deference. My own relatives, with whom I had been living, far from having shown me deference, had (so I imagined) felt I was a burden on their hands, and I am sure that I was, because no man in the frame of mind that I had been in for the past year could be anything other than a burden to all with whom he came into contact.

As the bellboy left the room, I instructed him to bring me some good cigars. Shortly, he returned with a box of cigars priced two for a quarter. I started to take a couple when my 'other self' sharply commanded me to send the boy back for some better cigars, which I did.

He brought another box priced at thirty-five cents each. I started to take two cigars when my 'other self' again commanded me to take a handful. Again I obeyed. It seemed like a wanton waste as I had never in all my life smoked a cigar costing as much as that, nor had I ever occupied a suite of rooms costing as much as the suite I now occupied.

It was becoming apparent that my 'other self' was determined to wean me away from the inferiority complex which I had developed.

I tossed the bellboy a dollar, lighted one of the cigars and seated myself in a big overstuffed chair. I started to estimate what my hotel bill would be by the end of the week when my 'other self' commanded me to get my mind entirely off of all thoughts of limitation and to conduct myself for the time being just as I would if I had all the money I wanted in my pockets.

The experience I was passing through was both new and strange to me. In all my life I had never done any "four-flushing," nor had I ever posed as being anything other than what I believed myself to be.

For nearly half an hour, this "other self" gave orders which I followed to the letter during the subsequent period of my stay in Philadelphia. The instructions were given through the medium of thoughts which presented themselves in my mind with such force that they were readily distinguishable from my ordinary self-created thoughts.

I RECEIVE STRANGE "ORDERS" FROM A STRANGE SOURCE

My instructions began in this fashion:

"You are now completely in charge of your 'other self.' You are entitled to know that two entities occupy your body, as in fact two similar entities occupy the body of each living person on earth.

"One of these entities is motivated by and responds to the impulse of fear. The other is motivated by and responds to the impulse of faith. For more than a year, you have been driven, like a slave, by the fear entity.

"Night before last, the faith entity gained control over your physical body, and you are now motivated by that entity. For the sake of convenience, you may call this faith entity your 'other self.' It knows no limitations, has no fears, and recognizes no such word as 'impossible.'

"You were directed to select this environment of luxury, in a good hotel, as a means of discouraging the return to power of the fear entity. That fear-motivated 'old self' is not dead; it has merely been dethroned and it will follow you around wherever you go, awaiting a favorable opportunity to step in and take charge of you again. It can gain control of you only through your thoughts. Remember this, and keep the doors to your mind tightly closed against all thoughts which seek to limit you in any manner whatsoever, and you will be safe.

"Do not permit yourself to worry about the money you will need for your immediate expenses. That will come to you by the time you must have it.

"Now, let us get down to business. First of all, you should know that the faith entity now in charge of your body performs no miracles, nor does it work in opposition to any of Nature's laws. As long as it is in charge of your body, it will guide you when you call on it, through impulses of thought which it will place in your mind, in carrying out your plans through the most logical and convenient natural media available.

"Above everything else, get this fact clearly fixed in your mind, that your 'other self' will not do your work for you; it will only guide you intelligently in achieving for yourself the objects of your desires.

"This 'other self' will aid you in translating your plans into reality. Moreover, you should know that it begins, always, with your major or most pronounced desire. At this time, your major desire— the one which brought you here—is to publish and distribute the results of your research into the causes of success and failure. You estimate that you will need approximately $25,000.

"Among your acquaintances, there is a man who will supply you with this needed capital. Begin, at once, to call into your mind the names of all persons of your acquaintance whom you have reason to believe might be induced to furnish the financial aid you require.

"When the name of the logical person comes into your mind, you will recognize it immediately. Communicate with that person, and the aid you seek will be given. In your approach, however, present your request in terminology such as you would use in the usual course of business transactions. Make no reference whatsoever to this introduction you have had to your 'other self'. If you violate these instructions, you will meet with temporary defeat.

"Your 'other self' will remain in charge and continue to direct you as long as you rely upon it. Keep doubt and fear and worry, and all thoughts of limitation, entirely out of your mind.

"That will be all for the present. You will now begin to move of your own free will, precisely as you did before you discovered your 'other self.' Physically, you are the same as you have always been; therefore, no one will recognize that any change has taken place in you."

I looked around the room, blinked my eyes, and to make sure that I was not dreaming, I got up and walked over to a mirror and looked at myself closely. The expression on my face had changed from one of doubt to one of courage and faith. There was no longer any doubt in my mind that my physical body was in charge of an influence far different from the one which had been dethroned two nights before, as I walked around that schoolhouse in West Virginia.

A NEW WORLD IS REVEALED TO ME

Obviously, I had undergone a new birth by which I had been separated from all forms of fear. I now had courage such as I never before had experienced. Despite the fact that I had not as yet been shown how, or from what source, I would be able to secure the necessary funds which I was seeking; I had such absolute faith that the money would be forthcoming that I could see it already in my possession.

On but few occasions in my entire life have I experienced such faith. It was a feeling which one person cannot describe to another. There are no words in the English language suitable for such a description—a fact which all who have had similar experiences can easily verify. No others can.

I proceeded, immediately, to carry out the instructions I had received. All feeling that I had embarked upon an unavailing mission had now left me. One by one, I began to call into my mind the names of all of my acquaintances whom I knew to be financially able to supply me with the $25,000 which I needed, starting with the name of Henry Ford, and going over the entire list of more than three hundred people, ending finally with the name of Edwin C. Barnes, a business associate of the late Thomas A. Edison.

My reason told me that I might safely count on assistance from Mr. Barnes inasmuch as he and I had been close personal friends for more than twenty years, but my "other self" plainly said "keep on searching."

"THE DARKEST HOUR IS JUST BEFORE DAWN"

But I had to come to the end of my rope. My entire list of acquaintances had been exhausted, and with it my physical endurance as well. I had been at work concentrating my mind upon that list of names for the better part of two days and nights, having stopped only long enough to sleep for a few hours.

I leaned back in my chair, shut my eyes and went into a sort of doze for a few minutes. I was aroused by what seemed to be an explosion in the room. As I regained consciousness, the name of Albert L. Pelton came into my mind, and with it a plan which I knew instantly to be the plan through which I would succeed in getting Mr. Pelton to publish my books. I remembered Mr. Pelton only as an advertiser in *The Golden Rule Magazine* which I had formerly published.

I sent for a typewriter, addressed a letter to Mr. Pelton at Meriden, Connecticut, and described the plan just as it had been handed over to me. He answered by telegram, saying that he would be in Philadelphia to see me the following day.

When he came, I showed him the original manuscripts of my philosophy, and briefly explained what I believed its mission to be. He turned through the pages of the manuscripts for a few minutes, then stopped suddenly and fixed his eyes on the wall for a few seconds and said, "I will publish your books for you."

The contract was drawn; a substantial advance payment on royalties was given me, the manuscripts were turned over to him, and he took them back to Meriden.

I did not ask him at the time, and I have not done so since, what caused him to reach a decision to publish my books before he had read the manuscripts, but I do know that he supplied the necessary capital, printed the books and assisted me in selling many thousands of sets of them to his own clientele of book buyers who were located in practically every English-speaking country in the world.

MY "OTHER SELF" MAKES GOOD

Three months from the day that Mr. Pelton called on me in Philadelphia, a completed set of my books was placed on the table in front of me, and my income from the sale of the books began to run high enough for all my needs. These books are now in the hands of my students in practically every village, town and city throughout America, and in most of the foreign countries.

My first royalty check from the sale of my books was for $850. As I opened the envelope in which it came, my "other self" said, "Your only limitation is the one which you set up in your own mind!"

I am not sure that I understand just what this "other self" is, but I do know that there can be no permanent defeat for the man or the woman who discovers it and relies upon it.

MY "OTHER SELF' CONTINUES TO DIRECT

The day after Mr. Pelton came to see me in Philadelphia, my "other self" presented me with an idea which solved my immediate financial problem.

The idea flashed into my mind that automobile merchandising methods had to undergo a drastic change, and that future salesmen in this field would have to learn to sell automobiles instead of merely serving as buyers of used car "trade-ins," as most of them were doing at the time.

It also occurred to me that young men who had just finished college and who, therefore, knew nothing of the old "tricks" of automobile merchandising would be the material out of which this new brand of salesman could best be developed.

The idea was so distinct and impressive that I immediately called the Sales Manager of the General Motors Company on long distance telephone and briefly explained my plan to him. He too was impressed by it and referred me to the West Philadelphia branch of the Buick Automobile Company, which was then owned and managed by Earl Powell.

I went to see Mr. Powell, explained my plan to him, and he retained me at once to train fifteen carefully selected young college men, through whom the plan was put into operation.

My income from that retainer was more than enough to take care of all of my expenses for the following three months, until the returns from the sale of my books began to come in, including the cost of that expensive suite of rooms, over which I had at first been much concerned.

My "other self" had not disappointed me. The money I needed was in my hands at the proper time, just as I had been assured that money would be. By this time, I had been convinced that my trip to Philadelphia was by no means a fool's mission, as my reason had indicated it would be before I left West Virginia.

From that time right up to this very minute, everything I have needed has come to me, and this despite the fact that the whole world has recently passed through a period of economic depression, when the bare necessities of life have not always been available to all people. Sometimes the arrival of the material things I needed has been a little late, but I can truthfully say that my "other self" has always met me at the crossroads, when I have come to them, and indicated which path I should follow.

THE "OTHER SELF" RECOGNIZES NO LIMITATIONS

The "other self" follows no precedents, recognizes no limitations, and always finds a way to accomplish desired ends! It may meet with temporary defeat, but not with permanent failure. I am as sure of the soundness of this statement as I am of the fact of being engaged in writing these lines.

Meanwhile, I earnestly hope that some of the millions of men and women who have been wounded by the business depression and other unpleasant experiences will discover within themselves this strange entity which I have called my "other self," and that the discovery will lead them, as it has led me, into a closer relationship with that source of power which surmounts obstacles and masters difficulties, instead of being mastered by them. There is a great power to be discovered in your "other self"! Search sincerely and you will find it.

"FAILURE" A BLESSING IN DISGUISE

I have made another discovery as the result of this introduction to my "other self," namely, that there is a solution for every legitimate problem, no matter how difficult the problem may seem.

I have also discovered that there comes with every experience of temporary defeat, and every failure and every form of adversity, the seed of an equivalent benefit.

Mind you, I did not say that full-blown flower of success, but the seed from which that flower may be made to germinate and grow. I know of no exception to this rule. The seed of which I speak may not always be observed, but you may be sure it is there in one form or another.

I do not pretend to understand all about this strange force which reduced me to poverty and want, and filled me with fear, and then gave me a new birth of faith through which I have been privileged to extend help to tens of thousands of my fellowmen who found themselves slipping. But I do know that such a force has come into my life and that I am doing all I can to place others in communication with it.

I DO NOT BELIEVE IN SO-CALLED "MIRACLES", BUT—

I have never been inclined to believe in so-called miracles, and I am less inclined now to do so than ever before. By no stretch of one's imagination could anything I have related in this narrative be attributed to a miracle. My own explanation of the change that has taken place in my life is that I have mysteriously come upon a workable plan by which I am adapting myself to one of Nature's great laws in a spirit of harmony. It is, of course, the reader's privilege to ascribe the experience I have related to whatever cause he or she may choose. I will find no fault with anyone for doing this.

During my quarter of century of research into the causes of success and failure, I have discovered many principles of truth which have been helpful to me and to others, but nothing I have observed has impressed me more than the discovery that every great leader of the past whose record I have examined was beset by difficulties and met with temporary defeat before "arriving."

From Christ on down to Edison, the men who have achieved most have been those who met with the most stubborn forms of temporary defeat. This would seem to justify the conclusion that Infinite Intelligence has a plan, or a law, by which it hurdles men over many obstacles before giving them the privilege of leadership or the opportunity to render useful service in a noteworthy fashion.

I would not wish to be again subjected to the experiences through which I passed during that fateful Christmas Day in 1923, and since, on that eventful evening when I walked around the schoolhouse in West Virginia and fought that terrible battle with fear, but all the wealth in the world would not induce me to divest myself of the knowledge I have gained from those experiences.

"FAITH" HAS A NEW MEANING TO ME

I repeat that I do not know exactly what this "other self" is, but I know enough about it to lean upon it in a spirit of absolute faith in times of difficulty, when the ordinary reasoning faculty of my mind seems to be inadequate for my needs.

The business depression which started in 1929 brought misery to millions of people, but let us not forget that the experience also brought many blessings, not the least of these being the knowledge that there is something infinitely worse than being forced to work. It is being forced not to work.

In the main, that depression was more of a blessing than it was a curse, if analyzed in the light of the changes it brought to the minds of those who were wounded by it.

The same is true of every experience which changes men's habits and forces them to turn to the great "within" for the solution of their problems.

The year which I spent in seclusion in West Virginia was, by great odds, the most severe punishment of my life, but the experience brought blessings in the form of needed knowledge which more than offset the suffering which it cost me. These two results—the suffering and the knowledge gained from it—were inevitable. The law of Compensation which Emerson so clearly defined, made this result both natural and necessary.

What the future may hold for me in the way of disappointment, through temporary defeat, I of course have no way of knowing, but I do know that no experience of the future can possibly wound me as deeply as have some of those of the past, because I am now on speaking terms at least with my "other self."

Since this "other self" took charge of me, I have come by useful knowledge which I am sure I never would have discovered while my old fear entity was on the throne. For one thing, I have learned that those who meet with difficulties which seem insurmountable may, if they will do so, best overcome these difficulties by forgetting them for a time and helping others who have greater problems.

THE VALUE OF "GIVING"
BEFORE TRYING TO "GET"

I am sure that no effort which we extend to those who are in distress can go without some form of adequate reward. Not always does the reward come from those to whom the service is rendered, but it will come from one source or another.

I seriously doubt that any man can avail himself of the benefits of his "other self" as long as he is steeped in greed and avarice, envy and fear, but if I am wrong in this conclusion, then I still have the unusual honor of being one who has found peace of mind and happiness through a viewpoint that was not sound. I would prefer being thus wrong and happy to being right and unhappy! But this viewpoint is not wrong!

As long as I remain on good terms with my "other self", I shall be able to acquire every material thing that I need. Moreover, I shall be able to find happiness and peace of mind. What more could anyone else accomplish?

WHERE TO START WHEN YOU SEEK YOUR "OTHER SELF"

The sole motive which inspired me to write this book was a sincere desire to be helpful to others by sharing with them as much as they may be prepared to accept of the stupendous fortune which became mine the moment I discovered my "other self." This fortune, happily, is one that cannot be measured alone in material or financial terms, because it is greater than everything which such things represent.

Material and financial fortunes, when reduced to their most liquid terms, are measurable in terms of bank balances. Bank balances are no stronger than banks. This other fortune of which I speak is measurable not only in terms of peace of mind, contentment and happiness, but as well in materials which are bankable. Also, it is backed by Infinite Intelligence, and its repository is the whole of the universe.

You may share this fortune under very reasonable terms, without signing any promissory notes or incurring any other form of maturing obligations, by removing the impediment of fear which may stand between you and your "other self." You should begin by acquiring a better understanding of the power of faith.

FEAR VERSUS FEAR!

Faith is a state of mind, and it is a condition precedent to the discovery of one's "other self." The opposite of faith is fear. It, too, is a state of mind which sometimes is induced by realities and at other times by imaginary causes.

Let us examine the nature of these two states of mind so that we may better understand why we must embrace one and repel the other, if we are to place ourselves on speaking terms with this "other self."

Faith permits one to approach within communicating distance of Infinite Intelligence (or God, if you prefer that term). Fear holds one at arm's length and makes communication impossible.

When I left West Virginia and started for Philadelphia to secure the funds with which to publish the philosophy of achievement, I had not the slightest idea who was going to supply those funds, but there was one fact which stands out indelibly in my mind: I had complete faith that someone would supply the money.

Before leaving West Virginia, I dismissed from my reasoning mind all thought as to the plan by which I would secure the funds I was seeking, concentrating my entire thought upon the purpose of obtaining the money! This statement of fact will be most significant to anyone who is adept at prayer.

My "other self" has taught me to concentrate upon my purpose and to forget about the plan by which it is to be attained, when I go to prayer.

I am not suggesting that material objects may be acquired without plans. What I am saying is that the power which translates one's thoughts or desires into realities has its source in an Infinite Intelligence which knows more about plans than the one doing the praying.

Stating the case in another way, may it not be wise, when praying, to trust to the Universal Mind to hand over the plan best suited for the attainment of the object of that prayer?

My experience with prayer has taught me that so often all which results from prayer is a plan (if the prayer is answered at all)—a plan that is suited for the attainment of the object of the prayer though natural and material media. The plan must be transmuted, through self-effort action.

I know nothing about any sort of prayer that will bring favorable results through "miracles." I know nothing about any form of prayer that will cause either the violation or cessation of natural laws.

In all of my research, I have never found one scintilla of evidence that any prayer ever was answered or fulfilled through other than natural forces.

I know nothing about any form of prayer which can be induced to work favorably in a mind that is colored, in the slightest degree, by fear.

A NEW WAY TO PRAY

Since becoming better acquainted with my "other self", my way of praying is different from what it was before. I used to go to prayer only when facing difficulty. Now I go to prayer before difficulty overtakes me, when possible.

I now pray, not for more of this world's goods and greater blessings, but to be worthy of that which I already have. I find that this plan is better than the old one.

Infinite Intelligence seems not at all offended when I give thanks and show that I am grateful for the blessings which have crowned my efforts.

I was astounded, when I first tried this plan of offering a prayer of thanks for what I already possessed, to discover what a vast fortune I had owned without being appreciative of it.

For example, I discovered that I possessed a sound body which had never been seriously damaged by illness.

I discovered that I had a mind which was reasonably well balanced.

I discovered that I had a creative imagination through which I could render useful service to great numbers of people.

I discovered that I was blessed with all the freedom I desired, in both body and mind.

I discovered that I was a citizen of the best all-round country civilization has yet evolved.

I discovered that I possessed an imperishable desire to help others who were less fortunate.

I discovered that happiness, the highest aim of mankind, was mine for the taking, business depression or no business depression.

Last, but by no means least, I discovered that I had the privilege of approaching Infinite Intelligence, either for the purpose of offering thanks for what I already possessed or to ask for more and for guidance.

May it not be helpful if every reader of this book will take inventory of his or her intangible assets? Such an inventory may disclose possessions of priceless value.

SOME SIGNS WE HAVE OVERLOOKED

Just now the whole world is undergoing a change of such stupendous proportions that millions of people have become panic-stricken with worry, doubt, indecision and fear! It seems to me that now is a splendid time for those who have come to the crossroads of doubt to endeavor to become acquainted with their "other selves."

All who wish to do so will find it helpful if they take a lesson from Nature. Observation will show that the eternal stars shine nightly in their accustomed places; that the sun continues to send down its rays of warmth, causing Mother Earth to yield an overabundance of food and clothing; that water continues to flow downhill; that the birds of the air and the wild animals of the forest receive their accustomed requirements of food; that useful day follows restful night; that busy summer follows the inactive winter; that the seasons come and go precisely as they did before the 1929 depression began; that, in reality, *only men's minds have ceased to function normally*, and this because men have filled their minds with fear.

Observation of these simple facts of everyday life may be helpful as a starting point for those who wish to supplant fear by faith.

I am not a prophet, but I can, with all due modesty, predict that every individual has the power to change his or her material or financial status by first changing the nature of his or her beliefs.

Do not confuse the word *belief* with the word *wish*. The two are not the same! Everyone is capable of "wishing" for financial, material, or spiritual advantages, but the element of faith is the only sure power by which a wish may be translated into a belief, and a belief into reality.

"FAITH" IS THE BEGINNING OF ALL GREAT ACHIEVEMENT

If Edison had stopped by merely wishing for the secret with which electric energy might be harnessed and made to serve through the incandescent lamp, that convenience to civilization would have remained among Nature's multifarious secrets. He met with temporary defeat more than ten thousand times before wrestling this secret from Nature. It was finally yielded up to him because he believed it would be and kept on trying until he had the answer.

Edison uncovered more of Nature's secrets (they might have been called "miracles" at an earlier period) in the realm of physics than did any other man who ever lived, and this because he became acquainted with his "other self."

I have his own word for this, but even if I did not have it, his achievements of themselves have disclosed the secret in their unfoldment.

Nothing within reason is impossible to the man who knows and relies upon his "other self." Whatever man believes to be true has a way of becoming true.

AN IMPROVED CONCEPTION OF DEITY

I have heard many people speak of a personal God upon whom they believed they could call for help through prayer and receive it.

During the early part of my life, when I had less courage to speak what I believed to be truth, I made a pretense of imagining that out there somewhere in the boundless cosmos was a *personal God* who made it His business to interfere with the petty problems of human beings, and that His decisions could be influenced through prayer; that He was an arbitrary being.

I never seriously believed that! I do not believe it now!

I have long since discarded even the pretense of belief in such a God, having supplanted it by another which offers the very great advantage of being demonstrably sound and practical.

This newer belief discards the personal God and substitutes in His place an all-prevailing force or law known as Infinite Intelligence or the Universal Mind.

My conception of this force is that it permeates every atom of matter and every unit of energy throughout the universe; that it is the form of energy throughout the universe; that it is the form of energy with which people think; that it voluntarily begins at once to help one to transmute into physical reality every thought (or prayer) which is released in a spirit of absolute faith, and by the most economical and convenient natural media available in each instance.

MY CONCEPTION OF PRAYER

This belief is more acceptable to me than the old orthodox pretense of belief in a personal God because I have applied it with a provable degree of success.

Moreover, it simplifies matters for both the one doing the praying and the source of power to which the prayer is offered, because that power has become a part of the mind of the one doing the praying.

This conception of prayer relieves God of all the unnecessary, petty annoyances to which He would be subjected if He had to arbitrate the differences which arise between human beings and hear all of their troubles.

This belief, even if it be no more than a theory, answers to my own satisfaction the question as to why prayer sometimes works, while on most occasions it does not.

A prayer is a released thought, sometimes expressed in audible words and at other times expressed silently. I have observed by experience that silent prayer is as efficacious as the one which is expressed in words. I have observed also *that one's state of mind is the determining factor* when prayer works, as well as when it does not.

From these observations (not opinions), I have reached the conclusion that the force or power which answers a prayer favorably is exactly the same force or power that converts an acorn into an oak tree, awakens the bird which sleeps in the egg, or develops two tiny cells into that marvelously organized form known as a human being.

My conception of the "other self" which I have tried to describe is that it merely symbolizes a newly discovered approach to Infinite Intelligence; an approach which one may control and direct through the simple process of mixing faith with one's thoughts.

This is only another way of saying that I now have greater faith in the power of prayer than I had when I depended upon a God who was supposed to exist in the form of a person, in some distant world of which I knew nothing, because this newer conception of the source from which prayer is answered places it within my own mind, where it remains constantly on duty, ready and willing to do my bidding when I approach it in the language which it understands, which is the language of faith.

The Gods dwell no longer on high Olympus, but in the mind of man.

The state of mind known as faith apparently opens to one the medium of sixth sense through which one may communicate with sources of power and information far surpassing any available through the five physical senses.

There comes to your aid and to do your bidding, with the development of the sixth sense, a strange power which, let us assume, is a guardian angel who can open to you at all times the door to the Temple of Wisdom.

The author is not a believer in nor an advocate of "miracles," for the reason that he has enough knowledge of Nature's laws to understand that Nature never suspends, countermands, or deviates from her established laws.

Some of her laws, however, are so incomprehensible that they produce what appear to the uninitiated to be "miracles." The "sixth senses" comes as near to being "miracles" as anything the author has ever experienced, and it appears so perhaps because the author does not understand the method by which this principle is operated.

This much the author does know—that there is a power or a first cause or an Intelligence which permeates every atom of matter and embraces every unit of energy perceptible to man; that this Infinite Intelligence converts acorns into oak trees, causes water to flow downhill in response to the law of gravity, follows night with day and winter with summer, each maintaining its proper place and relationship to the other. This Intelligence may aid in transmitting one's desires into concrete or material form. The author has this knowledge because he has experimented with it and has experienced it.

The author has for many years followed the habit of taking personal inventory of himself once a year, for the purpose of determining how many of his weaknesses he has bridged or eliminated, and to ascertain what progress, if any, he has made during the year.

On one of these occasions, before THE LAW OF SUCCESS philosophy had been reduced to textbooks and published, the inventory showed the author had not only slowed down during the year, but that he was becoming indifferent toward himself and toward life.

The discovery was alarming! The author made up his mind to do something about it—and do it at once! He was scheduled to deliver an address in Ohio, some two hundred miles from his home. The trip was made by automobile.

On the way, the author's "guardian angel" took her place beside him on the vacant front seat of the car. (This portion of the incident may, if the reader desires, be attributed entirely to the author's use of his imagination, or to daydreaming, or to any other cause one sees fit.)

The personage on the vacant seat beside the author seemed very real. There took place, almost immediately after the author observed by his "feelings" that some force or personality besides his own was in the car, the following interview, which resulted in the Compact described:

Voice speaking to me from within: "You have wasted more of your time in the past than you have used constructively. How long are you going to continue this waste?"

The author: "Yes, I know I have wasted too much time. What has been the cause of this waste, and how can I make amends for it in the future?"

Voice from within: "The time you have wasted in the main has been the time you have devoted to thinking and indulging too freely in physical pleasures. You should make amends for this waste by transmuting this vital energy into a service to others, through THE LAW OF SUCCESS philosophy."

The author: "Do I understand that my thoughts in the future should be devoted entirely to serving others through the LAW OF SUCCESS?"

Voice from within: "Not at all, but you should divert the major portion of your thoughts to the purpose suggested. If you fail to do so, you will bring misery to yourself, and deprive others of knowledge which you should impart to them through the LAW OF SUCCESS."

The author: "I haven't the money with which to publish the LAW OF SUCCESS philosophy."

Voice from within: "That is no excuse. You may have all the money you need for this, and for every other purpose, provided you are willing to accept advice and follow it."

The author: "I am willing to accept advice, and I will follow it. Give me instructions, and I will follow them to the letter."

Voice from within: "Very well, your willingness to follow instructions is all that you need for the present. Are you ready to receive your instructions now?"

The author: "I am ready."

Voice from within: "You will find it difficult at first to follow your instructions, because you will have to change completely your habits. The reward which awaits you, if you follow instructions faithfully, however, is worth all the effort you will devote to the task. Here are your instructions:

"First. In the future, you shall devote as much time and effort to serving others, through the LAW OF SUCCESS philosophy, as you have devoted in the past to indulgence in personal pleasures.

"Second. Proceed at once to the task of writing the LAW OF SUCCESS philosophy. When the manuscripts have been completed, you will receive further instructions for their publication.

"Third. Upon publication of the LAW OF SUCCESS philosophy, you will receive instructions for the writing of other books. Carry out those instructions as soon as you receive them.

"Fourth. As compensation for carrying out these and other instructions which will be given to you in the future, you may have your choice of any three things you wish."

The Author: "Do you mean that I may really have any three things I choose, in return for carrying out these instructions?"

Voice from within: "Yes, any three things you choose."

The author: "With whom am I dealing? Who will be responsible to me for the compensation I have been promised after I carry out the instructions?"

Voice from within: "You are dealing with Infinite Intelligence. I am the Individual Entity designated by Infinite Intelligence to bargain with you for your services. So you may proceed with your instructions with faith that you will receive your reward. I shall now give you the power to compensate yourself as soon as you earn your reward."

The author: "Very well. I shall choose (1) Wisdom through an understanding heart that will help me to relate myself to others in a spirit of harmony, (2) Health in both body and mind, and (3)

Wealth in such amounts as I may need to carry out the instructions you have given me."

Voice from within: "It is not enough. I cannot permit you to be cheated. You should modify your first choice to include happiness. Without happiness, you will not be an efficient worker. Infinite Intelligence is impending. You have been prepared to render useful service in connection with this crisis. Revise your first choice."

The author: "All right! My first choice shall be happiness through the wisdom of an understanding heart."

Voice speaking from within: "That is better! The terms of our compact are now satisfactory. You are now assuming the role of both master and servant. Your wages shall be paid as fast as the service is rendered. I shall explain the method by which you shall be paid, so that you will know you can neither collect without earning your pay, nor be cheated out of your reward after earning it.

"Happiness comes only from rendering useful service to others. You shall receive this portion of you reward as fast as you earn it.

"The wisdom of an understanding heart comes through intense desire for it. Take this portion of your reward as rapidly as you wish.

"Health of body and mind comes through positive thought. Keep your mind free from negative thoughts and claim this portion of your reward as fast as you earn it.

"Wealth of this sort, which will permit happiness, comes by rendering useful service to others. Through the LAW OF SUCCESS you may render such service. The money will be paid directly to you by those whom you serve, and in proportion to the amount of service you render, the quality of the service, and the number of people served.

"You will observe that Infinite Intelligence has very wisely made you your own supervisor, your own employer, your own servant, and your own paymaster. The compact is now in force. The extent to which it is carried out is limited only by you. The compact is irrevocable except by your default."

My visitor departed, leaving behind a "feeling" of aloneness, similar to that which one might have felt if a fellow traveler had opened the door of the car and stepped out. The experience was uncanny. I had never had such an experience before. For a time I was not sure what had happened.

Many thoughts ran through my mind. The first was that I had been daydreaming. Another was that I had been overworking my imagination. Subsequent events proved both conclusions to be wrong.

Briefly, the following took place, after that experience on the twenty-sixth of October, 1923 (my birthday):

1. Upon my return home the following day, I began to organize the data I had been gathering on the LAW OF SUCCESS philosophy for nearly fifteen years previously. On the following Christmas evening, I began the actual writing of the LAW OF SUCCESS.

2. Late in the year 1928, the manuscripts had been completed, after many revisions, and they were published by A.L. Pelton of Meriden, Connecticut, through circumstances which fully harmonize with the terms of the compact already described.

3. In 1929, the worldwide "Business Depression" began, creating a state of chaos throughout the civilized world. Examination of the LAW OF SUCCESS philosophy will disclose the fact that it is perfectly suited to the needs of millions of people who have been injured by loss of faith, and in other ways, by the depression.

4. The LAW OF SUCCESS philosophy now has a following in all cities, towns and villages in America, and in practically every country on earth. The mean of distribution of the philosophy (which I

have described in other books recently written) came through media which harmonize perfectly with the terms of the compact.

5. Last, but by no means least, I am healthy in both body and mind; I am happier than I have ever been before in my entire life, and I have not wanted for the money necessary to carry out my instructions.

The part of this experience which impresses me most is the ingenuity with which the compact was so designed that it gave me both the *privilege* of becoming the master, and the *responsibility* of being the servant. Literally, this compact made me the "Master of my own fate, the Captain of my own soul."

DOES EDISON SPEAK FROM THIS GRAVE?

While I was passing through the age of "hero worship," I found myself trying to imitate those whom I most admired. Moreover, I discovered that the element of faith, with which I endeavored to imitate my idols, gave me great capacity to do so quite successfully.

I have never quite divested myself of this habit of hero worship, although I have passed the age commonly given over to such state of being. My experience has taught me that the next best thing to being truly great is to emulate the great, by feeling and action, as nearly as possible. I have never known of this habit doing anyone any harm.

Long before the LAW OF SUCCESS philosophy was completed, before I had ever written a line for publication or endeavored to deliver a speech in public, I followed the habit of reshaping my own character by trying to imitate the nine men whose lives and lifeworks had been most impressive to me. These nine men were Emerson, Paine, Edison, Darwin, Lincoln, Burbank, Napoleon, Ford and Carnegie. Every night, over a long period of years, I held an imaginary council meeting with this group, whom I called my "Invisible Counselors.".

The procedure was this: Just before going to sleep at night, I would shut my eyes and see, in my imagination, this group of men seated with me around my council table. Here, I had not only opportunity to sit among those whom I considered to be great, but I actually dominated the group by serving as the chairman and leader.

I had a very definite purpose in indulging my imagination through these nightly meetings. My purpose was to rebuild my own character so it would represent a composite of my imaginary counselors. Realizing, as I did early in life, that I had to overcome the handicap of a lowly birth in an environment of ignorance and superstition, I deliberately assigned myself the task of voluntary rebirth through the method here described.

REBUILDING CHARACTER THROUGH AUTO-SUGGESTION

Having been an earnest student of psychology, I knew of course that all people become what they are because of their dominating thoughts and desires. I knew that every deeply seated desire may be transmuted into its physical counterpart. I knew that self-suggestion was a powerful factor in the building of character; that it was in fact the sole principle through which character is builded!

With this knowledge of the principles of mind operations, I was fairly well armed with equipment needed in rebuilding my character. In these imaginary council meetings, I called on my Cabinet members for the knowledge and the traits of character I wished each to contribute, addressing myself to each member, in audible words, as follows:

"Mr. Emerson, I desire to acquire from you the marvelous understanding of Nature which distinguished your life. I ask that you make an impress upon my subconscious mind of whatever qualities you possessed which enabled you to understand and adapt yourself to the laws of Nature. I ask that you assist me in reaching and drawing upon whatever sources of knowledge are available to this end.

"Mr. Burbank, I request that you pass on to me the knowledge which enabled you to so harmonize the laws of Nature that you caused the cactus to shed its thorns, and become an edible food. Give me access to the knowledge which enabled you to make two blades of grass grow where but one grew before, and helped you to blend the coloring of the flowers with more splendor and harmony. For you alone have successfully painted the lily.

"Napoleon, I desire to acquire from you, by emulation, the marvelous ability you possessed to inspire men and to arouse them to a greater and more determined spirit of action. Also to acquire the spirit of enduring faith which enabled you to turn defeat into victory, and to surmount staggering obstacles. Emperor of Fate, King of Chance, Man of Destiny, I salute you!

"Mr. Paine, I desire to acquire from you the freedom of your thought and the courage and clarity with which to express your convictions, which so distinguished you!

"Mr. Darwin, I wish to acquire from you the marvelous patience and ability to study cause and effect, without bias or prejudice, so exemplified by you in the field of natural science.

"Mr. Lincoln, I desire to build into my own character the keen sense of justice, the untiring spirit of patience, the sense of humor, the spirit of human understanding, and the tolerance which were your distinguishing characteristics.

"Mr. Carnegie, I am already indebted to you for my choice of a lifework, which has brought me great happiness and peace of mind. I wish to acquire a thorough understanding of the principles of organized effort which you used so effectively in the building of a great industrial enterprise.

"Mr. Ford, you have been among the most helpful of the men who have supplied much of the material out of which the philosophy of achievement is being built. I wish to acquire your spirit of persistence, your determination, your poise, and your self-confidence, with which you have mastered poverty, organized directness, unified and simplified human effort, so I may help others to follow in your footsteps.

"Mr. Edison, I have seated you nearest to me, at my right, because of the personal cooperation you have given me during my research into the causes of success and failure. I wish to acquire from you the marvelous spirit of faith with which you have uncovered so many of Nature's secrets, and the spirit of unremitting toil with which you have so often wrested victory from defeat."

My method of addressing the members of my imaginary Cabinet would vary, according to the traits of character in which I was, for the moment, most interested in acquiring. I studied the records of their lives with painstaking care. After some three months of this sort of nightly procedure, I was astounded by the discovery that these imaginary figures became apparently real.

Each of these nine men developed individual characteristics which surprised me. For example, Lincoln developed the habit of being always late, then walking around the table in a solemn parade. When he came, he walked slowly, with his hands clasped behind him, and once in a while, he would stop at my seat as he passed and rest his hand, momentarily, upon my shoulder. He always wore an expression of seriousness upon his face. Rarely did I see him smile. The cares of a sundered nation had made him grave.

That was not true of the others. Burbank and Paine often indulged in witty repartee which seemed at times to shock the other members of my Cabinet.

One night Paine suggested that I prepare a lecture on "The Age of Reason" and deliver it from the pulpit of a church which I formerly attended. Many around the table laughed heartily at the suggestion. But Napoleon did not. He drew his mouth down at the corners and groaned so loudly that they all turned and looked at him with amazement. To him, the Church was but a pawn of the State, not to be reformed, but to be used as a convenient inciter to mass activity by the people.

On one occasion, Burbank was late. When he came, he was excited with enthusiasm and explained that he had been delayed because of an experiment he was making, through which he hoped to be able to grow apples on most any sort of tree.

Paine chided him by reminding him that it was an apple which started all the trouble between man and woman.

Darwin chuckled heartily as he suggested that Paine should watch out for little serpents when he went out into the forest to gather apples, as they had the habit of growing into big snakes.

Emerson observed, "No serpents, no apples." And Napoleon remarked, "No apples, no state!"

Once I had a love affair with a young lady whose name was Josephine. We had a misunderstanding and agreed to discontinue our love affair. That evening at the meeting, Napoleon smiled as he reminded me that he too had given up a cherished possession whose name was Josephine, and he admonished me to re-establish myself in the young lady's good graces. I did not follow the advice.

Years later, I met the young lady, after she had married another man, and she told me that shortly after she and I had our break, she had a dream in which Napoleon appeared and strongly urged her to recant and invite me to do the same.

Lincoln developed the habit of being always the last one to leave the table after each meeting. On one occasion, he leaned across the end of the table on his folded arms, and remained in that position for several minutes. I made no attempt to disturb him. Finally he lifted his head slowly, got up and walked to the door, then turned around, came back and laid his hand on my shoulder and said, "My boy, you will need much courage if you remain steadfast in carrying out your purpose in life. But remember, when difficulties overtake you, that the common people have common sense. Adversity will develop it."

One evening, Edison arrived ahead of all the others. He seated himself at my left, where Emerson was accustomed to sit, and said, "You are destined to witness the discovery of the secret of life. When the time comes, you will observe that life consists of great swarms of energy, or entities, each as intelligent as human beings believe themselves to be.

"These units of life group themselves together like hives of bees, and remain together until they disintegrate, through lack of harmony. These units have differences of opinion, just as do human beings, and often they fight among themselves.

"These meetings which you are conducting will be very helpful to you. They will bring to your rescue some of the same units of life which served the members of your Cabinet, whose physical bodies have been discarded. These units are eternal. They never die!

"Your own thoughts and desires serve as the magnet which attracts units of life, from the great ocean of life. Only the friendly units which harmonize with the nature of your desires are attracted."

The other members of the Cabinet began to enter the room. Edison rose and slowly walked around to his own seat. Edison was still living when this happened. It impressed me so greatly that I went to see him and told him about the experience. He smiled broadly, and said, "Your dream was more a reality than you may imagine it to have been." He added no further explanation to his statement.

These meetings became so realistic that I became fearful of their consequence and discontinued them for several months. The experiences were so uncanny that I was afraid my mind might become unbalanced if I continued them, or that I would become a fanatic on the subject and lose sight of the fact that these meetings were purely experiences of my imagination.

Some six months after I had discontinued the practice, I was awakened one night, or thought I was, when I saw Lincoln standing by my bedside. He said, "The world will soon need your services. It is about to undergo a period of chaos which will cause men and women to lose faith and become panic-stricken. Go ahead with your work and complete your philosophy. That is your mission in life. If you neglect it, for any cause whatsoever, you will be reduced to a primal state and be compelled to retrace the cycles through which you have passed during thousands of years."

I was unable to tell when morning came whether I had dreamed this, or had actually been awake, and I have never since found out which it was, but I do know that the dream—if it were a dream—was so vivid in my mind the next day that I resumed my meetings the following night and have ever since continued them.

At our next meeting, the members of my Cabinet all filed into the room together and stood at their accustomed places at the council table, while Lincoln raised a glass and said, "Gentlemen, let us drink a toast to a friend of man. He has returned to the fold."

After that, I began to add new members to my Cabinet, until now it consists of more than fifty, among them Galileo, Copernicus, Aristotle, Plato, Socrates, Homer, Voltaire, Bruno, Spinoza, Drummond, Kant, Schopenhauer, Newton, Confucius, Elbert Hubbard, Brann, Ingersoll, Wilson and William James.

This is the first time that I have had the courage to mention this chapter of my life. Heretofore, I have remained quiet on the subject because I knew, from my own attitude in connection with such matters, that I would be branded as a pious fraud if I described my unusual experiences.

I have been emboldened by time to reduce my experiences to the printed page because the philosophy of achievement which I have had the privilege of organizing has been accepted as being sound and practical by a great army of men and women in practically every walk of life.

Also, I am now less concerned about what *"they will say"* than I was in the past. One of the blessings of maturity is that it sometimes brings one greater courage to be truthful, regardless of what those who do not understand may think or say.

Lest I be misunderstood, I wish here to state most emphatically that I still regard my Cabinet meetings as being purely imaginary, but I feel entitled to suggest that, while the members of my Cabinet may be purely fictional, and the meetings entirely existent in my own imagination, they have led me into glorious paths of adventure, rekindled an appreciation of true greatness, encouraged creative endeavor, and emboldened the expression of honest thought.

CHAPTER TWO

◆

AN INTERVIEW WITH MY "INVISIBLE COUNSELORS"

MY STRANGEST EXPERIENCE

Somewhere in the cell structure of the brain is located an organ which receives vibrations of thought ordinarily called "hunches." So far, science has not discovered where this organ of the sixth sense is located, but this is not important. The fact remains that human beings do receive accurate knowledge through other than the five physical senses.

Such knowledge generally is received when the mind is under the influences of some form of *extraordinary stimulation*.

Any emergency which arouses the emotions and causes the heart to beat more rapidly than normal may, and generally does, bring the sixth sense into action. Anyone who has experienced a near accident while driving an automobile, knows that on such occasions the sixth sense often comes to one's rescue and aids, by split seconds, in avoiding accident.

These facts are mentioned preliminary to a statement of fact which I shall now make: namely, that during my meetings with my "Invisible Counselors", I find my mind most receptive to ideas, thoughts, and knowledge which reach me through the sixth sense.

I am known to my friends as an "inspired" writer. I can truthfully say that I owe entirely to my "Invisible Counselors" full credit for such ideas, facts, or knowledge as I received through "inspiration."

The better part of the LAW OF SUCCESS philosophy, which now has a following throughout the civilized world, was revealed to me through my "Invisible Counselors." On more than a score of occasions, when I have faced emergencies, some of them so grave that actually my life seemed in jeopardy, I have been miraculously guided past these difficulties through the influence of my "Invisible Counselors."

I wish the reader to have these facts in mind before reading an actual transcript of a meeting with one of my "Invisible Counselors," which I shall enter in a few minutes.

What this meeting will reveal I have no way of knowing in advance, nor can I foretell its length. It may deal with subjects entirely foreign to the purpose of this book, but come what may, it will bring the reader as close to the source of my "inspiration" as I can take him. Any further knowledge of this subject must be gained by actual experimentation.

My original purpose in conducting council meetings with imaginary beings was solely that of impressing my own subconscious mind, through the principle of auto-suggestion, with certain qualities of character I desired to acquire.

In more recent years, my experimentation has taken on an entirely different trend. I now go to my imaginary counselors with every sort of problem which confronts me.

For the purpose of giving a better understanding of how I proceed in these meetings with my "Invisible Counselors", I shall now conduct an interview in which I shall direct questions to the late Thomas A. Edison, a member of my imaginary council.

My first question:

Q. Mr. Edison, where did you go when you died?

A.   Nowhere! I am not dead. I have merely shed the worn-out body which I no longer needed. It had worn out anyway.

Q.   Did you take with you your memory of your experiences during life?

A.   Yes, and I am still working on my experiments with synthetic rubber. As soon as I find someone who will lend me the use of his physical body, I shall help him to give the world the benefit of my work.

Q.   In what form do you now exist, as an individual, and where do you reside?

A.   I exist in the form of a group of organized units of intelligence, and I reside wherever I choose. I am not bothered about transportation. I can travel from one part of the universe to another at a speed inconceivably greater than the speed of light. Most of my time is spent near those who worked with me before I shed my physical body.

Q.   Did you find a God over there where you now live?

A.   Over here, every individual is a God, but that is not the name by which we are known. Here we are known as servants. All of us are rendering service to those who are still burdened with physical bodies. We enter the physical bodies of others through the medium of thought, whenever we find individuals who are capable of giving our thoughts admission. Sometimes, we individually enter the minds of others; at other times, we group ourselves together and as many as a dozen of us come over together when we have some special message of importance to deliver. When we come over together, we have less difficulty in conveying our meaning to an individual.

Q.   How do you communicate with others on your plane?

A.   That is easy. We communicate when we desire by the mere will to communicate. Distance makes no difference. We can communicate at any distance, at the same rate of speed that we travel.

Q. What is life?

A. Your meaning is not clear.

Q. What is it that gives one living on the physical plane the power to live and to think?

A. What you call life is a form of intelligence consisting of countless numbers of units or swarms. On the physical plane, these swarms increase in number as one grows older. They remain together as long as the physical body functions harmoniously. They disengage themselves and go about their business when the physical body ceases to function.

Sometimes these swarms of unit intelligence separate themselves into smaller groups, each moving as it chooses. When we communicate through physical bodies on your plane, we usually do so by sending over a small swarm of our individual units, the number depending upon the capacity of the body we visit to receive us.

Often we admit new units on this plane, very much the same as a hive of bees might admit to its number a group of strange bees. Mutual interest serves to attract new units to our individual groups.

Q. When was the earth on which we live during our physical existence created?

A. The earth was not created. It was thrown off a spinning cosmos about fifty million years ago.

Q. How did human beings and other forms of physical life find their way to the earth?

A. All physical life now on the earth on which you live is the outgrowth of swarms of units of life which took up their residence there about forty million years after the earth became a separate body.

Q. Do the units of energy which give life to vegetation and to the animals lower than man come back to your plane when they discard their physical places of abode?

A. All units of life come back. There is no difference whatsoever between the units of life. Each is endowed with exactly the same capacity for intelligence as are all others.

The units of life in a dog are as intelligent as those in a man. It is their numbers and experience which give to a physical being greater or less intelligence. The only difference in intelligence between a man and a stalk of grass is the difference in the number of units of intelligence residing in each.

The units of life in all animals lower than man travel in smaller swarms. When they come back to this plane, they often separate and lose their group individuality altogether, some of them joining larger groups and others floating around through space looking for an opportunity to express themselves on the physical plane again.

Q. Is this earth on which we live the only planet inhabited by life in physical form?

A. No! Man on earth is still in kindergarten stage.

Q. What other secrets in the field of natural law has man yet to discover?

A. The greatest of these cannot be explained to you because your swarm of intelligence units, at the present, is too small to comprehend, but you are learning rapidly. Within the next three years, you will be competent to receive a full description of one of these secrets, and you will be permitted to do so if you continue to harmonize yourself with the visiting units with which you are now communicating.

Q. If all units of life are gifted with the same degree of intelligence, why do some men indulge in destructive efforts toward others?

A. It will be difficult for me to explain this so you will understand it. I shall do my best. When I become too deep for you, stop me. The destructive tendency in man which you ask about is due to wars among the units of intelligence which man brings about by his emotional treatment of these units. When a swarm of intelligence units enters a man's body, they become imprisoned there, and cannot escape until the transformation which you call death takes place. During their imprisonment, they are under the control of the individual and are subject to the individual's commands. Through his thoughts, he can make them positive or negative. They are his servants. They follow his instructions until they are released through death.

Q. Will there ever be a time when life will survive over death on earth?

A. No! That would not be wise. The individual units of intelligence which give life to the physical body become dissatisfied with their physical existence. After a time, we on this plane come to their rescue and give them their freedom. Nothing of a physical nature can ever prevent this.

Q. Why do you who exist on your plane wish to release the swarms of intelligence units which have become dissatisfied on this earthly plane?

A. For various reasons, the most common of them being the fact that we are affected by the dissatisfaction of those units living on the physical plane.

Q. What sorts of individual activities do these units of intelligence engage in while embodied in the physical world?

A. They are divided into many groups, each group specializing in its own particular physical function. Some of them attend to the adornment of the physical body, while others mix and distribute the food which is taken into the body. Others manipulate the heart and vital organs of the body. Some of them look after the organs of reproduction. Each of the six senses is controlled and operated by a different group of intelligence units.

Q. I always understood there were but five of the physical senses. You speak of six.

A. The sixth sense is one which is not often understood. It operates through a group of brain cells which serve as organs of reception for impulses of thought which cannot be conveyed through any of the five senses. It is through this group of intelligence units that we on this plane communicate with those dwelling on the physical plane.

Q. In what physical forms did life on this earth first make its appearance?

A. In the form of vegetation which grew in the seas. Every other physical form on earth was evolved from that beginning.

Q. It is not true then that man was placed on earth a completed physical being, in his present form?

A. No! That story was pure fiction. It has no basis in fact. Such a thing would have been an impossibility.

Q. Is the language in which you are answering my questions your own?

A. No! I am communicating in your own language. My language is that of universal thought. It requires no words. You are receiving my thoughts, through your sixth sense, and translating them into your own words and phrases. Some of your translations are inaccurate. There is no way I can prevent this.

Q. Is it possible for others living on my plane to communicate with me through the sixth sense?

A. Yes! Impulses of thought may pass directly from one physical brain to another, through the sixth sense. This group may send to or receive from other minds vibrations of thought. You are translating this inaccurately, but you are as close to the right answer as may be at the present.

Q. Does the season of the year or the date of one's birth have anything to do with one's material or financial status?

A. Not the slightest. You have no proof that the time of one's birth has any influence whatsoever over one's material status. All truth is capable of proof. Any statement of an alleged truth which cannot be proved by natural laws may be discounted as nonexistent.

Q. Do you mean by this that there are no miracles?

A. The word 'miracle' is a mere term of speech which describes something that is not capable of proof because there is nothing to be proved, or something that is not understood.

Q. Can anyone on this earthly plane gain for another any advantage on your plane?

A. Only by such procedure as will induce one to seek direct communication with the units of intelligence of this plane.

Q. Can one human being pray effectively for another?

A. All prayers which bring about any form of change on the physical plane are answered only through the sixth sense of the mind of the one praying. Prayer, when properly conducted, opens the mind of the one praying to additional units of intelligence. These units, when they gain admittance, may effectively change the material status of the one praying.

Q. Then God does not answer prayer?

A. I have already informed you that we know of no power on this plane which corresponds to what you call God.

Q. What is that form of energy which we call by the name 'electricity?'

A. It is a collection of groups of unit intelligence which serve as conveyors of energy over which all other units travel.

Q. Are the units of intelligence with which men think the same as the units of intelligence known as electricity?

A. They are practically the same. They serve different purposes.

Q. What happens to the units of intelligence of a man who commits suicide?

A. These swarms usually break away from one another when they get back to this plane, each individual unit seeking an alliance with some strange swarm. The same thing happens to a man who commits murder, and to others who are guilty of gross injustices toward their fellow men on earth. Peace of mind and harmony with one's fellow men, at the time of death, are the only influences, generally speaking, which send the individual units of intelligence back to this plane in a friendly group. Permanence is born of cooperative association.

Q. Did the individual units of intelligence which lived in Lincoln's body come back to your plane as a group?

A. You ought to know. You are in communication with that group every day.

Q. Have you searched, unsuccessfully, for the individual groups of unit intelligence of any of your friends whom you knew on the earth plane?

A. Yes, many of them.

Q. Are some men inspired by the influence of units of intelligence which have gone back to your plane?

A. If they were not, you would not be in communication with my group now.

Q. If I understand you correctly, some individuals who undergo the transformation known as death go back to that plane as individual groups of intelligence and maintain their identity as such, with ability to remember their physical experiences, while others lose their identity. Is that correct?

A. Yes, I have already explained this to you. The individual units of intelligence never die, but they do not always remain together, as they were during their physical experience. If they separate at death, they lose their identity as swarms, retaining only their individual identity.

Q. Is there no form of authority to which individual units of intelligence become subject when they return to your plane, after death?

A. They are always subject to what you would call natural law. Nothing transcends harmony and ordered relation, which is the deathless force of all law. It is the essence of Infinite.

Q. Do you understand my thoughts?

A. That is all I do understand. You could not communicate with me through any other medium.

Q. Would you understand my thoughts if they were formed in terms other than the English language?

A. There is no language on this plane, save the language of thought. All thought is universally understood.

Q. Why are the majority of prayers not answered?

A. All prayers are answered. Not all prayers bring to those praying the material things for which they pray because some prayers seek, in effect, the suspension of natural law, while others are released in states of mind which are not in harmony with natural law.

Q. What is the purpose of life? Why do units of intelligence seek temporary dwelling in physical bodies?

A. There is no major purpose in life alone. The individual units of intelligence seek expression on physical planes for the purpose of growth into greater degrees of intelligence.

Q. I understood you to say that all individual units of intelligence on your plane were endowed with the same degree of intelligence. Did I misunderstand you?

A. You understood me correctly. The degree of intelligence on this plane is evenly divided between all individual units of intelligence. This degree of intelligence is increasing all the time. That is the purpose of physical experience, the only purpose.

Q. Are you becoming tired or annoyed by these questions?

A. On this plane, we know of no such experience as fatigue, and we never become annoyed by those who seek knowledge as you are doing.

Q. Was the 1929 business depression caused by any influence on your plane, or was it caused by man?

A. The experience which you call a business depression was caused by millions of swarms of intelligence units which were sent back to this plane as disorganized units, at the death of men who were engaged in the World War.

These units brought back to this plane with them the experiences of fear with which they were endowed when released. In 1929, they discovered a worldwide state of mind on this physical plane which was favorable to their return.

When they came back, they brought with them their fears and inharmonies, and it is from these that the world is now suffering.

The depressions will continue for approximately the same number of hours that the bloody conflict of World War lasted. Nothing can prevent this. All ebb and flow of tides leads but to balance. The lesson which the world is now learning is one that it needed to learn.

The lesson is being taught by the intelligence units which were sent back to this plane by force, before they were ready to return. The measure of suffering and damage experienced by the world during the depression will be in proportion to that experienced by the World War.

The world will not resume normal and ordered ways until 1933. After that year, the inhabitants of the earth will adjust themselves in a spirit of harmony. From 1933 to 1943, the world will discover more of Nature's secrets than it has discovered during the entire past.

The punishment which human beings are now undergoing will prepare them to rely more upon the spiritual forces available to individuals and less upon the material forces to which they have been submitting themselves since the beginning of the World War. Continue your preparation to render useful service. You will be needed.

Q. Are you happy and contented where you are?

A. Everyone here is happy. No one is contented.

Q. Has the natural law of biology ever been suspended for the purpose of bringing a human being into the physical plane through other natural methods of reproduction?

A. Never! Such an experience would be an impossibility.

Q. Did God authorize anyone to write the Bible?

A. I have stated to you before that we know of no such being as God on this plane. The Bible to which you refer is a collection of essays, some fictional and some factual and historical, which were written by many different writers.

These essays were copied many times before they were published in their present form. Many of those who did the copying made changes in the original manuscripts to suit their own tastes.

These essays never were intended by their original writers as being anything more than their own personal opinions.

Some of the books of the Bible were written in the same spirit that fictional writers now write stories, and for the same purpose, to amuse or to confound the minds of others. Some were written as poetry, others as philosophy.

Q. Am I to understand from what you say that there are no special rewards on your plane for individual units which return after having been of constructive service on this plane?

A. Their only reward is their own growth and development through physical experience.

Q. Then there is no such place as hell on your plane?

A. Not on this plane. The only hell that I know anything about is the one which exists there on the physical plane, and those similar to it on their worldly planes. These hells are man-made affairs. They exist only in the thoughts and deeds of man.

Q. What should my conduct on this plane be in order to gain for myself the greatest benefits both on this plane and on the one you now occupy, when I return there?

A. So live that you are at peace with yourself and with others.

Q. Can you modify that answer?

A. I might lengthen it so you would better understand it, but I could not improve it otherwise. Your individual intelligence units will come back to this side with whatever experiences you submit them to on the earth plane. They will come back as an organized group and maintain their identity as such only if you so live that you are at peace in your own mind when they separate themselves from your physical body. You should make of your intelligence an harmonious whole.

Q. When will my intelligence cells return to the other plane?

A. I will answer that if you insist upon an answer, but my answer will be of no help to you because it will be conditioned on your future experiences. Your best work is yet to be done. Continue your task and do not concern yourself about your future. It will take care of itself if you will properly attend to the present. You should be happy to know that the intelligence units of more than a hundred of the most distinguished men who ever lived on the earthly plane are seeking expression through you daily. Some of these swarms have joined with yours permanently.

Q. Why do I find this life so difficult at times and so pleasant and easy at other times?

A. The difficulties you encounter are caused by your negligence in responding to the efforts which intelligence units on this plane are making to serve through you.

Q. What is the nature of the influence I discovered in my physical body which I called my other self?

A. That was a group of intelligence units which joined you permanently at a time when you were in great distress. These units are now with you. They are guardians of your destiny. Others are now trying to gain admission.

Q. How can I best acquire the material and financial resources that I need on this earthly plane?

A. By rendering the greatest amount of service to the greatest number of people possible, through whatever media that present themselves to you.

Q. Am I engaged in the sort of service which will enable me to be of the greatest good to the world and to myself?

A. Yes! Continue in your present work no matter where it may lead you.

Q.   Will men's relationships, socially, financially and professionally, be the same after the business depression as before?

A.   The entire economic and social foundation of the world is now undergoing an ordered change. The new order of civilization will, as near as it can be described to you, be based on mutual interdependence in a community of coordinated endeavors.

This new civilization will be based upon the principle of cooperative effort. No individual will be permitted to suffer because of lack of wealth.

The churches will merge into one universal activity. The clergy will prepare itself to render temporal as well as spiritual aid.

Bank depositors will be insured by the State against loss. When losses occur, they will be covered by a levy which the State will lay against certain accumulated wealth.

The public schools will discontinue the habit of teaching classes en masse and start developing each individual student according to his or her physical, mental and spiritual needs.

It will be unlawful for newspapers to print anything detrimental to the reputation of anyone.

Moving pictures will teach as well as entertain. It will be unlawful for anyone to teach any child under the age of fourteen anything concerning life after death except that which is subject to proof.

Children will be permitted to develop their own minds and to think for themselves on all subjects connected with religion.

Transportation facilities will be greatly improved. All passenger traffic will be through the air, with equipment that is safer than any now in existence. Air traffic will be controlled by the principle of radio, which will eliminate most of the chances of collision.

Prisons will be converted into schools, and the services of prisoners will be paid for, the State deducting from each prisoner's earnings the cost of his keep.

Capital punishment will be eliminated entirely.

Warfare will be outlawed. Differences between nations will be settled in courts of arbitration. Finally, there will come to be no such thing as separate nations. This will follow from an evolutionary process. This change will so reduce useless expense and competition that the returns from one hour of daily labor will support an average family.

Causes of disease will be so thoroughly understood and controlled that every man may be free from its ravages, and the transformation known as death will take place naturally and without pain or fear.

New sources of energy will be uncovered which will be inexhaustible. One of these newly discovered sources will be announced within five years.

Crime will practically be unknown because there will be no cause for committing crime.

Q. Do you remember where I first met you and by whom we were introduced?

A. You were introduced to me by Ed Barnes, at my laboratory. I remember what a difficult time you had in communicating with me because of my deafness. I also remember that you delivered an address before our men. Mrs. Edison said it was very interesting. Of course I did not hear it. Tell Ed Barnes it is time for him to go back to work. He has played long enough.

Q. Can you see me?

A. On this plane, we communicate entirely through a form of energy which you would call thought. We do not need any of the five senses. I cannot see you, but I remember how you looked when I last saw you. At that time, you were dressed in a blue serge coat and white flannel trousers. I remember telling Mrs. Edison that you looked as well in your clothes as Ed Barnes. You know that Barnes has enough clothes to start a clothing store.

Q. Can you explain to me why some children become geniuses while others who are born of the same parents are lacking in normal intelligence?

A. That is very easily explained. The degree of an individual's intelligence is determined by the number of intelligence units which his physical brain can accommodate, and the character of the intelligence units which seek expression through the individual.

I have already explained to you that there are specialists among the units of intelligence. For example, the intelligence units which occupy the body of a literary genius, such as Homer, Shakespeare, or Emerson, often seek expression through others on your plane, after they return to this plane.

You may be interested in knowing that some of your best work in the literary field was inspired by units of intelligence which Elbert Hubbard sent over to help you.

Hubbard finds in you his most favorable physical medium of expression. He says that you will be of great help on your plane when you gain the courage to give free expression to the intelligence units which now use you as a medium of expression.

Q. Does Elbert Hubbard send his intelligence units to the aid of any other person?

A. He is constantly in communication with his son, Bert, at East Aurora. He is trying to bring you and Bert together in a business alliance. He has inspired you to write to Bert about this alliance. You will have a reply to your letter in a few days. It will be favorable.

Hubbard wants you to continue writing where he left off, as his untimely departure stopped work he was doing on his most important document, which was destroyed when he went down on the Lusitania.

He will pass over to you the contents of this document and direct you in completing it. He wants Bert to help you take it to the world. Hubbard will give you his own instructions the next time you open your mind to him.

Q. Is there any reason why I should not make known to others the information I acquire through my communication with you?

A. It is your duty to use this information for the benefit of others. By doing so you will influence other people to become more receptive to the units of intelligence which are seeking expression through every available individual on your plane.

Our most difficult task is to get people to recognize the difference between impulses of thought which we inspire and those which they believe they create.

Most people who recognize our attempts to communicate with them call these attempts 'hunches' and make no effort to discover their source or purpose. The night that you discovered your 'other self' you were influenced by a composite group of intelligence units which were sent over by Elbert Hubbard, Emerson, Napoleon and Andrew Carnegie.

It was Napoleon who gave the military command which brought you to attention and placed you in a physical posture favorable to reception of the instructions which sent you to Philadelphia.

Q. What is the state of mind known as faith? What takes place when one yields to the feeling of faith?

A. Faith is a state of feeling which one experiences when the physical brain has been voluntarily cleared of all forms of emotional conflict.

When the brain is free from all conflict between the emotions, it becomes a favorable organ of expression for any units of intelligence which may be seeking admittance.

When an individual on your plane is in distress, the individual units of intelligence which have been imprisoned in that individual communicate with those on our plane and call for help. They can send out the call for assistance, but they cannot escape, unless the emotional conflict becomes great enough to cause death.

If the individual units of intelligence succeed in organizing themselves into a harmonious cooperative group, they thereby open the way for aid from units of intelligence on our plane. The result is a state of mind known as faith.

During this state of mind, there is unity of effort between intelligence units on this plane and those on the physical plane. Through this form of cooperation, ways and means are easily found for the attainment of any desired purpose which is not out of harmony with natural laws.

Q. Most people are skeptical as to the possibility of communications such as the one I am conducting with you. I admit a certain degree of skepticism. How can this form of doubt be overcome?

A. Only by experimentation such as you are conducting. You are less skeptical now than you were before you discovered your "other self." You are developing very fast.

Within the next three years, you will be prepared to receive positive evidence that you are in communication with intelligence units outside of those which serve in your physical body. You are being prepared now to take this discovery to the world.

Q. Why have I not been permitted to receive that knowledge before?

A. Because of your personal vanity and egotism.

Q. Do I understand you to say that people who are vain or ego-tistical cannot communicate with or receive information from units of intelligence of your plane?

A. They could, but they will not. In their eagerness to indulge their vanity, they attribute to their own intelligence all impulses of thought which they experience.

Q. Why do I find communication with you so much less difficult than it is with others on your plane?

A. Because you believe this to be true. It is all in your own mind. My units of intelligence communicate with you more freely be-cause you invite them to do so.

You have greater faith when you are in communication with me. Faith is a state of mind which makes communica-tion easy. Without faith, there could be no communication whatsoever between the units of intelligence on this plane and those on your physical plane. Lack of faith closes all doors of communication.

Q. Has civilization been retarded by the business depression?

A. No. Civilization has not been retarded by the depression. On the other hand, it has been advanced. The depression served as a needed moral physic to the world. It will have the effect of re-establishing cooperation between the physical and the spiri-tual forces of man.

Q. Could I earn $100,000during a year if I made up my mind to do so, and if so, how?

A. You will earn more than $100,000.00 during a year, and you will receive the money after you earn it. You will earn the mon-ey from the sale of books on which you are now at work.

Q. Is the philosophy of individual achievement on which I have been at work for nearly a quarter of a century now complete?

A. No, it is not complete. As a matter of fact, it is merely a foundation upon which you are building a philosophy of achievement which will be complete. The experience you are now receiving from the plane on which I am located will help you to add the spiritual factors which you neglected in your earlier writings.

You had to undergo a lot of personal punishment before you were made to recognize this deficiency. Until quite recently, you imagined your writings were created by yourself. They were, in part, because you were not amenable to guidance by the units of intelligence which were sent over to help you.

You paid too much attention to your head and too little attention to the messages which were trying to reach you through your sixth sense.

You have now reversed yourself. This accounts for the great improvement in your work. Your readers were quick to sense this improvement and to give you credit for it.

Q. Is it true that impulses of thought which are mixed with emotion have a tendency to translate themselves into their physical equivalent?

A. No! Impulses of thought are not physical in nature. Matter cannot be created out of nothing. It is true, however, that thought may, and often does, influence people to accumulate or organize its equivalent in the form of physical matter.

For illustration, you have the desire to accumulate $100,000 during a year. Your desire is very definite, and that desire will be realized, but its realization will come about through perfectly natural means. In this instance, your impulse of desire for $100,000 will be transmuted into its monetary equivalent through your own efforts, by the publication and distribution of your books to large numbers of people who will be willing to pay for them.

Thought cannot translate itself into physical matter, but it can, and does, cause individuals to shape matter into forms which correspond to the nature and objects of thoughts.

Desires which are conceived in faith become all-consuming in nature. They drive individuals both consciously and unconsciously to seek the attainment of their physical equivalent.

Moreover, desires which are backed by faith have the advantage of being supported by intelligence units which are best suited to the task of translating them into their physical equivalent.

You will receive the $100,000 you desire, and more besides, because you have such faith in the attainment of this end that you see yourself already in possession of the money. You will receive it.

No power in the universe can withhold this money from you unless you cease to have faith. As a matter of fact, you have already completed the labor from which this money will be received.

Only one more step remains to be taken, and that is the distribution of your books to those who want them. This is being attended to for you. Go to bed and go to sleep if you wish. The money will be in your hands just the same.

(NOTE: I am now going to ask a question which may prove conclusively, to my mind at least, that these answers are coming either from my own subconscious mind, or from the mind of some living person with whom I may be in communication.)

Q.   Who kidnapped the Lindbergh baby?

A.   I have no way of answering this question. I can communicate only with minds which are receptive to my units of intelligence.

It would be impossible for anyone continuing as individual entity on this plane to communicate with the kidnapper of the Lindbergh child because of the disharmony of criminal minds, which are antisocial and disunited on the earthly plane, and become separated and sundered into fragmentary units of intelligence.

(NOTE: That answer was a surprise to me. I expected there would be no answer. The answer seems quite logical, although it does not prove that these flashes of intelligence have not originated in the mind of some living person.)

Q. What was the cause of Samuel Insull's downfall? (Mr. Insull was once Mr. Edison's secretary.)

A. The same as the one which brought you the reprimand I have just given you.

Insull became too much absorbed in material values and lost contact with the spiritual forces which were his main asset during the earlier days of his career.

When a man becomes consumed by the desire for material possessions and personal power over his fellow men and forgets that his greatest privilege on the earth plane is that of rendering useful service to others, he is creating a weapon of self-destruction.

High silk hats and swallowtail coats and dazzling displays of jewels at opera functions are physical translations of impulses of desire which originate on the earth plane. They do not come from this side.

Q. Will Henry Ford experience financial disaster before death?

A. No! Ford is using his fortune in a constructive way. Before he is through, he will convert it into a successful demonstration of the principle of cooperative effort. The Ford fortune is being accumulated for this purpose. Through its use (before and after his death) such huge fortunes will ultimately become both unpopular and impossible of accumulation.

Q. What was wrong with Herbert Hoover's administration of the Presidency of the United States?

A. Hoover's mistakes were not as great as they were represented. He was a victim, in common with other leaders all over the world, of an upheaval in civilization out of which will come a redistribution of the material advantages available to mankind. Time will bring his recognition.

Q. Will Roosevelt meet with greater success than Mr. Hoover experienced?

A. Yes. Roosevelt is by nature more adaptable to the rapid changes which are taking place in civilization. He will be popular with the people because he likes people. Roosevelt also has the advantage of coming into office at a time when the whole world is approaching a period of harmony and prosperity which will be conspicuous. Roosevelt will receive credit for virtues he does not possess, even in greater proportion than Hoover was charged with faults which were not his.

Q. At what period will I begin to collect my $100,000 income?

A. Why do you not profit by the suggestion I have already offered you and forget about yourself?

Q. It is not of myself I am thinking when I inquire about my income. I am thinking of those to whom I may render useful service through the use of this money. Does this fact alter or modify your answer?

A. Forget about yourself entirely. Ways and means by which you will be privileged to render useful service have already been prepared for you.

Go about your work day by day just as if you had in hand everything you need. There are more than 50,000 men and women in the world who will supply you with all the material aid you need. They are the men and women who have profited by your philosophy. Some of them are already giving you the cooperation you need. The others will come to your aid when you need them.

Q. What is the best way of meeting difficulties which cause worry and suspense?

A. Find some other person who has greater difficulties and lose yourself in trying to assist him or her.

Q. Is that always the best rule to follow?

A. Not always, but generally it will work. Give it a trial.

Q. Some people will doubt that I have established contact with you. How shall I prove that I have?

A. Do not try to prove anything. Only your own thoughts should be of real concern to you.

Some people did not believe in the teachings of Christ, but Christianity has continued to extend its influence for almost two thousand years.

Go right ahead with your work, following your promptings with courage, and you will have no need to worry about what other people will think of you. Give the skeptics no concern, save that you do not emulate them.

(NOTE: At this point, I was interrupted by a delivery of mail, in which I found a letter from Elbert Hubbard, Jr., of East Aurora, New York. I have adequate evidence that this letter was received several hours after the reference to it which you have read. The letter was favorable, and negotiations are now under way for the alliance between Elbert Hubbard, Jr., and myself which the reference mentioned. I have no explanation to offer as to this apparent coincidence.)

Q. Does Elbert Hubbard wish to communicate further with me at this time?

A. He wishes to communicate directly with you. He has further instructions to offer you. He says that many fields of potentially productive thought lie fallow because yet unbroken by trenchant pen.

Q. Do you have a form of judgement of your plane?

A. Yes, everyone who comes over is carefully judged on merit and give a chance to correct any wrongs that may have been committed on the earth plane.

Q. Who supplies the evidence of one's deeds?

A. Everyone who returns here brings back a complete record of all his or her earthly deeds. The record is literally a part of the swarm of intelligence units. It cannot be altered in any way and it cannot be falsified.

Q. Who sits as the judge?

A. We have courts which measure intelligence in the larger sense. They are very accurate.

Q. How do these courts function?

A. With unfailing exactness and self-executing judgements. There is no lost motion. There are no delays, no mistakes. All sentence imposed upon those who have erred on the earth plane are corrective, but never punitive.

For example, your late antagonist, _____, who has just come over, will not be punished for his wrongs to you and his similar wrongs to others. He will be given an opportunity to correct the damage he has done. Until his debt has been entirely wiped out, by his own efforts, no other individual intelligence unit will give him any cooperation.

We need no one to enforce sentences over here. The enforcement is done by the one on whom sentence is passed.

Emerson wishes you to communicate with him. Come back to me at your convenience. This has been an extensive visit. I hope it will be profitable to you, profitable in terms of knowledge.

I addressed another question to Edison, but there was no answer. Only the walls resounded with the echo of my voice.

The interview was over.

NOTE: This interview with Edison took place while Napoleon Hill was on the staff of President Franklin D. Roosevelt, in 1933, and it was written in the White House while work on *Think and Grow Rich* was in progress. The manuscript was read by the President who expressed great interest in it and requested that he be given a copy of it. A copy of it was also sent to Dr. J.B. Rhine, of Duke University, with whom Napoleon Hill has been exchanging information on ESP (extra sensory perception) for nearly a quarter of a century.

◆

REFLECTIONS ON MY STRANGE INTERVIEW

◆

A FRANK ANALYSIS

Here we are, at the end of one of the strangest experiences of my life.

When I began these translations, I had nothing in mind except a mere description of my meetings with my imaginary cabinet members. When I got into the subject, I was seized by an impelling desire to continue, which was so strong that I could not resist it.

I was something like a fly which ventures inquisitorially on to a sheet of flypaper, except that I did not wish to escape from my task.

A strange feature of this interview has been the peculiar physical condition of my body, which appeared to be stepped up by some form of stimulation such as I had never before experienced, and my mind was never so keen and alert before.

The stimulation of both mind and body was so great that I found it impossible to continue my work on the translations longer than a few minutes at a sitting without becoming so fatigued that my whole body trembled and my nervous energy seemed almost exhausted.

I felt as if I had been engaged in some form of strenuous exercise. At times, during the translations, my pulse became so rapid that I was compelled to stop and rest.

Time passed so rapidly during this experience that I could not account for it except by consulting my watch.

One of my business associates remarked, after reading a few pages of the translations, "You surely must have done some very deep thinking before you wrote this." To which I replied truthfully, "Quite to the contrary, I did no thinking at all. Everything on those pages, both the questions and the answers, poured into my mind so rapidly and so spontaneously that it was not necessary or possible for me to use my reasoning faculty most of the time."

Going back over the questions and answers, in the coolness of the aftermath of the experience, I doubt that I could sit down and quietly create even the questions through my reasoning faculty, let alone the answers. The spontaneity and the rapidity with which those questions and answers poured into my mind was the most astounding part of the whole experience.

WHERE SCIENCE STOPS, I ALSO HESITATE

Over a long period of years, while organizing the LAW OF SUCCESS philosophy, I had the privilege of close contact with Thomas A. Edison, Dr. Alexander Graham Bell, Dr. Elmer R. Gates, and more than a dozen others of equal recognition in the field of science.

This association taught me to stick very closely to the paths hewn by science, in all of my own research in the field of mind stimuli. Metaphysics and Occultism never tempted me except in a very limited way, and in a *spirit of caution.*

In all of my public career, I have never indulged in what might be termed "soapbox" or radical, unorthodox activities of any nature. For these reasons I am perhaps less credulous than the average person. I believe only that which can be supported by reasonably substantial evidence. "Miracles" and all manner of activity based upon so-called supernatural phenomena have never made favorable impression on my mind.

I have been indiscreet enough to criticize those who pretended to believe in such things. I mention these facts so those who do not know me will understand that I am not a person who would be apt to be greatly impressed by any form of unusual phenomena, and above all, that I am not a person who would be likely to deliberately deceive himself.

Candidly, however, my experience in connection with the translations described leads me to the conclusion that perhaps after all I am not really as smart as I have believe myself to be about such matters.

For nearly ten years I carefully observed a great number of groups of so-called Spiritualists, and my close friends will vouch for my statement that I came away from every meeting of this sort that I ever attended more convinced than I was before I went in that all I had witnessed had been a stock of legerdemain or professions of a form of pious fraud.

I have never believed in anything that savored of the supernatural, and I am still of that same frame of mind. I want this clearly understood. At the same time, I am, I hope, honest enough with myself to admit that I cannot attribute all that took place during these translations to any natural cause with which I am familiar. The experience was uncanny.

There is quite enough superstition and ignorance in this world without my trying to add to the stock of either. All of my life, I have been a seeker after truth. The task of finding it is not an easy one, no matter how sincere one may be in one's effort or how willing one may be to investigate persistently all sources of truth. I shall not begin, at my age, either to willingly deceive myself or to endeavor to deceive others.

The facts described in these translations have in no way been altered or colored. Without a question of doubt, I have unwittingly and by accident stumbled upon a new experience which has opened to me a marvelous source of inspiration.

This source may be merely my own mind, or it may be something outside of my own mind. As to that, I cannot say definitely, but there is one thing of which I am perfectly sure: this newly discovered source of mind stimulation has given me a keenness of imagination and a quickening of the spiritual forces within me which I never knew before.

I am aware, of course, that the whole world is now passing through a series of events which have confounded the minds of the shrewdest of men.

I have heard hundreds of intelligent people analyze the recent business depression in general terms, but I have yet to find the first person who claims to be able to state definitely what was its cause.

I want it clearly understood that I am not claiming, either by direct statement or by inference, to be able to interpret the cause of this strangest of all business depressions the world has ever experienced.

NOT IMPRESSED BY "ISMS" OR PSEUDO "SCIENTISTS"

Times almost without number I have warned my own students against a great variety of "isms," including Numerology, Astrology,

Fortune Telling, Palmistry, and other systems whose exponents claim the power to foretell the future.

I doubt that any human being can foretell what will happen one second in advance of the event, except by deductive reasoning based upon known facts, or by pure guesswork.

I do not believe that even Infinite Intelligence can foretell the future, and this for the reason that chance and the law of averages are realities from which no one can escape.

The laws of Nature grind all grist which chance brings to the mill. Moreover, human beings have inherent powers of choice of thought and of action which would seem to make accurate foresight into the future an impossibility.

I am not one who becomes "hot and bothered" because someone accidentally prophesies some event which later happens. The law of chance, or shrewd guesswork, could cover such happenings.

Without this explanation, I would not permit the translations which I have described to appear in this or any other book under my name.

Now, with equal emphasis, I wish to state that the translations I have described may have come from the source indicated in the translations for all I know. I do not say that they did not. I only say I do not believe they came from any source excepting my own mind.

For more than a quarter of a century, I have been engaged in a work of research in the field of mind stimuli. My labor has covered every known field of such stimuli. My labor was prompted by a sincere desire to organize into a philosophy all the dependable forms of mind stimuli which would cause people to use their talents more intelligently.

I have never expected to find anything that would be helpful toward this and in the realm of so-called "miracles." Consequently, if I stumbled upon discoveries which savor of the miraculous, you may be sure the discovery was a genuine surprise to me.

LET US BE OPEN-MINDED

In fairness to myself, and to my thousands of loyal friends and students who are influenced by my work and who believe in my integrity, I am compelled to recognize that this is an age of unfoldment and discovery which staggers the imagination.

Surely, this is not an age favorable to the skeptic of the Doubting Thomas. It is an age which has practically changed the meaning of the word "impossible."

Within the past fifty years, man has conquered the air above him, the sea beneath him and many of the things on the earth's surface which, prior to that time, had puzzled him.

An age which permits man to send the whisper of his voice around the earth in a fraction of a second, with the aid of a carrying agency which he had not previously known to exist, surely is not an age favorable to skepticism and doubt.

I shall continue my contact and experiment with my friends of the "unseen plane of intelligence." If there is such a plane, I shall probably find more substantial evidence of its existence than any I have thus far received. Meanwhile, it can do no harm if any reader of this book chooses to experiment, as I have been doing with the "Invisible Counselors."

Whether my mentors have been real or imaginary, they have led me to wide fields of thought which I could not have reached without them.

Perhaps you may accomplish similar results through experimentation. I recommend that you prove to your own satisfaction, through experiments similar to those I have mentioned, that one may gain unmistakable benefits from such a practice.

HOW OFTEN ARE WE THE VICTIMS OF ILLUSION?

I know that the five physical senses are not reliable. I have proved this many times. Through experiments, I have deceived my own physical senses over and over again.

Many have been the times that I have caused an audience to smell the fumes of oil of cloves which I poured from a bottle on a handkerchief right in front of their own eyes, when in reality the bottle contained only pure water.

Many have been the times that I have drawn a few straight lines on a blackboard in front of an audience, arranging the lines in such a fashion that despite the fact they were all exactly the same length, the audience believed them to be of different lengths.

Many, also, have been the times that I have placed an ordinary marble in the hand of another person, under the tips of the first and second fingers, which had been crossed, with the result that the person holding the marble felt two marbles where his eyes clearly showed that only one existed.

In a similar fashion, I have deceived every one of the five senses. Therefore, I know that they are not always reliable.

May it not be that much of the reality which we believe to be such is illusory? Optical illusions are multitudinous. Everyone is familiar with them.

My contention is that most of the experiences through which the world passed during the 1929 business depression are nothing but illusions. They exist only in the minds of people. The mind can, and does make illusions appear real. What is the essential nature of reality?

While engaged in a most exhaustive study of the religion known as Mormonism, I went in person to the birthplace of Joseph Smith, the founder of the religion.

I stood on the very spot where he alleged that an angel revealed to him the hiding place of the gold plates which he alleged he used in translating the Book of Mormon.

I walked over the very spot where he alleged the plates were uncovered. I stood in the room where he alleged the translations took place. I read the Book of Mormon through very carefully, and despite the fact that it is a literary document far surpassing, in many ways, most books of the Bible, I saw nothing that I would accept as reasonable evidence that Joseph Smith was communicating with any angel, or that he actually had possession of any plates of gold from which the Book of Mormon was translated.

My own theory of that unusual man's experience is that he had, by intensive study of the Bible and other books on religion, so surcharged his own mind with their contents that he created in his mind a spiritual or mental picture, or entity, which might easily have deceived him, no matter how conscientious he might have been in his beliefs.

My own experience with "Invisible Counselors" has proved to me that any thought which a man cherishes deeply and on which he directs his conscious mind daily has a tendency to translate itself, through practical methods, into reality as far as his own mind is concerned.

And right here is an appropriate place at which to call attention to a real benefit which anyone may experience by deliberately focusing attention upon any form of constructive desire. The mind acts upon one's dominating or most pronounced desires. There is no escape from this fact. It is a fact indeed. "Be careful what you set your heart upon, for it surely shall be yours."

CHAPTER THREE

◆

A STRANGE INTERVIEW
WITH THE DEVIL

While you are reading the interview with the Devil, you will recognize from the brief description I have given you of the history of my life what a desperate effort the Devil made to muzzle me before I gained public recognition. You will understand also, after reading the interview with the Devil, why the interview had to be preceded by this personal history of my background.

Before you begin to read the interview, I want you to have a clear picture of the final fling His Majesty had at me, and be it remembered with profit that it was this final fling which gave me my chance to turn and twist the Devil's tail until he squealed out his confession!

The Devil's undoing began with the depression in 1929. Through that fortunate turn of the Wheel of Life, I lost my six hundred-acre estate in the Catskill Mountains; my income was entirely cut off, as the Harrison National Bank in which all my funds were deposited, folded up and was wiped out.

Before I realized what was happening, I found myself caught in the throes of a spiritual and economic hurricane which evolved into a worldwide catastrophe of such force that no individual or group of individuals could withstand it.

While waiting for the storm to cease and the stampede of human fear to stop, I moved to Washington, D.C., the city from which I made my start after my first meeting with Andrew Carnegie, nearly a quarter of a century previously.

There seemed nothing for me to do except sit down and wait. All I had was Time. After three years of waiting without tangible results, my restless soul began to push me back into service.

There was little opportunity for me to teach a philosophy of success when the whole world around me was in the midst of abject failures and men's minds were filled with the fear of poverty.

This thought came to me one evening while I was sitting in my automobile, in front of the Lincoln Memorial on the Potomac River, within the shadow of the Capitol. With it came another thought: The world had staged an unprecedented depression over which no human being had control. With that depression had come to me an opportunity to test the philosophy of self-determination, to the organization of which I devoted the better portion of my adult life.

I now had the opportunity to learn whether my philosophy was practical or mere theory.

I realized too the opportunity had come to test a claim I had made hundreds of times, that "every adversity brings with it the seed of an equivalent advantage." What, if any, I asked myself, were the advantages to me of a world depression?

When I began to look for a direction in which I might move to test my philosophy, I made the most shocking discovery of my life. I discovered that through some strange power which I did not understand, I had lost my courage; my initiative had been demoralized; my enthusiasm had been weakened; and worst of all, I was sorely ashamed to acknowledge that I was the author of a philosophy of self-determination, because down deep in my heart I knew, or thought I knew, that I could not make my philosophy pull me out of the hole of despair in which I found myself.

While I floundered in a state of mental bewilderment, the Devil must have been dancing a jig of rejoicing. At last, he had "the author of the world's first philosophy of individual achievement" pinned under his thumb and paralyzed with indecision.

But, the Devil's opposition must have been at work too!

As I sat there in front of Lincoln's Monument, reviewing in retrospect the circumstances which had so many times previously lifted me to great heights of achievement, only to let me drop to equal depths of despair, a happy thought was handed over to me in the form of a definite plan of action by which I believed I could throw off that hypnotic feeling of indifference with which I had been bound.

In the interview with the Devil, the exact nature of the power by which I had been deprived of my initiative and courage has been described. It is the same power with which millions of others were bound during the 1929 depression. It is the chief weapon with which the Devil ensnares and controls human beings.

The sum and substance of this thought which came to me was this: Despite the fact that I had learned from Andrew Carnegie and more than five hundred others of equal business and professional achievements that noteworthy achievements in all walks of life come through the application of the Master Mind (harmonious coordination of two or more minds working toward a definite end), I had failed to make such an alliance for the purpose of carrying out my plan to take the philosophy of individual achievement to the world.

Despite the fact I had understood the power of the Master Mind, I had neglected to appropriate and use this power. I had been laboring as a "lone wolf" instead of allying myself with other and superior minds.

Let us now briefly analyze the strange interview you are about to begin. Some who read will want to ask, after they finish it, "Did you really interview the Devil, or did you merely interview an imaginary Devil?" Some may wish the answer to this question before they begin the interview.

I will answer in the only truthful way I could answer, by saying the Devil I interviewed may have been real, just as he claimed to be, or he may have been only the creation of my own imagination. Whichever he was, whether real or imaginary, is of little importance compared with the nature of the information conveyed through the interview.

The important question is this: Does the interview convey dependable information which may be helpful to people who are trying to find their places in the world?

If it conveys that sort of information, no matter whether it is conveyed in the form of fact or fiction, then it is worthy of serious analysis through careful reading.

I believe it does convey information of practical benefit to all who have not found Life to be friendly, and the reason I believe so is the fact that I have made the central theme of this book yield to me all the happiness I need, in the form best suited to my nature.

I am not concerned in the least as to the real source of the information, or as to the real nature of the Devil whose astounding story you are about to read.

I am concerned only with the fact that the Devil's confession squares perfectly with what I have seen of Life.

I have had the experience with enough of the principles mentioned by the Devil to assure me that they will do exactly what he says they will.

That is enough for me. So I pass the story of the interview on to you for whatever you may be able to make it pay in useful dividends.

Perhaps you will get the greatest values if you accept the Devil as being what he claims himself to be, relying upon his message for whatever it may bring you that you can use, and not worrying as to who the Devil is or whether he exists.

If you want my honest, personal opinion, I believe the Devil is exactly what he claims to be. Now let us analyze his strange *confession*.

THE DEVIL IS FORCED TO CONFESS!

After forcing his way into the consciousness of the Devil, Mr. Earthbound began the unwilling interview with questions which could not be evaded.

Q. I have uncovered the secret code by which I can pick up your thoughts. I have come to ask you some very plain questions. I demand that you give me direct and truthful answers Are you ready for the interview, Mr. Devil?

A. Yes, I am ready, but you must address me with more respect. During this interview you will address me as Your Majesty!

Q. By what right do you demand such royal respect?

A. You should know I control ninety-eight percent of the people of your world. Do you not think that entitles me to rate as royalty?

Q. Have you proof of your claim, Your Majesty?

A. Yes, plenty of it!

Q. Of what does your proof consist, Your Majesty?

A. Of many things. Some you will understand; some you will not. In order that you may get my viewpoint, I shall describe myself and correct the false notions people have of me and my place of abode.

Q. That is a fine idea, Your Majesty! Start by telling me where you live. Then describe your physical appearance.

A. My physical appearance? Why, my dear Mr. Earthbound, I have no physical body. I would be handicapped by such an encumbrance as those in which you earthbound creatures live. I consist of negative energy, and I live in the minds of people who fear me. I also occupy one half of every atom of physical matter and every unit of mental and physical energy. Perhaps you will better understand my nature if I tell you I am the negative portion of the atom.

Q. Oh, I see what you are preparing to claim. You are laying the foundation to say that if it were not for you, there would be no world, no stars, no electrons, no atoms, no human beings—nothing! Is that correct?

A. True! Absolutely true!

Q. Well, if you only occupy one half of energy and matter, who occupies the other half?

A. The other half is occupied by my opposition!

Q. Opposition? What do you mean?

A. The opposition is what you earthbound call God!

Q. So, you have the universe divided up with God! Is that your claim?

A. Not my claim, but the actual fact. Before this interview is finished, you will understand why my claim is true. You will also understand why it has to be true, or there could be no world such as yours, no earthbound creatures such as you. I am no beast with a forked tongue and a spike tail.

Q. But you do control the minds of ninety-eight out of every one hundred people. You said so yourself! Who causes all the misery in this ninety-eight percent Devil-controlled world, if you do not?

A. I have not said that I do not cause all the misery of the world. On the other hand, I boast of it! It is my business to represent the negative side of everything, including the thoughts of you earthbound people. How else could I control people? My opposition controls positive thought. I control negative thought. Ever since the first creature crawled out of the water on your earth, millions of years ago, I have specialized in the control of earthbound dwellers.

Q. How do you gain control of the minds of people?

A. Oh, that is easy! I merely move in and occupy the unused space of the human brain. I sow the seeds of negative thought in the minds of people so I can occupy and control the space!

Q. You must have many tricks and devices by which you gain and hold control of the human mind.

A. To be sure, I employ tricks and devices to control human thought. My devices are clever ones too. (The Devil begins to boast. Now we shall learn something of his real nature.)

Q. Go ahead and describe some of your clever tricks, Your Majesty.

A. I refuse to do so on the grounds that such a confession would destroy my control over all who hear of it.

Q. Then I shall take advantage of my knowledge of the secret passageway to your thoughts and describe your tricks in my own language.

A. No! no! Don't do that. You would only malign me, as all other earthbound people do when they speak of me. I shall confess in my own way, but you are taking unfair advantage.

Q. It is you who are on the defensive, Your Majesty. Tell us all about the tricks and devices you use in the control of people's minds, and remember I want the whole story—not just the part of it which is favorable to you. Why hedge about answering, Your Majesty? You who boast of controlling ninety-eight out of every hundred people on this earth should be proud of your record, and especially so in view of the fact that Omnipotence is your opposition.

A. One of my cleverest devices for mind control is fear. I plant the seed of fear in the minds of people, and as these seeds germinate and grow, through use, I control the space they occupy. The six most effective fears are: the fear of poverty, the fear of criticism, the fear of ill health, the fear of loss of love, the fear of old age, and the fear of death.

Q. Which of these six fears serves you most often, Your Majesty?

A. The first and the last—poverty and death! At one time or another during life, I tighten my grip on all people through one or both of these. I plant these fears in the minds of people so deftly that they believe them to be their own creation.

Q. Very, very clever, Your Majesty! Now tell us something more of your devices for the control of the human mind.

A. One of my tricks is the method by which I cause people to fear old age and death, so I occupy most of the space of their minds through these fears. I accomplish this by making people believe I am standing just beyond the entrance gate to the next life, waiting to claim them after death, for eternal punishment. Of course I cannot punish anyone, *except in that person's own mind* through some form of fear, but fear of the thing that does not exist is just as useful to me as fear of that which does exist. All forms of fear extend the space I occupy in the human mind.

Q. Your Majesty, I did not know your control over human beings was so great. Will you explain how you gained this control?

A. The story is too long to be told in a few words. It began over a million years ago, when the first man began to think. Up to that time, I had control over all mankind, but enemies of mine discovered the power of positive thought, placed it in the minds of men, and then began a battle on my part to remain in control. So far, I have done quite well by myself, having lost only two percent of the people to the opposition.

Q. I take it from your answer that men who think are your enemies. Is that right?

A. It is not RIGHT, but it is correct.

Q. Tell me something more about the world in which you live.

A. I live wherever I choose. Time and space do not exist with me. I am a force best described to you as energy. My favorite physical dwelling place, as I have told you, is the minds of the earthbound. I control a part of the brain space of every human being. The amount of space I occupy in each individual's mind depends upon how little, and what sort of, thinking that person does. As I have told you, I cannot entirely control any person who thinks!

Q. You say you exist in the form of force or energy. Will Your Majesty state whether this force is negative or positive?

A. The form of power in which I exist is negative! The opposition controls the positive forces, and I control the negatives. That is why I am so powerful. I control the forces of hate, fear, vanity, avarice, greed, revenge, superstition and lust. These are the forces which rule the world, and I control ninety-eight percent of the people of the world because I control these forces.

Q. You speak of your opposition. Just what do you mean by that?

A. My opponent controls all the positive forces of the world, such as love, faith, hope and optimism. My opponent also controls the positive factors of all natural law throughout the universe, the forces which keep the earth and the planets and all the stars balanced in their courses, but these forces are meek in comparison with those which operate in the human mind under my control. You see, I do not seek to control stars and planets. I prefer the control of human minds.

Q. Where did you acquire your power, and by what means do you add to it?

A. I add to my power by approaching the mind-power of the earthbound, as they come through the gate at the time of death. Ninety-eight out of every hundred who come back to my plane from the earth plane are taken over by me and their mind-power is added to my being. I get all who come over with any form of fear. You see, I am constantly at work, preparing the minds of people before death, so I can appropriate them when they come back to my plane.

Q. Will you tell me how you go about your job of preparing human minds so you can control them?

A. I have countless ways of gaining control of human minds while they are still on the earth plane. My greatest weapon is poverty. I deliberately discourage people from accumulating material wealth because poverty discourages men from thinking and makes them easy prey for me. My next best friend is ill health. An unhealthy body discourages thinking. Then I have countless thousands of workers on earth who aid me in gaining control of human minds. I have these agents placed in every calling. They represent every race and creed, every religion.

Q. Do I understand Your Majesty to say you have workers in all religions?

A. Most of the churches are my greatest allies, although their leaders and members do not know it. Billy Sunday, for example, was a great worker of mine. If I had a hundred such men on earth at one time, I would control it in one generation.

Q. I always understood that Billy Sunday represented your opposition, that he fought you bitterly. How do you happen to claim him as one of your workers?

A. Mr. Earthbound, you give me a big laugh!

I can see that you know little or nothing about psychology. Of course, Billy Sunday fought me. I had him kick me all over the stage, throw me on the floor, jump on me, choke me, and go through all those silly antics of which he was so fond, to keep people from discovering he was my agent.

You may not know it, Mr. Earthbound, but the best way to advertise an idea is by attacking it.

Look what my agents did with the Anti-Saloon League. I had them fight the saloons. I had them pass the prohibition laws, and look what happened! As soon as liquor was forbidden by law, *almost everyone began to drink.*

Now I ask you to take a look at my modernistic, streamlined saloons which supplanted the old-style places. I have made the saloon a place for smart social gatherings.

I have taught women and young girls to go into the saloon by the front door and sit at the bar, where they drink and show off their physical charms to best advantage.

Take a walk down Broadway some day during cocktail hour and see what I have done to add women customers to my list, through the psychology of prohibition.

Q. I think I get your point of view, Your Majesty, but I fail to see how Billy Sunday helped your cause. Will you explain this?

A. Let me state it this way. Men come to resemble the thoughts that dominate their minds! By presenting Billy Sunday to the world in the name of opposition, to attack and vilify me, don't you see how simple it was for me to fix the attention of people on the negative side of life?

I had Billy Sunday talk about fear, and sin, and liquor, and lust, and all the other negatives until these influences became the dominating forces of the minds of his followers.

As fast as the Billy Sunday followers come over to this plane, I catch them at the gate because they come with their minds saturated with fear.

Q. Do you have other workers in the churches who are helping your cause?

A. Oh yes! Thousands of them. But most of them are not as effective as Sunday was. He was a great dramatist, with the ability to take possession of the imagination of those who listened to him. I seldom have more than one Billy Sunday on earth during a generation.

Q. Am I to understand, Your Majesty, that all church leaders who fill the minds of people with fear of you are your allies?

A. That is correct. Without these ignorant, but friendly, workers my cause would suffer.

Q. Why do say friendly allies? Surely you do not claim that church leaders who teach Christianity are your friendly allies?

A. They are my friendly allies because they teach what I want taught, but do it in the name of my opposition! Any person who serves my purpose is friendly. Church leaders could hardly serve me effectively if they praised me. Do you now get the idea?

Q. While we are on the subject of the churches, will you give me a brief description of what you think is wrong with them?

A. The main weakness of the churches is that the clergy is concentrating upon the dead past and the yet unborn future, while letting the realistic present go to hell.

Q. Is that the fault of the clergy entirely?

A. No! Emphatically not. Most preachers are preaching what their followers wish to hear more often than what they themselves believe. Their hands are tied by those who pay their salaries.

Q. You think in effect that preachers generally are perjuring themselves in order to satisfy their flocks?

A. I wouldn't put it just that way. I would rather say they are engaging in pious fraud. Moreover, anything a man repeats over and over again, he soon embraces as truth, although he may have known at the beginning that it was untrue.

Q. Who are your greatest enemies on earth, Your Majesty?

A.   All who inspire people to think and act on their own initiative are my enemies. Such men as Socrates, Confucius, Voltaire, Emerson, Thomas Paine, Abraham Lincoln, and the more recent Robert G. Ingersoll and Elbert Hubbard. And you are not doing me any good!

Q.   Is it true that you use men who have great wealth?

A.   As I have already told you, poverty is always my friend because it discourages independence of thought and encourages fear in the minds of men. Some wealthy men serve my cause while others do me great damage, depending upon how the wealth is used. The great Rockefeller fortune, for example, is one of my worst enemies.

Q.   That is interesting, Your Majesty. Will you tell me why you fear the Rockefeller fortune more than others?

A.   The Rockefeller money is being used to isolate and conquer diseases of the physical body, in all parts of the world. Disease has always been one of my most effective weapons. The fear of ill health is second only to the fear of poverty. The Rockefeller money is uncovering new secrets of nature in a hundred different directions, all of which are designed to help men take and keep possession of their own minds.

It is encouraging new and better methods of feeding, clothing, and housing people. It is wiping out the slums in the large cities, the places where my favorite allies are found.

It is financing campaigns for better government and helping to wipe out dishonesty in politics.

It is helping to set higher standards in business practice and encouraging business men to conduct business by the Golden Rule, and that is not doing my cause any good.

Q.   Who are some of the other wealthy men whom you believe are endangering your cause?

A. Henry Ford is not doing me any good. His horseless buggy has cost me millions of recruits, and it is destined to cost me additional millions. You see, Ford caused the world to become good-roads conscious. This wiped out frontiers and brought all people closer together.

When people get together, they talk, *and sometimes they think*! Ford hurt me in other ways—chiefly by setting higher wage scales and effectively fighting my allies who serve me through organized labor. But, I shall soon have him humbled. My chief labor racketeer will bring Ford to his knees. Watch and you will see.

Q. So, some of the labor leaders are on your side of the fence?

A. Oh, yes, but I suspect some of being too friendly with my opposition. That doesn't help my cause. What I need are men who rule by fear and determination; men who are not afraid to line up their entire following and sell it out to politicians in return for special class privilege laws, such as the Wagner Act.

Q. Your Majesty, what about these boys and girls who are said to be on the road to hell? Are you in control of them?

A. Well, I can answer that question only with yes and no. I have corrupted the minds of the young by teaching them to drink and smoke, but they have me baffled through their tendency to think for themselves.

I used to control young people through fear of their parents, but that is a thing of the past. Alas, boys and girls are learning to think and act on their own, and if this keeps up, I shall be ruined in another generation.

Q. I take it from your answer that young people are getting out from under your control.

A. Yes, they are, because they are learning to think for themselves.

Q. You say you have corrupted the minds of the young people with liquor and cigarettes. I can understand how liquor might destroy the power of independent thought, but I do not see what cigarettes have to do with helping your cause.

A. You are like millions of other people in this respect. You may not know it, but cigarettes break down the power of persistence; they destroy the power of endurance; they destroy the ability to concentrate; they deaden and undermine the imaginative faculty, and help in other ways to keep people from using their minds most effectively.

Do you know, I have millions of people, young and old, of both sexes, who smoke two packages of cigarettes a day? That means I have millions of people who are gradually destroying their power of resistance.

One day I shall add to their habit of cigarette smoking other thought-destroying habits, until I shall have gained control of their minds.

Habits come in pairs, triplets and quadruplets. Any habit which weakens one's willpower invites quadruplets. Any habit which weakens one's willpower invites a flock of its relatives to move in and take possession of the mind. The cigarette habit not only lowers the power of resistance and discourages persistence, but it invites looseness in other human relationships.

Q. How did you induce young people to take up this cigarette habit?

A. Ah, there is a story for you! Just after World War I, I saw that young boys and girls were beginning to think for themselves, and I had to think fast—do something to counteract this. I started by inducing them to drink liquor on the theory that it was smart.

The idea worked so well that I introduced cigarettes as being smart.

The trick was turned through clever psychology. Do you remember these advertisements in which were portrayed the scene of a young man and an attractive young women lying on the sand at the beach, in bathing suits, with the young men smoking a cigarette while the girl looked on with admiration?

Do you remember how the girl reclined in a suggestive manner, with bare legs?

At first, I dared not show the girl smoking a cigarette, but gradually I had her light the cigarette for her companion. After the public had accepted this advertisement, without tearing down the billboards and canceling newspaper subscriptions, I took another step and showed the girl lighting the cigarette in her own mouth and then handing it to her male companion, with plenty of sex suggestion in the posture of the two, in their clothing, in the look in their eyes. Then, I took the final step and came out boldly with advertising that showed young women smoking cigarettes. But I did it in such a way that I portrayed cigarette smoking as a smart habit. That is where I hooked the female cigarette smokers and converted millions of women to the habit.

High school girls, college girls, and women in all walks of life are rapidly taking up the smoking of cigarettes. Many of them are in the two-package-a-day class. It is no secret that this habit has not been beneficial to them. Young people may assert their rights to independence of action and thought, as far as their parents are concerned, but they are not smart enough to deceive me. I am gaining control over them through the cigarette habit.

Q. I never thought that cigarettes were a tool of destruction, Your Majesty, but your explanation throws a different light on the subject. How many converts to the habit do you now claim?

A. I am proud of my record. Millions are now victims, and the number is increasing daily. Soon I shall have most of the world indulging in the habit. In thousands of families, I now have followers of the habit including every member of the family. Very young boys and girls are beginning to take up the habit. They are learning how to smoke by observing their parents and older brothers and sisters.

Q. Which do you consider to be your greater tool for gaining control of human minds—cigarettes or liquor?

A. Without hesitation, I would say cigarettes. Once I get a young person to join my two-package-a-day club, I have no trouble in inducing that person to take on the habit of liquor, over-indulgence in sex, and all other related habits which destroy independence of thought and action.

You may not know it, but I have many cigarette companies working night and day turning out hundreds of millions of packages of cigarettes daily for my followers. These companies are cleaning up millions of dollars on profits annually, but I am hooking millions of followers of my cause.

Q. Tell me about some of the other traps through which you snare people.

A. Well, take the popular game of Bridge, for example. I have elevated this to a position of affluence so that it is now one of my greatest assets. I use it to convert wives and young girls into gamblers, thieves and gossipers.

Q. I never thought of Bridge as a vice. Wherein does it help your cause?

A. Any habit which is stronger than the human will is my friend. The gambling habit converts people into cheats, liars and the like. Bridge is one of my most ingenious devices. Through this growing fad, I take women away from running their homes and start them to gossiping about one another.

I teach them to gamble and to steal money from the household budget so they can pay their losses. I take them away from their children while they are playing Bridge, and I can then have a freer hand with the children.

I cause them to lose at their game so they will go home in a bad humor and make things unpleasant for their husbands. All this tends to upset the household and set everyone's nerves on edge. It is one of my cleverest tricks, and you might be surprised to know how many converts I have won through it, mostly women.

Q. Your Majesty, I am interested in your clever scheme to break down willpower through the cigarette habit. I would like for you to tell me why so many professional people, like moving picture stars and stage celebrities, endorse cigarettes.

A. That is a natural question. Many people who endorse cigarettes are liars for a price. For a hundred dollars I can get many people to endorse almost anything. My friends, the advertising men, have a regular catalogue of prices they pay for such endorsers. The price depends upon the popularity of the endorser.

Q. Your Majesty, when I began this interview, I had you all wrong. I thought you were a fraud and a fake, but I see now that you are quite real, and very powerful.

A. Your apology is accepted, but you need not have bothered. Millions of people have questioned my power, and I got most of them at the gate as they came over.

I ask no person to believe in me. I prefer that people fear me.

I am no beggar! I take what I want by cleverness and force. Begging people to believe is the business of my opposition, not mine.

All I ask is the privilege of entering people's minds and planting there the seed of my negative philosophy. All I want is to be permitted to retain this privilege of entertaining minds at will. Once I get in, I will attend to my own business and win a convert to my cause.

Q. Your Majesty will please pardon my rudeness, but I would not be able to look myself in the face again if I did not tell you, here and now, that you are the damnedest fiend ever to be turned loose on innocent people.

I always had the wrong conception of you, Your Majesty. I thought you were kind enough to let people alone while they were living, that you merely tortured their souls after death. Now I learn, from your own brazen confession, that you destroy their right to freedom of thought and cause them to go through a living hell on earth. What do you have to say to that?

A. His Majesty, the Devil, *never loses self-control*!

Q. Is that all you have to say?

A. Is that not enough? I got what I want by exercising self-control. It is not so good for my own business, but I suggest that your business on earth can best be attended to if you emulate me instead of criticizing me. You call yourself a thinker, and you are. Otherwise you would never have forced this interview on me. But you will never be the sort of thinker that frightens me unless you gain and exercise greater control over your own emotions. Now, if that be treason, then make the most of it!

Q. Let us get away from personalities, Your Majesty. I came here to learn more about you, not to discuss myself. Please go ahead with your story and tell me of the many tricks you have devised for gaining control of the human mind. What is your most powerful weapon just now?

A. That is a difficult question to answer. I have so very many devices for entering human minds and controlling them that it is difficult to say which are the most powerful.

Right at the moment, I am trying to bring about another world war. My friends here in Washington are helping me to involve America in the war. If I can start the world to killing on a wholesale basis, I shall be able to put into operation my favorite device for mind control. It is what you may call mass fear.

I used this device to bring about the other world war in 1914. I used it to bring about the Republican depression in 1929, and if my opposition had not double-crossed me, I would now be in possession of every man, woman and child in the world. You can see for yourself how near I came to world domination—the thing I have been struggling to attain for thousands of years.

Q. Yes, I see your point, Your Majesty. Who wouldn't? You are a very ingenious manipulator of the minds of people. Is your devilish business carried on only through people of high position and great influence?

A. Oh, no! I use minds of people in all walks of life. As a matter of fact, I prefer the type of person who makes no pretense of thinking. I can manipulate that sort of person without difficulty. I could not control ninety-eight percent of the people of the world if all people were skilled in thinking for themselves.

Q. I am interested in the welfare of those ninety-eight out of every hundred people whom you claim to control. Therefore, I wish you to tell me all of the tricks by which you enter and control their minds. I want a complete confession from you, so begin with your cleverest trick, Your Majesty.

A. This is suicide you are forcing on me, but I am helpless! So settle down and I will place in your hands the weapon by which millions of your fellow-earthbound will defend themselves against me.

CHAPTER FOUR

◆

DRIFTING WITH THE DEVIL

Q. Go right ahead now, and tell me first about your most clever trick—the one you use to ensnare the greatest number of people.

A. If you force me to give away this secret, it will mean my loss of millions of people now living and still greater numbers of millions as yet unborn. I beg of you to permit me to pass this one question unanswered. (We have His Majesty on the run. Now let us watch him squirm.)

Q. So, His Majesty, the Devil, fears a mere humble earthbound creature! Is that right?

A. It is not right, but it is true! You have no right to rob me of my most necessary tool of trade. For millions of years, I have dominated earthbound creatures through fear and ignorance. Now you come along and destroy my use of these weapons by forcing me to tell how I use them. Do you not realize that you will break my grip on every person who heeds this confession you are forcing from me? Have you no mercy? Have you no sense of humor? Have you no sportsmanship? Have you no pride in minding your own business?

Q. Stop stalling, Your Majesty, and start confessing. Who are you to ask mercy of one whom you would destroy if you could?

Who are you to talk of sportsmanship and a sense of humor? You, who by your own confession, have set up a living hell on earth, where you punish innocent people through their fears and their ignorance? As for minding my own business, that is just what I am doing when I force you to tell how you control people through their own minds. My business, if it can be called a business, is helping to unlock doors of the self-made prisons in which men and women are confined because of the fears you have planted in their minds. Now let us come to the point and begin your dethronement.

A. My greatest weapon over human beings consists of two secret principles by which I gain control of their minds. I will speak first of the principles of habit, through which I silently enter the minds of people. By operating through this principle, I establish the habit of (I wish I could avoid using this word) the habit of drifting! When a person begins to drift on any subject, he is headed straight toward the gates of what you earthbound call Hell!

Q. Describe all the ways in which you induce people to drift. Define the word and tell us exactly what you mean by it.

A. I can best define the word drift by saying that people who think for themselves never drift, while those who do little or no thinking for themselves are drifters. A drifter is one who permits himself to be influenced and controlled by circumstances outside of his own mind.

A drifter is one who would rather let me occupy his mind and do his thinking than go to the trouble of thinking for himself. A drifter is one who accepts whatever Life throws in his way, without making a protest or putting up a fight. A drifter is one who doesn't know what he wants from Life, and spends all of his time getting just that. A drifter has lots of opinions, but they are not his own. Most of them are supplied by me. A drifter is one who is too lazy mentally to use his own brain.

That is the reason I can take control of people's thinking and plant my own ideas in their minds.

Q. I think I understand what a drifter is, Your Majesty. Go ahead now and tell me the exact habits of people by which you induce them to drift through life. Start by telling me when and how you first gain control of a person's mind.

A. My control over the mind of a human being is obtained while the person is young! Sometimes I lay the foundation for my control of a mind before the owner of it is born, by manipulating the minds of that person's parents. Sometimes I go further back than this and prepare people for my control through what you earthbound call physical heredity. You see, therefore, I have two approaches to the mind of a person.

Q. Yes, Your Majesty, go on and describe these two doors by which you enter and control the minds of human beings.

A. As I have stated, I help to bring people into your world with weak brains by giving to them, before birth, as many as possible of the weaknesses of their ancestors. You call this principle physical heredity. After people are born, I make use of what you earthbound call environment as a means of controlling them. This is where the principle of habit enters. The mind is nothing more than the sum total of one's habits! One by one, I enter the mind and establish habits which lead finally to my absolute domination of the mind.

Q. That is interesting, Your Majesty. Go on now and tell me of the most common habits by which you control the minds of people. Go into details. Tell me exactly how you operate in other people's minds without them detecting your presence!

A. That is one of my cleverest tricks! (His Majesty starts to brag again.) I enter the minds of people through thoughts *which they believe to be their own.* This is where physical heredity comes in handy. You see, people are born with certain traits brought over at birth, which they have inherited from their ancestors, dating back to primitive beginning in the animalistic world. Through these traits of instinct and physical character, I can easily deceive people into believing that my thoughts are their own.

Q. What are some of these inborn traits of people of which you make such effective use in controlling them?

A. Those most useful to me are fear, superstition, avarice, greed, lust, revenge, anger, vanity and plain laziness! Through one or more of these, I can enter any mind, at any age, but I get my best results when I take charge of a mind while it is young, before its owner has learned how to close any of these nine doors. Then I can set up habits which keep the doors ajar forever.

Q. I am catching on to your methods, Your Majesty. Now let us go back to the habit of drifting. Tell us all about that habit since you say it is your cleverest trick in controlling the minds of people.

A. As I said before, I start people drifting during their youth! I induce them to drift through school without knowing what occupation they wish to follow in life. Here I catch the majority of people. Habits are related. Drift in one direction and soon you will be drifting in all directions. Often I send people into the world so handicapped physically that they are forced to drift on all subjects. But I do not depend upon physical heredity alone to gain control of people and cause them to drift into my control. I use environmental habits to give me a definite grip on my victims.

Q. I see! Your Majesty, you make it your business to train children in the habit of drifting by inducing them to go through school without aim or purpose. Now tell me of some of your other tricks with which you cause people to become drifters.

A. Well, my second best trick in developing the habit of drifting is one that I put into operation with the aid of parents and public school teachers and religious instructors. I warn you not to force me to mention this trick. If you do so, you will be hated by my co-workers who help me use this trick. If you publish this confession in book form, your book will be barred from the public schools.

It will be blacklisted by most of the religious leaders. It will be hidden from children by many parents. The newspapers will not dare to give reviews of your book. Millions of people will hate you for writing the book. In fact, no one will like you or your book except those who think, and you know how very few there are of this sort! My advice to you is to let me skip the description of my second best trick.

Q. So, for my own good, you wish to withhold the description of your second best trick. No one will like my book except those who think, eh? Very well, go ahead and answer.

A. You'll regret this, Mr. Earthbound, but the joke is on you. By this mistake of yours you will divert attention from me to yourself. My co-workers, of whom there are millions, will forget about me and hate you for uncovering my methods.

Q. Never mind about me, Your Majesty. Go ahead and tell me all about this second best trick of yours with which you induce people to drift with you to Hell.

A. My second best trick is not second at all. It is first! It is first because without it, I never could gain control of the minds of the youths.

Q. That is interesting. It seems that I have stumbled upon something very important, so proceed.

A. Parents, schoolteachers, religious instructors and many other adults unknowingly serve my purpose by helping me to destroy in children the habit of thinking for themselves. They go about their work in various ways, never suspecting what they are doing to the minds of children, or the real cause of their mistakes.

Q. I can hardly believe you, Your Majesty. I have always believed that children's best friends were those closest to them, their parents, their schoolteachers and their religious instructors. Where would children go for dependable guidance if not to those who have charge of them?

A. Ah! *There is where my cleverness comes in.* There is the exact explanation of how I control ninety-eight percent of the people of the world.

I take possession of people during their youth, before they come into possession of their own minds, by using those who are in charge of them. I especially need the help of those who give children their religious instruction, because it is here that I break down independent thought and start people on the habit of drifting, by confusing their minds with unprovable ideas concerning a world of which they know nothing. It is here, also, that I plant in the minds of children the greatest of all fears—the fear of Hell!

Q. I understand how it is easy for you to frighten children with threats of Hell, but how do you continue to make them fear you and your Hell after they grow up and learn to think for themselves?

A. Ah! Children grow up, but they do not always learn to think for themselves! Once I capture the mind of a child, through fear, I weaken that child's ability to reason and to think for himself, and that weakness goes with the child all through life.

Q. Is that not taking unfair advantage of a human being, contaminating his mind before he comes into full possession of it?

A. Everything is fair that I can use to further my ends. I have no foolish limitations of right and wrong. Might is right with me. I use every known human weakness to gain and keep control of the human mind.

Q. I understand your devilish nature! Now let us get back to further discussion of your methods of inducing people to drift to Hell here on earth. From your confession, I see that you take charge of children while their minds are young and pliable. Tell me more of how you use parents, teachers and religious leaders to ensnare people into drifting.

A. One of my favorite tricks is to coordinate the efforts of parents and religious instructors so they work together in helping me destroy the children's power to think for themselves. I use religious instructors to undermine the courage and power of independent thought of children, by teaching them to fear me; but I use parents to aid the religious leaders in this great work of mine.

Q. How do parents help religious leaders destroy their children's power to think for themselves? I never heard of such a monstrosity!

A. I accomplish this through a very clever trick. I cause the parents to teach their children to believe as they (the parents) do in connection with religion, politics, marriage, and other important subjects. In this way, as you can see, when I gain control of the mind of a person I can easily perpetuate the control by causing that person to help me fasten it upon the minds of his offspring.

Q. In what other ways do you use parents to convert children into drifters?

A. I cause children to become drifters by following the example of their parents, most of whom I have already taken over and bound eternally to my cause. In some parts of the world, I gain mastery over children's minds and subdue their willpower in exactly the same way that men break and subdue animals of lower intelligence. It makes no difference to me how a child's will is subdued; as long as it fears something, I will enter its mind through that fear and limit the child's power to think independently.

Q. It seems that you go out of your way to keep people from thinking?

A. Yes! Accurate thought is death to me. I cannot exist in the minds of those who think accurately. I do not mind people thinking as long as they *think in terms of fear, discouragement, hopelessness and destructiveness.* When they begin to think in constructive terms of faith, courage, hope and definiteness of purpose, they immediately become allies of my opposition, and are therefore lost to me.

Q. So, you want people to think so long as they think your way! Is that correct?

A. Oh, yes, I not only want them to think, but I keep them busy believing that they think. Only in this way can I make them believe my ideas are their own.

Q. I am beginning to understand how you gain control of the minds of children through the help of their parents and religious instructors, but I do not see how the schoolteachers help you in this damnable work.

A. Schoolteachers help me gain control of the minds of children, not so much by what they teach the children as because of what they do not teach them. The entire public school system is so administered that it helps my cause by teaching children almost everything except how to use their own minds and think independently! I live in fear that some day some courageous person will reverse the present system of school teaching and deal my cause a death blow by allowing the students to become the instructors, using those who now serve as teachers only as guides to help the children establish ways and means of developing their own minds from within. When that time comes, the schoolteachers will no longer belong to my staff.

Q. I was under the impression that the purpose of all schooling was to help children to think.

A. That may be the purpose of schooling, but the system in most of the schools of the world do not carry out the purpose. School children are taught, not to develop and use their own minds, but to adopt and use the thoughts of others. This sort of schooling destroys the capacity for independent thought, except in a few rare cases where children rely so definitely upon their own willpower that they refuse to allow others to do their thinking.

Q. As I understand you, the churches, the schools and the homes of the world are all allied with your cause, to a degree, and all of them are helping you to convert people into drifters. Is that your claim?

A. Not merely my claim, but the actual fact!

Q. If your claim is correct, you control almost everything civilization represents. If your allies are found in the homes, in the public and private schools, in the churches, where could one turn for dependable help in learning how to think accurately?

A. Accurate thought is the business of my opposition, not mine!

Q. What relationship, if any, has your opposition with the homes, the churches and the schools? Your reply to this question should be interesting.

A. Here is where I make use of some more of my clever tricks. I cause it to appear that everything done by the parents, the schoolteachers and the religious instructors is being done by my opposition.

This diverts attention from me while I manipulate the minds of the young. When religious instructors try to teach children the virtues of my opposition, they generally do so by frightening them with my name.

That is all I ask of them. I kindle the flame of fear into proportions which destroy the child's power to think accurately. In the public schools the teachers further my cause by keeping the children so busy cramming nonessential information into their minds they have no opportunity to think accurately or to analyze correctly the things their religious instructors teach them.

In the homes, the parents say family prayers and ready the family Bible and talk vaguely in the name of my opposition, of the glories to come after death, but they restrain their children from doing any independent thinking on the subject of Life and Death. This leads to indecision, fear and the fixed habit of drifting!

Q. Do you claim, for your cause, all those who are bound by the habit of drifting?

A. No! Drifting is only one of my tricks through which I take over the power of independent thought. Before a drifter becomes my permanent property, I must lead him on and ensnare him with another trick. I will tell you about this other trick after I finish describing my methods of converting people into drifters.

Q. Do you mean you have a method by which you can cause people to drift so far away from self-determination that they can never save themselves?

A. Yes, a definite method! And it is so effective it never fails.

Q. Do I understand you to claim your method is so powerful your opposition cannot reclaim those whom you have permanently ensnared through drifting?

A. I claim just that! Did I not tell you in the beginning that I control ninety-eight out of every hundred people living? Do you think I would control so many people if my opposition could prevent me? Nothing can stop me from controlling people *except people themselves.*

Nothing can stop me except the power of accurate thought. People who think accurately do not drift on any subject. They recognize the power of their own minds. Moreover, they take over that power and yield it to no person or influence.

Q. I understand, from your claims, that your opposition controls very few people.

A. My opposition controls only two out of every hundred—the two who think for themselves.

Q. Go ahead and tell me more of the methods by which you cause people to drift to Hell with you!

A. I cause people to drift on every subject through which I can control independent thought and action. Take the subject of health, for example. I cause most people to eat too much food and the wrong sort of food. This leads to indigestion and destroys the power of accurate thought. If the public schools and the churches taught children more about proper eating, they would do my cause irreparable damage.

Marriage: I cause men and women to drift into marriage without plan or purpose designed to convert the relationship into harmony. Here is one of my most effective methods of converting people into the habit of drifting.

I cause married people to bicker and nag one another over money matters.

I cause them to quarrel over the bringing up of their children.

I engage them in unpleasant controversies over their intimate relationships.

I engage them in disagreements over friends and social activities.

I keep them so busy finding fault with one another that they never have time to do anything else long enough to break the habit of drifting.

Occupation: I teach people to become drifters by causing them to drift out of school into the first job they can find, with no definite aim or purpose except to make a living. Through this trick, I keep millions of people in fear of poverty all their lives. Through this fear, I lead them slowly but surely onward until they reach the point beyond which no individual ever has broken the drifting habit.

Savings: I cause people to spend freely and to save sparingly or not at all, until I take complete control of them through their fear of poverty!

Environment: I cause people to drift into inharmonious and unpleasant environments in the home, in their place of occupation, in their relationship with relatives and acquaintances, and to remain there until I claim them through the habit of drifting.

Dominating Thoughts: I cause people to drift into the habit of thinking negative thoughts. This leads to negative acts and involves people in controversies and fills their minds with fears, thus paving the way for me to enter and control their minds. When I move in, I do so by appealing to people through negative thought in the minds of people through the pulpit, the newspapers, the moving pictures, the radio and all other popular methods of appeal to the mind. I cause people to allow me to do their thinking for them because they are too lazy and too indifferent to think for themselves.

Q. I conclude, from what you say, that drifting and procrastination are the same. Is that true?

A. Yes, that is correct. Any habit which causes one to procrastinate—to put off reaching a definite decision—leads to the habit of drifting.

Q. Is man the only creature who drifts?

A. Yes. All other creatures move in response to definite laws of nature. Man alone defies nature's laws and drifts when he will.

The stars and planets are fixed in their courses. They move in response to laws from which they cannot deviate. If nature permitted the stars to drift, there would be chaos throughout the universe. There could be no world and no man to drift through it.

Everything outside the minds of men is controlled by my opposition, by laws so definite that drifting is impossible. I control the minds of men solely because of their habit of drifting, which is only another way of saying that I control the minds of men only because they neglect or refuse to control and use their own minds.

Q. This is getting to be pretty deep stuff for a mere human being. Let us get back to the discussion of something less abstract. Please tell me how this drifting habit affects people in the everyday walks of life, and tell me in terms the average person can understand.

A. I would prefer to keep this interview up among the stars!

Q. No doubt you would. That would save you from being exposed. But let us come back to earth. Tell me now what drifting is doing to us as a nation here in the United States.

A. It is a bitter pill you have asked me to swallow.

Q. What is bitter about it? Do you not like to discuss the people of the United States?

A. Frankly, I may as well tell you that I hate the United States as only the Devil can hate.

Q. That is interesting. What is the cause of this hatred?

A. The cause was born on July 4, 1776, when fifty-six men signed a document which destroyed my chances of controlling the nation. You know that document as the Declaration of Independence. Had it not been for the influence of that damnable document, I would now have a dictator running the country and I would stop this right to free speech and independent thought that is threatening my rule on earth.

Q. Am I to understand, from what you say, that nations controlled by self-appointed dictators belong in your camp?

A. There are no self-appointed dictators. I appoint them all. Moreover, I manipulate them and direct them in their work. Nations run by my dictators know what they want and take it by force! Look what I have done through Mussolini in Italy! Look what I am doing through Hitler in Germany! Look what I am doing through Stalin in Russia. My dictators run those nations for me because the people have been subdued through the habit of drifting. My dictators do no drifting. That is why they rule for me the millions of people under their control.

Q. What would happen if Mussolini, Stalin and Hitler turned traitors and disavowed you and your rule?

A. That will not happen because I have them too well-bribed. I am paying each of them *with the sop of his own vanity*, by making him believe he is acting on his own account. That is another trick of mine.

Q. Let us come back to the United States and learn something of what you are doing to convert people into the habit of drifting.

A. Right now, I am paving the way for a dictatorship by sowing the seeds of fear and uncertainty in the minds of the people.

Q. Through whom are you carrying on your work?

A. Mainly through the President. I am destroying his influence with the people by causing him to drift on the question of a working agreement between employers and their employees. If I can induce him to drift for another year, he will be so thoroughly discredited I can hand over the country to a dictator. If the President continues to drift, I will paralyze personal freedom in the United States just as I destroyed it in Spain, Italy, Germany and England.

Q. What you say leads me to the conclusion that drifting is a weakness which inevitably ends in failure, whether among individuals or nations. Is that your claim?

A. Drifting is the most common cause of failure in every walk of life. I can control anyone whom I can induce to form the habit of drifting on any subject. The reason for this is two-fold. First, the drifter is just so much putty in my hands, to be molded into whatever pattern I choose, because drifting destroys the power of individual initiative. Second, the drifter cannot get help from my opposition, because the opposition is not attracted to anything so soft and useless.

Q. Is it not possible for a drifter to attain success in the world through the law of chance?

A. The drifter may come into possession of advantageous opportunity through the law of chance, but he will not attain success through it because he will lose it to another who does not drift.

Q. Is that why a few people are wealthy while the majority of people are poor?

A. That is exactly the reason. Poverty, like physical illness, is a contagious disease. You find it always among the drifters, *never among those who know what they want and are determined to get just that*! It may mean something to you when I call your attention to the fact that the non-drifters which I do not control, and those who possess most of the wealth of the world, happen to be the same people.

Q. I have always understood that money was the root of all evil, that the poor and the meek would inherit heaven, while the wealthy would pass into your hands. What have you to say of that claim?

A. I have this to say—men who know how to get the material things of life generally know how to keep out of the hands of the Devil as well. The ability to acquire things is contagious. Drifters acquire nothing except that which no one else wants. If more people had definite aims and stronger desires for material and spiritual riches, I would have fewer victims.

Q. I assume, from what you say, that you do not claim fellowship with the industrial leaders. Evidently they are not friends of yours.

A. Friends of mine? I'll tell you what sort of friends of mine they are. They have belted the entire country with good roads, thus bringing into close communion the people of both city and country.

They have converted ores into steel, with which they have built the skeletons of great skyscrapers.

They have harnessed electrical power and converted it into a thousand uses, *all designed to give man more time to think*! They have provided through the automobile personal transportation to the humblest citizen, thus giving everyone the freedom of travel.

They have provided every home with instantaneous news of what is happening in all parts of the world, through the aid of the radio.

They have reared libraries in every city, town and hamlet, and have filled them with books giving to all who read a complete outline of the most useful knowledge mankind has gathered from his experiences.

They have given the humblest citizen the right to express his own opinion on any subject, at any time, anywhere, without fear of molestation, and they have seen to it that every citizen may help make his own laws, levy his own taxes, and manage his own country through the ballot.

These are but some of the things the industrial leaders have done to give every citizen the privilege of becoming a non-drifter. Do you think these men have helped my cause?

Q. Who are some of the present-day non-drifters over whom you have no control?

A. I have control over no non-drifter, present or past. I control the weak, not those who think for themselves.

Q. Go ahead and describe a typical drifter. Give your description point by point so I can recognize a drifter when I see him.

A. The first thing you will notice about a drifter is his total lack of major purpose in life.

He will be conspicuous by his lack of self-confidence. He will never accomplish anything requiring thought and effort.

He spends all he earns and more too, if he can get credit.

He will be sick or ailing from some real or imaginary cause, and calling to high heaven if he suffers the least physical pain.

He will have little or no imagination. He will lack enthusiasm and initiative to begin anything he is not forced to undertake, and he will plainly express his weakness by taking the line of least resistance whenever he can do so.

He will be ill-tempered and lacking in control over his emotions.

His personality will be without magnetism and it will not attract other people.

He will have opinions on everything, but accurate knowledge of nothing.

He may be jack of all trades, but good at none.

He will neglect to cooperate with those around him, even those on whom he must depend for food and shelter.

He will make the same mistake over and over again, never profiting by failure.

He will be narrow-minded and intolerant on all subjects, ready to crucify those who may disagree with him.

He will expect everything of others, but be willing to give little or nothing in return.

He may begin many things, but he will complete nothing.

He will be loud in his condemnation of his government, but he will never tell you definitely how it can be improved.

He will never reach decisions on anything if he can avoid it, and if he is forced to decide, he will reverse himself at the first opportunity.

He will eat too much and exercise too little.

He will take a drink of liquor if someone else will pay for it.

He will gamble if he can do it on the cuff.

He will criticize others who are succeeding in their chosen calling. In brief, the drifter will work harder to get out of thinking than most others work in earning a good living. He will tell a lie rather than admit his ignorance on any subject.

If he works for others, he will criticize them to their backs and flatter them to their faces.

Q. Judging from your description of a drifter, there is nothing for which he is suited.

A. You are wrong there, my friend. A drifter is good for many things. He makes an excellent prep for a shovel in a WPA crew. He makes a fine agitator in a labor union if the agitation is for shorter hours and longer pay.

He makes an excellent window display for the modern barroom.

He is an excellent dreamer of fantasy and impractical things.

He makes a good husband for the woman who has more money than brains.

He keeps up with all the dope on prize fights and baseball, and he knows the moving picture stars by their first names.

He makes excellent cannon fodder in time of war, providing he cannot squirm out of service.

Think what a hard time Hitler, Mussolini and Stalin would have if they were forced to do their own soldiering.

Last, but not least, the drifter makes it possible for me to control ninety-eight percent of the people of the world. Without the drifter I would be sunk!

Q. You have given me a graphic description of the drifter. Please now describe the non-drifter so that I may recognize him on sight.

A. The first sign of a non-drifter is this: He is always engaged in doing something definite, through some well-organized plan which is definite.

He has a major goal in life toward which he is always working, and many minor goals, all of which lead toward his central scheme.

The tone of his voice, the quickness of his step, the sparkle in his eyes, the quickness of his decisions clearly mark him as a person who knows exactly what he wants and is determined to get it, no matter how long it may take, or what price he must pay.

If you can ask him questions, he gives you direct answers, and never falls back on evasions or resorts to subterfuge.

He extends many favors to others, but accepts favors sparingly or not at all.

He will be found up front, whether he is playing a game or fighting a war.

If he does not know the answers, he will say so frankly.

He has a good memory, never offers an alibi for his shortcomings.

He never blames others for his mistakes, no matter if they deserve the blame.

He used to be known as a go-getter, but in modern times he is called a go-giver. You will find him running the biggest business in town, living on the best street, driving the best automobile, and making his presence felt wherever he happens to be.

He is an inspiration to all who come into contact with his mind. The major distinguishing feature of the non-drifter is this: He has a mind of his own and uses it for all purposes.

Q. Are non-drifters always successful?

A. That depends upon what you mean by the term success. If by that term you have reference to the ability to procure whatever material thing one wants, the answer is yes, the non-drifter is successful.

Henry Ford is a non-drifter. If he had been a drifter, he would have said, I wonder why someone does not build a popular-priced, dependable, self-propelled vehicle, but he never would have undertaken to build such a machine.

If he had been a drifter, he might have said, I would like to build automobiles, but I cannot do it because I do not have the capital.

If Ford had been a drifter, he might have offered the alibi that he was born poor, or that he lacked sufficient schooling to become the world's number one automobile builder, and his alibi would have been based on truth.

Instead of giving the world a truthful alibi, he gave it the world's best low-priced automobile, and the world gave him a fortune. Non-drifters are like that! They have an uncanny way of surmounting obstacles and mastering opposition, no matter in what form it may appear. That is one reason why I have no non-drifters among my earthly allies. They build instead of destroy.

Q. Is the non-drifter born with some mental, physical, or spiritual advantage not available to the drifter?

A. No! The major difference between the drifter and the non-drifter is something equally available to both. It is simply the prerogative right of each to use his own mind and think for himself.

The non-drifter exercises this right; the drifter does not.

That is all there is to distinguish between the two.

You understand, of course, I am speaking of people born with normal bodies and brains. Those who come into the world with physical afflictions may become drifters through no fault of their own.

Physical afflictions which do not weaken the brain need not force one to become a drifter. Many people with such afflictions have achieved noteworthy success in occupations of their own choosing.

Q. Is the non-drifter a handicap to the drifter?

A. He may be, where their interests clash and they are in competition with one another, but more often, the non-drifter aids rather than hinders the drifters he influences.

Again, take Henry Ford as an example and observe that he supplies profitable employment and a source of livelihood to many thousands of people, most of whom belong in the drifting class.

Here the non-drifter's initiative, imagination, self-reliance, and definiteness of purpose help to increase the earning capacity of thousands of drifters, many of whom could not earn a living without his cooperation.

Q. What brief message would you send to the typical drifter if you wished to cure him of this evil habit?

A. I would admonish him to *wake up and give*!

Q. Give what?

A. Some form of service useful to as many people as possible.

Q. So, the non-drifter is supposed to give, is he?

A. Yes, if he *expects to get*! And he must give before he gets!

Q. Some people doubt that you exist.

A. I wouldn't worry about that if I were you. Those who are ready to be converted from the habit of drifting will recognize the authenticity of this interview by its soundness of counsel. The others are not worth the trouble it would take to convert them.

Q. Why do you not try to stop me from publishing this confession I am wringing from you?

A. Because that would be the surest of all ways to guarantee you will publish it. I have a better plan than trying to suppress publication of my confession. I will urge you to go ahead with the publication, then sit back and watch you suffer when some of my faithful drifters begin to make things hot for you.

I will not need to deny your story. My followers will do that for me—see if they don't.

Q. What makes you think I care what your earthbound allies think or say of me?

A. Frankly, this has me worried. I don't think you give a damn whether people believe your story or not, because you are seeking nothing at the hands of others, and therefore do not need their cooperation or their approval.

Q. Who among your allies on earth do you believe will make things hot for me, as you put it?

A. My allies in the churches will pin no medals on you because of what you are doing to me. Remember well this truth: the world deals harshly with pioneers who bring to the world new ideas or expound new truths.

The millions of my earthbound followers who have trembled with fear when my name was spoken will not look with favor on your efforts when you disclose to them the secret of how they became my dupes.

Q. What about your victims in the churches who are ready and willing to know the truth about you, and have the courage to throw off the habit of drifting and begin the habit of thinking for themselves? Do you think they will hate me for breaking your hold on their minds?

A. I admit you will swing some of my victims away from me, but the number will be small compared with the total I control.

Q. Your boastfulness reminds me of the professional politician seeking office. You and the professional politicians have a lot in common, chiefly the fact that both you and they are optimistic liars, even in the face of sure defeat. You know you are on your way out, so why do you hedge and resort to subterfuge and bait me with your challenge? Why do you not take off your false whiskers, step up to the block and have yourself beheaded, just as a brave man would?

A. That is where you are wrong again. I am not on my way out because I am not a drifter. I know my business and I shall run it successfully as long as the world continues to give birth to people who drift. I admit you would hurt my business if you lived long enough, but you will not be here long enough to convert more than a negligible few of my drifters.

Q. If this confession of yours stopped right here, your statement would be sound, but fortunately for millions of your victims who will gain their release because of your confession, this interview will continue until you have supplied me with the weapon by which you will eventually be restrained from domination of people through their fears and superstitions.

Remember, Your Majesty, your confession has just begun. After I wring from you a description of the methods by which you control people, I will force you also to give the formulas by which your control can be broken at will.

It is true I shall not remain here long enough to defeat you, but the published word I leave behind me will be deathless because it will consist of truth! You fear the opposition of no individual because you know it will be short, but you do fear truth.

You fear truth and nothing else, for the reason it is slowly but definitely giving human beings freedom from all manner of fear. Without the weapon of fear, you would be helpless and entirely unable to control any human being! Is that true or false?

A. I have no alternative but to admit that what you say is true.

Q. Now that we understand each other, let us go ahead with your confession. But before we continue, I may as well take time out to do a little boasting on my own account, now that you have had your fling at it. I will confine myself to one question, the answer to which will give me all the satisfaction I want. Is it not true that you control only the minds of those who have allowed the drifting habit to be fixed upon them?

A. Yes, that is true! I have already admitted this truth in a dozen or more different ways. Why do you tantalize me by repeating the question?

Q. There is power in repetition! I am forcing you to repeat the highlights of your confession in as many different ways as possible so your victims may check this interview and determine its soundness by their own experiences with you. That is one of my little tricks, Your Majesty. Do you approve of my method?

A. It is your privilege to use your knowledge any way you choose. I am powerless to stop you.

Q. That is an interesting confession, Your Majesty. Why are you powerless to control me?

A. You couldn't be setting a trap for me for the purpose of doing some more boasting, could you, Mr. Earthbound?

Q. I am asking the questions and you are doing the answering! Go ahead now and confess why you are powerless to stop me from forcing this confession from you. I want your confession for aid and comfort to victims of yours whom I intend to release from your control the moment they read your confession.

A. I am powerless to influence or control you because you have found the secret approach to my kingdom. You know that I exist only in the minds of people who have fears.

You know that I control only the drifters who neglect to use their own minds.

You know that my hell is there on earth and not in the world that comes after death. And you know also that drifters supply all the fire I use in my hell.

You know that I am a principle or form of energy which expresses the negative side of matter and energy, and that I am not a person with a forked tongue and spiked tail.

You have become my master because you have mastered all your fears.

Lastly, you know that you can release all of my earthbound victims whom you contact, and this definite knowledge is the blow with which you will deal me the greatest damage.

I cannot control you because you have discovered your own mind and you have taken charge of it! There now, Mr. Earthbound; that confession should feed your vanity to the bursting point.

Q. That last dart was unnecessary, Your Majesty. Knowledge of the sort I have used to master you does not contaminate itself with vulgar indulgence in vanity.

Truth is the one, and only, thing in the world that can stand ridicule. I am hoping that the hundred million or more drifters you control in the United States alone will seek my shrine to scoff at my interview with you. Some of them will remain to pray!

Now let us continue with your confession. What is wrong with the principle of flattery? You use it, do you not?

A. Do I use it? Man alive! Flattery is one of my most useful weapons. With this deadly instrument I slay the big ones and the little ones.

Q. Your admission interests me. Go ahead now and tell me how you make use of flattery.

A. I make use of it in so many ways it is difficult to know where to begin. I warn you, before I answer in detail, that my answers will bring down an avalanche of ridicule on your head for bringing up the question.

Q. I'll take the responsibility. Proceed!

A. Well, I may as well here admit that you have stumbled onto the major secret of how I convert people to the habit of drifting!

Q. That is a startling admission. Go ahead with your confession, and stick strictly to this subject of flattery! No more side remarks, and no more facetiousness for the present. Tell me all about your use of flattery in gaining control over people.

A. Flattery is a bait of incomparable value to all who wish to gain control over others. It has powerful pulling qualities because it operates through two of the most common human weaknesses—vanity and egotism. There is a certain amount of vanity and egotism in everyone. In some people, these qualities are so pronounced they literally serve as a rope by which one may be bound. The best of all ropes is flattery!

Flattery is the chief bait through which men seduce women. Sometimes, in fact, frequently, women use the same bait to gain control of men, especially men who cannot be mastered through sex appeal. I teach its use to both men and women. Flattery is the chief bait with which my agents weave their way into the confidence of people from whom they procure information needed to foment and carry on warfare.

Wherever anyone stops to feed his vanity on flattery, I move in and begin to build another drifter! Non-drifters are not easily flattered.

Now comes the part of my confession that may put you on the spot if you are foolish enough to publish it: Flattery is the bait of major importance used by my allies in most of the religions of the world.

Did you ever hear a prayer that did not begin with an attempt to flatter God?

Did you ever know of one of those flattering prayers being answered? No, of course not! Infinite Intelligence is not impressed favorably by begging and flattery!

That is why I like to see men begin their prayers with an attempt at flattery.

Q. I am beginning to see your point! You inspire people to approach Infinite Intelligence through flattery so their prayers will not be answered. Is that your only purpose?

A. My goodness, no! I inspire people to use flattery in every human relationship where its use is possible, because those who are influenced by it become easy victims of the drifting habit!

Q. Can you control anyone who is amenable to flattery?

A. Very easily! As I have already told you, flattery is of major importance in alluring people into the habit of drifting.

Q. At what age are people most susceptible to flattery?

A. Age has nothing to do with one's susceptibility to flattery.

People respond to it, in one way or another, from the time they become conscious of their own existence until they die.

Q. Through what motive can women be most easily flattered?

A. Their vanity! Tell a women she is pretty, or that she wears clothes well, or that her eyebrows are arched properly, and she will take off her shirt and give it to you.

Q. What motive is most effective in harpooning men?

A. Egotism, with capital E! Tell a man he has a strong Herculean body, or that he is a great business tycoon, and he will purr like a cat and smile like an opossum! After that, you know what happens.

Q. Are all men like that?

A. Oh, no. Two out of every hundred have their egotism so thoroughly under control that even an expert flatterer couldn't get under their skins with a double-edged butcher knife!

Q. How does a cunning woman apply her art of flattery in attracting men?

A. Great heavens, man, do I have to draw a picture of her method for you? Have you no imagination?

Q. Oh, yes, I have imagination enough, Your Majesty, but I am thinking of the poor dupes of the world who need to understand the exact technique with which they may be flattered into the habit of drifting. Go on and tell us how a woman can harpoon rich, and presumably, smart men.

A. This is a devilish trick to play on women, but since you demand the information I am helpless to withhold it. Women influence men through a technique consisting (1) of ability to inject soft, cooing baby tones into their voices, and (2) by closing their eyes into a half-closed position which registers hypnotism in connection with the flattery of men.

Q. Is that all there is to the business of flattery?

A. No, that is only the technique! Then comes the motive a woman uses as a lure. The type of woman you perhaps have in mind never sells a man herself or anything she can give him. Instead, she sells him his own egotism!

Q. Is that all that women use when they wish to flatter men?

A. That is the most effective thing they use. It works when sex appeal fails!

Q. So, I am to believe that big, strong, smart men can be wound up and manipulated through flattery, just as if they were so much putty? Is that possible?

A. Is it possible? It is happening every minute of the day. Moreover, unless they are non-drifters, the bigger they come, the harder they fall when the expert flatterer moves in on them.

Q. Tell me of some of your other tricks with which you cause people to drift in life.

A. One of my most effective devices is failure! The majority of people begin to drift as soon as they meet with opposition, and not one out of ten thousand will keep on trying after failing two or three times.

Q. So, it is your business to induce people to fail whenever you can. Is that correct?

A. You have it right! Failure breaks down one's morale, destroys self-confidence, subdues enthusiasm, dulls imagination, and drives away definiteness of purpose.

Without these qualities, no one can permanently succeed in any undertaking, The world had produced thousands of inventors with ability superior to that of the late Thomas A. Edison. But these men have never been heard of, while the name of Edison will go marching on because Edison converted failure into a stepping stone to achievement while the others used it as an alibi for not producing results.

Q. Is the capacity to surmount failure without being discouraged one of Henry Ford's chief assets?

A. Yes, and this same quality is the chief asset of every man who attains outstanding success in any calling.

Q. That statement covers lots of territory, Your Majesty. Do you not wish to modify it or tone it down a bit for the sake of accuracy?

A. No modification is necessary because the claim is none too broad. Search accurately into the lives of men who achieve enduring success and you will find, without exception, that their success has been in exact proportion to the extent that they surmounted failure.

The life of every successful person loudly acclaims that which every true philosopher knows: Every failure brings with it the seed of an equivalent success.

But the seed will not germinate and grow under the influence of a drifter. It springs to life only when it is in the hands of one who recognizes that most failures are only temporary defeat and never, under any circumstances, accepts defeat as an excuse for drifting.

Q. What is the strongest factor in converting temporary defeat into failure?

A. The habit of drifting!

Q. If I understand you correctly, you claim there is virtue in failure. That does not seem reasonable. Why do you try to induce people to fail if there is virtue in failure?

A. There is no inconsistency in my claims. The appearance of inconsistency is due to your lack of understanding. Failure is a virtue only when it does not lead one to quit trying and begin drifting. I induce as many people as I can to fail as often as possible for the reason that not one out of ten thousand will keep on trying after failing two or three times. I am not concerned about the few who convert failures into stepping stones because they belong to my opposition anyway. They are the non-drifters and therefore they are beyond my reach.

Q. Your explanation clears up the matter. Now go ahead and tell me of some of your other tricks with which you allure people into drifting.

A. One of my most effective tricks is known to you as propaganda. This is the instrument of greatest value to me in setting people to murdering one another under the guise of war.

The cleverness of this trick consists mainly of the subtlety with which I use it.

I mix propaganda with the news of the world. I have it taught in public and private schools. I see that it finds its way into the pulpit.

I color moving pictures with it. I see that it enters every home where there is a radio. I inject it into billboard, newspaper and radio advertising.

I spread it in every place of business where people work. I use it to fill the divorce courts and I make it serve to destroy business and industry.

It is my chief instrument for starting runs on banks. My propagandists cover the world so thoroughly that I can start epidemics of disease, turn loose the dogs of war, or throw business into a panic at will.

Q. If you can do all that you claim with propaganda, it is little wonder that we have wars and business depressions. Give me a simple description of what you mean by the term propaganda. Just what is it and how does it work? I wish to know particularly how you cause people to drift through the use of this devilish device.

A. Propaganda is any device, plan, or method by which people can be influenced without knowing that they are being influenced, or the source of the influence.

Let me show you how it can be used to undermine competition in business. A manufacturer desired to destroy one of his competitors, so he sent out a whispering squad of men and women who dropped the word here, there and everywhere that the Health Department had found an employee suffering with leprosy working in the plant of his competitor.

The news spread like wildfire. Bad news always does. The trick cost the victim the loss of millions of dollars, and just barely missed breaking him financially. Now, what do you think of that for cleverness?

Q. I think it is very clever indeed, Your Majesty! Did the plan cause the victim to drift into failure?

A. No, not exactly. The competitor caught up with the trick before it had gone too far, and set into motion a counter trick which saved his business.

Q. Nice fellows, aren't they, Your Majesty?

A. Propaganda is used in business for the purpose of discouraging competition. Employers use it to gain advantage over their employees. The employees retaliate by using it to gain advantage over their employers.

The railroads use it to pave the way for rate increase.

The public utility men use it to justify the rates they charge for services. In fact, it is used so universally and through such a smooth and beautiful streamlined technique that it looks harmless even when it is detected.

Q. I suppose some of your boys are now engaged in preparing the minds of the American people to drift into some form of dictatorship. Tell me how they work.

A. Yes! Millions of our boys are preparing Americans to become Hitlerized.

Our best boys are working through politics and labor organizations. We intend to take over the country with ballots instead of bullets.

Americans are so sensitive they would never stand the shock of seeing their form of government changed with the aid of machine guns and tank cars.

So our propaganda boys are serving them a diet they will swallow, by stirring up strife between employers and employees and turning the government against business and industry.

When propaganda does its work thoroughly, one of my boys will move in as dictator and these Nine Old Men with their silly notions of the Constitution will move out!

Everybody will be given a job or fed from the government treasury. When men's bellies are filled, they drift freely with one who does the filling. Hungry men get out from under control.

Q. I have often wondered who invented the clever trick which you call propaganda. From what you tell me of its source and nature, I understand why it is so deadly. Only one as clever as Your Majesty could have invented such a device with which to dull the reason, dethrone the will, and lure men into drifting.

A. Yes, I admit its cleverness. Through the aid of this trick, I can use a person's own close friends and relatives to bring about his failure or lure him into drifting. For proof of what I claim, take a look at the President of the United States and observe how I clipped his wings during his second term of office, by the simple trick of causing him to drift on all of his polices of administration.

Observe also that I cut him down to the right size with the help of the very people from whom he got his influence. I could have disposed of him as a politician when the South was disposed of, but that would have given him and his plans the status of martyrdom. I cut him down more effectively through the aid of propaganda.

Q. Why do you not use your powerful propaganda to gain control of your victims instead of subduing them through fear and annihilating them through warfare?

A. What is fear of the Devil except propaganda? You have not observed my technique very carefully or you would have seen that I am the world's greatest propagandist! I never attain an end by direct, open means, which I can achieve through subterfuge and subtlety.

What do you suppose I am using when I plant negative ideas in the minds of men and gain control of them through what they believe to be their own ideas? What would you call that except the cleverest of all forms of propaganda?

Q. I see your point. Also I see your hellishness! The person who pours poison in one's drinking water is a murderer, but you, who poison millions of people by planting the germ of negative thoughts in their minds, are an artist! Is that your purpose?

A. You have catalogued me correctly. I never do anything clumsily. That is one reason—the major reason, I admit—why I control ninety-eight percent of the people of the world.

Some of my victims are smart people, too! But smartness of the average type is no match for perfection in the art of the use of propaganda. If you understand what I am here confessing, you know why and how I control all but two percent of the people of the world, despite the fact that my opposition is clothed with the power of Omnipotence!

Q. Your admission is most enlightening. I am sure millions of people have wondered how it is that the evil forces of the world so overwhelmingly outweigh the forces for good. Your side is in the lead because you stoop to use tricks your opposition will not employ. Is that correct?

A. In a way that is correct, but you are trying to do me an injustice. You are charging me with all the evils of the world and giving me no credit for the good I do.

Q. We will skip your virtues for the present. I want to hear more about your faults. The only virtue I have observed in studying you is the cleverness of your technique. Tell me more of your technique in gaining objectives through the use of propaganda. The whole world is interested right now in knowing more about how propaganda works. You say you use propaganda to lure people into the habit of drifting. Just how do you accomplish this shocking result?

A. I use so many methods it is impossible for me to describe them all, but I will explain some of my favorites. I shall begin by telling you how I gain control over individuals by using their own minds for propaganda purposes.

Q. Surely you are not going to tell me that you destroy people through their own help without them realizing what you are doing?

A. That is exactly what I wish you to understand. Moreover, I will show you exactly how the trick is performed.

Q. Now we are getting somewhere, Your Majesty! Exactly how do you convert human beings into propagandists and lure them into self-imprisonment? Give me the story with all its lurid details. This is the most important part of your confession and I am consumed with eagerness to gain control of your secret, I can hardly blame you for stalling about answering my question because you know so well that your answer will snatch millions of innocent victims from your control. You also know that your answer will protect other countless millions of yet unborn people from being victimized by you. It is little wonder you are hedging about answering.

A. Your deductions are correct! This part of my confession will do me more damage than all the remainder of it.

Q. Stating your headache in a better way, this part of your confession will save more millions of people from your control than all the remainder of it.

A. All I can say is that you have me in a hell of a situation!

Q. Splendid! Now you shall know how the millions of your victims feel. Let's have it.

A. I make my first entry into an individual's mind by bribing him.

Q. What do you use as a bribe?

A. I use many things, all of them pleasant things the individual covets.

Q. Tell me about these pleasant things with which you bribe individuals while you are teaching them the habit of drifting.

A. Well, you might say I use the same sort of bribes that individuals use when they bribe one another. That is, I use for bribes the things people most want. My best bribes are:

1. Love

2. The thirst for sex expression

3   Covetousness for money

4.   The obsessional desire for something for nothing—gambling

5.   Vanity in women; egotism in men

6.   Desire to be the master of others

7.   Desire for intoxicants and narcotics

8.   Desire for self-expression through words and deeds

9.   Desire to imitate others

10.   Desire for perpetuation of life after death

11.   Desire to heroize and worship others

12.   Desire for physical food

Q. That is an imposing list of bribes, Your Majesty. Do you use others?

A. Yes, plenty of them, but these are my favorites. Through some combination of them I can enter the mind of any human being, at will, at any age from birth until death.

Q. You mean that these bribes are the keys with which you can silently unlock the door to any mind you choose?

A. That is exactly what I mean, and I can do it too.

Q. What is the first thing you do when you enter a person's mind?

A. That depends upon who the person is, and how I wish to use him.

Q. Do I understand you to claim you can enter the mind of anyone you choose, and use that person's own mind as a weapon with which to enslave him?

A. No, I never made so broad a claim as that. I can enter any mind I choose, with the aid of some combination of bribes, but I can gain control of only ninety-eight out of every hundred people—the ones who can be induced to form the habit of drifting! I can enter the minds of the two out of every hundred who are non-drifters, but I cannot remain there. They throw me out and shut the door in my face.

Q. There is advantage then in being a non-drifter?

A. In exact proportion that there is disadvantage in being a drifter!

Q. What happens when you enter the mind of a person who is not yet in the habit of drifting, but belongs in the ninety-eight percent class as a potential drifter?

A. I go to work immediately to occupy as much of that person's mind as I can master.

If the individual's greatest weakness is the desire for money, I begin to dangle coins before him, figuratively speaking. I intensify his desire and induce him to go after money. Then when he gets near it, I snatch it away from him.

This is an old trick of mine. After the trick has been repeated a few times, the poor fellow gives in and quits. Then I take over a little more space in his mind and fill it with the fear of poverty! That is one of my best mind fillers.

Q. Yes, I admit your method is very clever, but what happens if the victim fools you and gets his hands on a lot of money? You don't fill his mind with fear of poverty then, do you?

A. No, I don't. I take over the space by filling it with something which serves my purpose just as well. If my victim converts his desire for money into large sums, I start to overfeeding him with the things he can buy with it.

For example, I cause him to stuff himself with rich foods.

This slows down his thinking capacity and starts him on the road to drifting.

Then I pester him with intestinal poisoning through the surplus food he eats. That also slows down his thinking and gives him a nasty disposition.

Q. What if the victim is not a glutton? What other follies can you induce him to pick up that lead to drifting?

A. If the victim is a male, I can usually snare him through his sex appetite. Overindulgence in sex starts more men to drifting toward failure than all other causes combined.

Q. So, food and sex are two of your sure-fire baits! Is that correct?

A. Yes. With these two lures I can take over a majority of my victims.

Q. What a pity! And these two things which you use to control people happen to be the two essentials of major importance in perpetuating life itself.

A. Oh, yes. That is the very reason I can use them so effectively. You may have observed that I never use non-essentials or mere trash as bait with which to lure human beings. I promise them the finest of the land!

Q. Yes, you do, and in return the poor victims give you—what? Don't answer. I'll tell you what they give you for your deceit and trickery. They give you the right to think their thoughts while they are living, and the privilege of taking over what is left of them after they die. That is all you ask of your victims, is it not?

A. That is all! It is none too much when you consider how much cleverness I put into my profession.

Q. I am beginning to think that wealth is more dangerous than poverty, if your story is to be believed.

A. That altogether depends upon who has the wealth, and how it was acquired!

Q. What has the manner in which money is acquired to do with its being a blessing or a curse?

A. Everything! If you don't believe me, take a look at those who acquire a large amount of money quickly, without time to get wisdom along with it, and observe how they use it.

Why do you suppose rich men's sons seldom equal the achievements of their fathers?

I'll tell you why. It is because they have been deprived of the self-discipline which comes from being forced to work.

Look into the records of moving picture stars who suddenly find themselves in possession of big money and over-fulsome praise from the public. Observe how quickly I move in and take them over in many cases, mainly through sex, gambling, food and liquor.

With these, I catch and control the biggest and the best of people as soon as they get their hands on big money.

Q. What about those who acquire money slowly, by rendering some form of useful service? Are they easily snared too?

A. Oh, I get them all right, but I generally have to change my bait. Some of them want one thing and others want something else.

Where my purpose is best served, I see to it that they get what they want most, but I manage to wrap in the package something they don't want.

This is another very clever trick of mine. For example, Mr. Roosevelt wanted to be President of the United States for a second term.

I let him have the object of his desire, but I gave him John L. Lewis and an endless labor problem along with it. The thing I gave him which he did not want is the definite thing that made him a drifter. Do you see how I work?

Q. And very clever work it is. You lure people through their natural desires, but you slip your deadly poison into the object of
those desires wherever you can.

A. Now you are catching on! You see, I play both ends against the
middle, so to speak. For example, I enter the mind by whetting
one's appetite for money. If my victim stumbles and falls over
any of the hurdles I set up between him and money, he loses
courage, quits and drifts into failure. If he surmounts the handicaps and gets money, I take him over just the same, through his
unwise use of the money.

Q. What happens if your victim successfully runs all your hurdles,
acquires money in large amounts and refuses to be interested
in any of your other baits? Can you induce that person to drift
with you into failure?

A. Not that person! He belongs in the non-drifter class.

Q. From all you say, I infer that you cannot induce a non-drifter
to help you gain control of his mind by baiting him with your
bribes. Is that correct?

A. That is exactly correct. I can, and I do, interest non-drifters in
my bribes, because I use for the purpose of bribery the things all
people naturally desire, but the non-drifter resembles a fish that
steals the bait from your hook but refuses to take the hook.

The non-drifter takes from Life whatever he wants, *but he
takes it on his own terms!* The drifter takes whatever he can get,
but he takes what he gets on my terms.

Stating the matter in another way, the non-drifter borrows
money from a legitimate banker, if he wants it, and pays a legitimate rate of interest. The drifter goes to the pawn shop, hocks
his watch and pays a suicidal rate of interest for his loan.

This sort of discrimination distinguishes the non-drifter
from the habitual drifter all through life, in all human relationships. Everybody wants to do something to help the non-drifter.

He can borrow money at will. He can get all the credit he wants.

He is invited to join the best clubs and associate with the best people. He can get public office for the asking. But all the drifter gets is a stiff kick in the pants, and he gets it from his closest friends and relatives the same as from others. Look around you, take inventory of all whom you know, and see for yourself that I am stating the facts.

Q. So, I draw from your claims the conclusion that your hand is mixed up somehow in all of people's troubles and miseries, even though your presence may not be visible?

A. That is certainly a reasonable conclusion. If I am not there in person, I see to it that one of my propagandists attends to my interest. As I have already told you, my propagandists, both willing and unwilling, run well into the millions.

Q. I had no idea you control unwilling workers.

A. Oh, yes! My unwilling workers are often my best workers. You see, my unwilling workers are those whom I cannot control with some combination of bribes. People whom I have to master by fear or through some form of misfortune. They do not wish to serve me, but they cannot avoid it because they are eternally bound to me by the habit of drifting!

Q. Now I am beginning to better understand your technique. You bribe your victims through their natural desires, and lead them astray while you induce them to become drifters if they respond to your lure. If they refuse to respond, you plant the seed of fear in their minds, or trap them through some form of misfortune, and hog-tie them while they are down. Is that your method?

A. That is exactly the way I work! Clever, don't you think?

Q. Which do you prefer to serve as your propagandists—the young or the old?

A. The young, of course! They can be influenced by most bribes more easily than people of mature judgement. Moreover, they have longer to remain in my service.

Q. What happens to old people who no longer respond to your bribes and are in no position where you can use them to carry on your destruction?

A. They go over the hill to the poor farm.

THIS WAY TO PREVENT DRIFTING

Q. Your Majesty has given me a clear description of drifting. Tell me what must be done to insure against the habit of drifting. I want a complete formula that anyone can use.

A. Protection against drifting lies within easy reach of every human being who has normal body and a sound mind. The self-defense can be applied through these simple methods:

1. Do your own thinking on all occasions. The fact that human beings are given complete control over nothing save the power to think their own thoughts is laden with significance.

2. Decide definitely what you want from life, then create a plan for attaining it, and be willing to sacrifice everything else, if necessary, rather than accept permanent defeat.

3. Analyze temporary defeat, no matter of what nature or cause, and extract from it the seed of an equivalent advantage.

4. Be willing to render useful service equivalent to the value of all material things you demand of life, and render the service first.

5. Recognize that your brain is a receiving set that can be attuned to receive communications from the universal storehouse of Infinite Intelligence, to help you transmute your desires into their physical equivalent.

6. Recognize that your greatest asset is time, the only thing except the power of thought which you own outright, and the one thing which can be shaped into whatever material things you want. Budget your time so none of it is wasted.

7. Recognize the truth that fear generally is a filler with which the Devil occupies the unused portion of your mind; that it is only a state of mind which you can control by filling the space it occupies with faith in your ability to make Life provide you with whatever you demand of it.

8. When you pray, do not beg! Demand what you want and insist upon getting exactly that, with no substitutes.

9. Recognize that Life is a cruel taskmaster, that you either master it or it masters you. There is no half-way or compromising point. Never accept from Life anything you do not want! If that which you do not want is temporarily forced upon you, you can refuse, in your own mind, to accept it and it will make way for the thing you do want.

10. Lastly, remember that your dominating thoughts attract, through a definite law of nature, by the shortest and most convenient route, their physical counterpart. Be careful what your thoughts dwell upon.

Q. That list looks imposing, Your Majesty. Give me a simple formula combining all the ten points. If you had to combine all ten in one, what would it be?

A. Be definite in everything you do and never leave unfinished thoughts in the mind. Form the habit of reaching definite decisions on all subjects!

THE SECOND AND
LAST STAGE OF DRIFTING

Q. Can the habit of drifting be broken, or does it become permanent once it has been formed?

A. The habit can be broken if the victim has enough willpower, providing it is done in time. There is a point beyond which the habit can never be broken. Beyond that point, the victim is mine. He resembles a fly that has been caught in a spider's web. He may struggle, but he cannot get out. Each move he makes entangles him more securely. The web in which I entangle my victims permanently is a law of nature not yet isolated by, or understood by, men of science.

Q. What is this mysterious law through which you take permanent control of people's bodies even before you take over their souls? The whole world will want to know more about this law and how it operates.

A. It will be hard to describe the law so you will understand it, but you may call it Hypnotic Rhythm! It is the same law through which people can be hypnotized.

CHAPTER FIVE

◆

HYPNOTIC RHYTHM

Q. So, you have the power to use the laws of nature as a web in which you bind your victims in eternal control. Is that your claim?

A. That is not only my claim. It is the truth!

Q. Then you can, and do, take over the souls of people after they die?

A. That isn't the half of it. I take over their minds and bodies before they die whenever I lure them or frighten them into hypnotic rhythm!

Q. Describe hypnotic rhythm. What is it? How do you use it to gain permanent mastery over human beings?

A. I will have to go back into time and space and give you a brief elementary description of how nature uses hypnotic rhythm. Otherwise, you will not be able to understand my description of how I use this universal law to control human beings.

Q. Go ahead, but keep your story confined to simple illustrations which come within the range of my own experience and knowledge of natural laws.

A. Very well, I shall do my best! You, of course, know that nature maintains a perfect balance between all the elements and all the energy in the universe.

You can see that the stars and the planets move with perfect precision, each one keeping its own place in time and space. You can see that the seasons of the year come and go with perfect regularity.

You can see that an oak tree grows from an acorn and a pine grows from the seed of its ancestor. An acorn never produces a pine and a pine seed never produces an oak.

These are simple things which anyone can understand. What one cannot see is the universal law through which nature maintains perfect balance throughout the myriad of universes.

You earthbound caught a fragmentary glimpse of this great universal law when Newton discovered that it holds your earth in its position and causes all material objects to be attracted toward the center of the earth. He call the law gravitation.

But he did not go far enough in his study of the law. If he had, he would have discovered that the same law which holds your earth in position and helps nature to maintain a perfect balance over the four dimensions in which all matter and energy are contained is the web in which I entangle and control the minds of human beings.

Q. That is a shocking claim you have made. If science discovers your claim to be true, the discovery will change all human relationships for the betterment of mankind. The discovery would wipe out poverty! It would release human beings from all fear! It would remove the causes of crime by enabling people to supply their needs without fighting among themselves. Tell me more of this astounding law of hypnotic rhythm.

A. Shall I go back and describe how this law is the connecting link between the four dimensions, or do you prefer that I keep within the range of man's everyday knowledge?

Q. Keep your story confined to established knowledge. Otherwise it will be of no benefit.

A.   As I have already stated, there is a universal form of energy with which nature keeps a perfect balance between all matter and energy.

She makes specialized use of this universal building material by breaking it up into different wavelengths. The breaking up process is carried on through habit.

You will better understand what I am trying to convey if I compare it with the method by which one learns to play music. At first the notes are memorized in the mind. Then they are related to one another through melody and rhythm. By repetition the melody and rhythm become fixed in the mind. Observe how relentlessly the musician must repeat a tune before he masters it. Through repetition, the musical notes blend and then you have music.

Any impulse of thought the mind repeats over and over through habit forms an organized rhythm. Undesirable habits can be broken. They must be broken before they assume the proportions of rhythm. Are you following me?

Q.   Yes.

A.   Well, to continue, rhythm is the last stage of habit! Any thought or physical movement which is repeated over and over through the principle of habit finally attains to the proportion of rhythm.

Then the habit cannot be broken because nature takes it over and makes it permanent. It is something like a whirlpool in water. An object may keep floating indefinitely unless it is caught in a whirlpool. Then it is carried round and round but it cannot escape. The energy with which people think may be compared with water in a river.

Thoughts may be compared with objects floating in the water.

If the same thought is held in the mind, or left there by neglect, for a certain length of time, nature takes it over, through the rhythm of habit, and makes it permanent.

Q. So this is the way in which you take control of the minds of people, is it?

A. Yes. All I have to do to gain control over any mind is to induce its owner to drift. (Drifting is any habit of the mind not deliberately controlled and directed to a definite end.)

Q. Am I to understand that the habit of drifting is the major danger through which people lose their prerogative privilege of thinking their own thoughts and shaping their own earthly destinations?

A. That, and much more. Drifting is not only the habit through which people lose control over their earthly destination, but it is also the habit through which I take over their souls after they give up their physical bodies.

Q. Then the only way a human being can be saved from eternal annihilation is by maintaining control over his own mind while he is on this earth. Is that true?

A. You have stated the truth perfectly! Those who control and use their own minds escape my web. I get all the others as naturally as the sun sets in the west.

Q. Is that all there is to the business of being saved from eternal annihilation? Doesn't what you call your opposition have anything to do with saving people?

A. I can see that you do think very deeply. My opposition has everything to do with the salvation of people from eternal annihilation, and for that reason, it is my opposition who provides every human being with the privilege of using his own mind.

You will better understand by the explanation that the energy with which people think is not generated in their own minds.

It is universal energy—the power you earthbound call God!

If you use that power, by maintaining control over your own mind, you become a part of it when you give up your physical body.

If you neglect to use it, then I have the privilege of taking advantage of the neglect, through the law of hypnotic rhythm.

Q. How much of a person do you take over when you gain control of him?

A. Everything that is left after he ceases to control and use his own mind.

Q. In other words, when you gain control of a person, you take over all there is of his individuality up to the time that he quits using his own mind? Is that correct?

A. That is how I operate.

Q. What do you do with people whom you control before death? Of what good are they to you while they live?

A. I use them, or what is left of them after I take charge, as propagandists to help me prepare the minds of others to drift!

Q. You not only fool people into destroying their power to control their own minds, but you use them to help you trap others?

A. Yes, I let no opportunity get away from me.

Q. Let us come back to the subject of hypnotic rhythm. Tell me more of how this law works. Show me how you use individuals to help you gain control over others. I want to know something of the most effective way you use hypnotic rhythm.

A. It is hard for me to say what is the most effective way I use this force, because I use it in so many ways.

Q. Tell me then what is the most desirable end you attain through its use.

A. Oh, that is easy! The thing I like best is to fill the minds of people with fear! Once I fill one's mind with fear, I have little trouble causing him to drift until I have entangled him in the web of hypnotic rhythm.

Q. What human fear best serves your purpose?

A. The fear of death.

Q. Why is the fear of death your favorite weapon?

A. Because no one knows, and by the very nature of the laws of the universe, no one can prove definitely what happens after death.

This uncertainty frightens people out of their wits. Here is where I make religion and religious teachers serve me.

Q. Which of the brands of religion serve you best?

A. Brands mean nothing to me. I use them all! Sectarianism, or brands of religion, are man-made. They are nothing but names. The important thing to me, concerning all religions, is something most people never suspect.

Q. What is that, Your Majesty?

A. It is the fact that all religions keep the minds of people centered on their fears, especially the fear of death. You never saw a deeply religious person who did not desperately fear something. People who give over their minds to fear—any sort of fear—neglect to use their minds and begin to drift. Eventually they drift into the whirlpool of hypnotic rhythm from which they may never escape.

Q. I have always been under the impression that the religious leaders of the world have been responsible for our civilization. Is that true, Your Majesty?

A. If it is true, they are welcome to the honor! I control ninety-eight out of every hundred of your civilization. Right here I may as well tell you the major credit for my control belongs to the religious leaders!

Q. That's an astounding claim. How have the religious leaders helped your cause?

A. By keeping people's minds filled with fear of me!

Q. But I was under the impression the religious leaders had found you out; that they no longer frighten people with tall stories of eternal punishment with fire and brimstone. Aren't the religious leaders gaining ground on you in this age of printing presses, radio, and scientific research?

A. Oh yes! I have lost some ground since the days when I could frighten people with a clap of thunder, but there is still enough of the uncertainty of what happens after death to make the very thought of death fill people's minds with fear.

To me, fear is an aid, no matter what one fears or what is the cause of the fear.

Q. I am astounded to hear you lay claim to the religions as an aid to your cause. It seems to me you would have been damaged by the warfare the churches have carried on against you.

A. Not in the least! If the religious leaders had stopped preaching about me and my wickedness two thousand years ago, and had put in their time studying the laws of nature, they would have discovered hypnotic rhythm, and the scientists would have uncovered the principles of beneficial use to mankind which they are just now finding. Instead of damaging me, the religious leaders have helped me by keeping people's minds occupied with unknown and unknowable hypotheses!

Q. Do you not fear the religious leaders will resent your charges and fight you still harder?

A. I am counting on that! Nothing helps my cause more than opposition.

Q. Then you do not mind what religious leaders think or say of you?

A. Not as long as they say something! If the churches should stop talking about me, my cause would receive a severe setback.

Every attack made against me fixes the fear of me in the minds of all who are influenced by it. You see, opposition is the thing that keeps some people from drifting! Providing they do not yield to it.

Q. Since you claim the churches help instead of hindering your cause, tell me what would give you cause to worry?

A. My only worry is that some day a real thinker may appear on earth!

Q. What would happen if a thinker did appear?

A. You ask me what would happen? I'll tell you what would happen!

People would learn the greatest of all truths—that the time they spend in fearing something would, if reversed, give them all they want in the material world and save them from me after death. Isn't that worth thinking about?

Q. What is keeping such a thinker from appearing in the world?

A. Fear!

Q. Fear of what or whom?

A. Fear of criticism! It may interest you to know that the fear of criticism is the only effective weapon I have with which to whip you. If you were not afraid to publish this confession after you wring it from me, I would lose my earthly kingdom.

Q. And, if I did surprise you and publish it, how long would it be until you lost your kingdom?

A. Just long enough for one generation of children to grow into understanding. You cannot take the adults from me. I have them too securely sewed up. But, if you published this confession, it would be sufficient to keep me from gaining control of the yet unborn and those who have not yet reached the age of reason. You wouldn't dare publish what I have told you about religious leaders. They would crucify you!

Q. I thought the savage practice of crucifixion went out of style two thousand years ago.

A. I don't mean crucifixion on a cross. I mean social and financial crucifixion. Your income would be shut off. You would become a social outcast. Religious leaders and their followers, alike, would treat you with scorn.

Q. What if I could get along without the approval of the religious leaders and their followers?

Being the wise Devil that you are, you know the world is peopled with many who belong to no church and fear neither you nor God.

You also know that great thinkers who have lived were affiliated with no religious group; such men as Socrates, Plato, Bruno, Newton, and our modern times scientists such as Edison, Franklin, and others of their type.

Suppose I should choose to throw my lot with the select few who make a pretense of using their own minds rather than fear the masses who do not—the masses of whom you claim ninety-eight percent?

A. If you have courage enough to do this, you will crimp my style.

Q. Why do you lay claim to no scientist? Don't you like scientists?

A. Oh yes, I like all people well enough, but scientists are out of my reach.

Q. Why?

A. Because they think for themselves and spend their time studying natural laws.

Q. Is that the reason scientists usually affiliate with no brand of sectarianism?

A. Scientists have no need for brands or sectarianism. They deal with cause and effect. They deal with facts wherever they find them. But do not make the mistake of believing scientists have no religion. They have a very definite religion.

Q. What is their religion?

A. The religion of Truth! The religion of natural law! If the world ever produces an accurate thinker with ability to fathom the deeply buried secret of life and death, you can be sure that science will be responsible for the catastrophe.

Q. Catastrophe to whom?

A. To me, of course!

A. Let's get back on the subject of hypnotic rhythm? I want to know more about it. Is it something like the principle through which people can hypnotize one another?

A. It is precisely the same thing. I have already told you so. Why do you repeat your questions?

Q. That is an old worldly custom of mine, Your Majesty! For your enlightenment I will tell you I am forcing you to repeat many of your statements for the sake of emphasis. I am also trying to see if I can catch you in a lie! Don't dodge the issue.

Get back to hypnotic rhythm and tell me all you know about it.

Am I a victim of it?

A. Not now, but you barely missed falling into my web. You drifted toward the whirlpool of hypnotic rhythm until you discovered how to force me into making this confession. Then I lost control of you!

Q. How interesting, Your Majesty! You are not trying to recapture me through flattery, are you?

A. That would be the best bribe I could offer you. It is the bribe I used on you effectively before you got the upper hand of me.

Q. With what did you flatter me?

A. With many things, chief among them sex and the desire for self-expression.

Q. What effect did your bribes have on me?

A. They caused you to neglect your major purpose in life, and started you to drifting.

Q. Was that all you did to me through your bribes?

A. That was plenty!

Q. But I am back on the track and out of your reach now, am I not?

A. Yes, you are temporarily out of my reach because you are not drifting.

Q. What broke your spell over me and released me from the habit of drifting?

A. My answer may humiliate you. Do you want to hear it?

Q. Go ahead and give it to me, Your Majesty! I wish to learn how much truth I can stand.

A. When you found a great love in the woman of your choice, I lost my grip on you.

Q. So, you are going accuse me of hiding behind a woman's skirts, are you?

A. No, not hiding! I wouldn't put it that way. I would say you have learned how to give yourself a solid background with the embellishment of a woman's mind.

Q. The woman's skirt has nothing to do with it then?

A. No, but her brain does! When you and your wife began to combine your two brains, through your habit of Master Minding every day, you stumbled upon the secret power with which you forced me into this confession.

Q. Is that the truth, or are you trying to flatter me again?

A. I could flatter you if I had you alone, but I cannot flatter you while you have the use of your wife's mind!

Q. I am beginning to catch on to something important. I am beginning to understand what was meant by the writer of the passage in the Bible which says, substantially, "When two or more meet together and ask for anything in My name, it shall be granted." It is true, then, that two minds are better than one.

A. It is not only true, it is necessary before anyone can continuously contact the great storehouse of Infinite Intelligence wherein is stored all that is, all that ever was, and all that can ever be.

Q. Is there such a storehouse?

A. If there had not been, you would not—could not—now be humiliating me with this silly forced confession.

Q. Can anyone contact the original source of all power and all knowledge?

A. No one can contact it alone. The approach can be made only where two or more minds are combined, in a spirit of perfect harmony, with a definite purpose.

Q. But I knew about the Master Mind principle, through which two or more minds may combine and tune in on Infinite

Intelligence, long before I ever knew my wife. Why didn't I discover how to use this principle before?

A. Because you did not have an alliance with a friendly, harmonious mind until you found your wife.

Q. May any two minds combine and contact Infinite Intelligence, at will?

A. No! The minds must be in perfect harmony and they must seek, simultaneously, the same end. Mere association of minds, alone, is not enough.

Q. Isn't it dangerous to give this sort of information to the world?

A. Sure, it is dangerous—to me! If I were you, I would not give it out!

Q. How does it happen that you have the power to control ninety-eight percent of the people of the world? What is your opposition doing while you are entangling people in your web of hypnotic rhythm? Why doesn't your opposition use the same law and take over all your victims for the other side?

A. How do you know that is not exactly what is happening right now? This is the first time anyone has forced me to tell my secrets.

Q. Let us get back now to the technique through which you fasten on your victims the habit of drifting. I want you to tell me, definitely, what is the point beyond which people who have the drifting habit cannot throw off the habit.

Where does one find that endless whirlpool you mentioned which fastens on its victims the law of hypnotic rhythm?

A. It will be difficult if not impossible for me to describe the exact point of a drifter's life beyond which he cannot throw off the habit and reclaim his right to use his own mind, but I will do my best. You see, the point beyond which the drifter cannot turn back differs with the individual.

Q. What is the very first step a drifter must take to break the habit?

A. A burning desire to break it! You of course know that no one can be hypnotized by another person without his willingness to be hypnotized. Neither can nature place one under the spell of hypnotic rhythm without his willingness to be hypnotized. The willingness may assume the form of indifference toward life generally, lack of ambition, fear, lack of definiteness of purpose, and many other forms. Nature does not need one's consent in order to place him under the spell of hypnotic rhythm. It needs only to find him off guard, through any form of neglect to use his own mind! Remember this—whatever you have, you use it or you lose it!

Q. I get the idea. Nature hates vacuums and idleness and unused things. Wherever she finds an empty, unused mind, she takes it over and puts it to work in her own way. Is that correct?

A. Yes, I see to it that no unused minds are neglected! I fill unused minds with the habit of drifting. After a while, natural law takes my job over and makes it permanent, through hypnotic rhythm. After that happens, there is no turning back for the individual. All successful attempts to break the habit of drifting must be done before nature makes the habit permanent, through hypnotic rhythm.

Q. As I understand you, hypnotic rhythm is a natural law through which nature fixes the vibration of all environments. Is that true?

A. Yes, nature uses hypnotic rhythm to make one's dominating thoughts and one's thought habits permanent. That is why poverty is a disease. Nature makes it so by fixing permanently the thought habits of all who accept poverty as an unavoidable circumstance.

Through this same law of hypnotic rhythm, nature will also fix permanently positive thoughts of opulence and prosperity.

Perhaps you will better understand the working principle of hypnotic rhythm if I tell you its nature is to fix permanently all habits, whether they are mental or physical! If your mind fears poverty, your mind will attract poverty. If your mind demands opulence and expects it, your mind will attract the physical and financial equivalents of opulence. This is in accordance with an immutable law of nature.

Q. Did the writer of that sentence in the Bible, "Whatsoever a man soweth, that shall he also reap" have in mind this law of nature?

A. He could have had nothing else in mind. The statement is true. You can see evidence of its truth in all human relationships.

Q. And that is why the man who forms the habit of drifting through life must accept whatever Life hands him. Is that correct?

A. That is absolutely correct. Life pays the drifter its own price, on its own terms. The non-drifter makes Life pay, on his own terms.

Q. Doesn't the question of morals enter into what one gets from life?

A. To be sure, but only for the reason that one's morals have an influence on one's thoughts. No one can collect what he wants from Life merely by being good, if that is what you want to know.

Q. Do I understand you to mean that the immoral person and the dishonest person can make Life pay in the same coin that Life pays the person who is honest and moral?

A. No, I made no such statement. Your question is answered by your own quotation from the Bible: Whatsoever a man soweth, that shall he also reap.

Q. Al Capone sowed beer and machine guns and reaped a fortune running into millions while men of sound morals, education, and a keen sense of justice were starving all around him.

What do you have to say to that?

A. Just this—Al Capone is now in durance vile, on a lonely island in the Pacific Ocean. Do you know of anyone who would take his place, his fears and his thoughts as well as his prison cell, in return for all the earthly possessions he has?

Q. No, I guess not! I see what you mean. We are all where we are and what we are because of our own deeds.

A. No, not exactly! You are where you are and what you are because of your thoughts and your deeds!

Q. Which is more important, one's thoughts or one's deeds?

A. All deeds follow thoughts! There can be no deeds without their having first been patterned in thought. Moreover, all thoughts have a tendency to clothe themselves in their physical counterpart.

One's dominating thoughts, that is, the thoughts one mixes with the emotions, desire, hope, faith, hate, greed, enthusiasm, not only have a tendency to clothe themselves in their physical equivalent, but they are bound to do so.

Q. How can a thought go about clothing or transmuting itself into its physical equivalent?

A. It proceeds through the most available natural means of attracting its physical counterpart. A thought may attract the physical thing it represents, or it may merely supply one with a plan and a motive for procuring the thing it represents.

Q. Where did you acquire all the understanding of Life which your confession shows you possess?

A. I acquired it from its original source, from facts and realities as they exist in all forms. The acquisition was not difficult because I am a part of Life, the negative part.

Q. That reminds me to ask you to tell me more about yourself. Where, in addition to the minds of people, do you dwell and operate?

A. I operate wherever there is something I can control and appropriate.

- I have already told you I am the negative portion of the electron of matter.

- I am the explosion in lightning.

- I am the pain in disease and physical suffering.

- I am the unseen General in warfare.

- I am the unknown Commissioner of Poverty and Famine.

- I am the executioner extraordinary at death.

- I am the inspirer of lust after the flesh.

- I am the creator of jealousy and envy and greed.

- I am the instigator of fear.

- I am the genius who converts the achievements of men of science into instruments of death.

- I am the destroyer of harmony in all manner of human relationships.

- I am the antithesis of justice.

- I am the driving force in all immorals. I am the stalemate of all good.

- I am anxiety, suspense, superstition, and insanity.

- I am the destroyer of hope and faith.

- I am the inspirer of destructive gossip and scandal.

- I am the discourager of free and independent thought.

- In brief, I am the creator of all forms of human misery, the instigator of discouragement and disappointment. My nature and my purpose is to destroy every living thing that uses energy and appropriate unto myself the energy of the vanquished!

Q. Nice fellow!

A. No, not nice fellow—powerful fellow!

Power is the thing that counts. Inmates of the poor house are nice enough, but they have no power. There is no virtue in being nice. Those who demand what they want from Life and make Life pay do so with power. Get this clearly fixed in your mind if you wish to make Life pay.

Q. Does one always have to be cruel, unjust, merciless, and cold-hearted to be powerful?

A. No! But one does have to be definite, courageous, persistent and above all else, know exactly what he wants! To such a person Life pays in his own coin. All others, Life hands over to me and I grind their bodies into dust and appropriate their souls to my own estates.

Q. And you do not call that cold and cruel?

A. I call that definite and dependable!

Q. What is the major difference between Henry Ford and any of the thousands of men who work for him?

A. The difference in appearance is slight. The unseen difference is great. Henry Ford knows what he wants of Life and has had the courage to make Life pay just that. The men who work for Ford have no such definite state of mind. That is the major difference between Ford and all men who cannot make Life pay in their terms.

Q. Was Ford born with this capacity to know what he wants and the ability to get it, or did he acquire it, through schooling or from his experience?

A. He was born with the potential capacity to know what he wants and the ability to get it. So is every other person! He was also born with the power of choice, to exercise his prerogative to demand what he wants of life or neglect to do so.

So is every other person.

Q. Is it not true that Ford's stupendous material achievements are due, in the main, to the fact he was born at a favorable time, when the world happened to need self-propelled vehicles of transportation, and he just happened to drift into contact with opportunity?

A. No one ever drifts into anything except failure! Where there was one opportunity to achieve material success when Ford began his business career, there are no fewer than a hundred equally advantageous opportunities today.

The world depression broke up the habits of men everywhere and redistributed the sources of opportunity in all walks of life on an unprecedented scale.

The drifter's pet alibi, with which he tried to explain away his undesirable position, is his cry that the world has run dry of opportunities.

Non-drifters do not wait for opportunity to be placed in their way. They create opportunity to fit their desires and demands of Life!

Q. Are non-drifters smart enough to avoid the influence of hypnotic rhythm?

A. No one is smart enough to dodge the influence of hypnotic rhythm! One could just as easily avoid the influence of the law of gravity.

The law of hypnotic rhythm fixes permanently the dominating thoughts of men, whether they be drifters or non-drifters.

There is no reason why a non-drifter would want to avoid the influence of hypnotic rhythm, because that law is favorable to him. It helps him convert his dominating aims, plans, and purposes into their physical replicas. It fixes his habits of thought and makes them permanent.

Only the drifter would wish to dodge the influence of hypnotic rhythm.

Q. For the better portion of my adult life, I have been a drifter. How did I manage to escape being swept into the whirlpool of hypnotic rhythm?

A. You haven't escaped! The major portion of your dominating thoughts and desires, since you reached adulthood, has been well-defined,definite desire to understand all the potentialities of the mind.

You may have drifted on thoughts of lesser importance, but you did not drift in connection with this desire. Because you did not drift in connection with this desire, you are now recording a document which gives you exactly what your dominating thoughts demanded of Life.

Q. Does hypnotic rhythm change or modify one's desires?

A. No, it only solidifies one's desires and makes them permanent.

Q. I see what you mean. Hypnotic rhythm is a sort of rope with which nature bundles one's habits and ties them in definite groups. Is that correct?

A. Yes! Another way to state the nature of hypnotic rhythm is to compare with cement which sets itself to conform with any desired pattern and hardens into permanency with time.

Q. Why doesn't your opposition use hypnotic rhythm to make permanent one's higher thoughts and nobler deeds? Why does your opposition permit you to use this stupendous force as a means of entangling people in a web of evil spun by their own thoughts and deeds? Why does your opposition not outwit you by binding people with thoughts which build and lift them above your influence?

A. The law of hypnotic rhythm is available to all who will use it! I make use of it more effectively than does my opposition, for the reason I offer people more attractive bribes to think my sorts of thoughts and indulge in my sorts of deeds!

Q. In other words, you control people by making negative thinking and destructive deeds pleasing to them. Is that correct?

A. That is the idea, exactly!

Q. If you speak the truth, why do you not make the churches more attractive, through programmes that compete successfully with the moving pictures and theatres and road houses and dance halls? Why are church programmes so dry and lacking in human interest?

A. The dryness of which you complain is no invention of mine. That is the work of my opposition. You see, I do not control the churches. I only use them to fight me and spread fear of me and to embarrass my opposition.

Q. I have often wondered why your opposition—what we earthbound call God—does not annihilate you? Can you tell me why?

A. Because the power which you earthbound call God is as much mine as his. It is as available to me as to him. That is what I have been trying to get over to you. The highest power in the universe can be used for constructive purposes, through what you call God, or it can be used for negative purposes, through what you call the Devil. And something more important still, it can be used by any human being just as effectively as by God or the Devil.

Q. That is a far-reaching claim you have made. Can you prove your claim?

A. Yes, but it would be better if you proved it for yourself. The Devil's word is not worth much among you earthbound sinners. Neither is God's word! You fear the Devil and refuse to trust your God; therefore, you have but one source available through which you may appropriate the benefits of universal power, and that is by trusting and using your own power of thought. This is the direct road to the universal storehouse of Infinite Intelligence. There is no other road available to any human being.

Q. Why have we earthbound not found the road to Infinite Intelligence sooner?

A. Because I have intercepted you and led you off the path by planting in your minds thoughts which destroy your power to use your minds constructively. I have made it attractive to you to use the power of Infinite Intelligence to attain negative ends, through greed, avarice, lust, envy, and hatred. Remember, your mind attracts that which your mind dwells upon. To divert you away from my opposition I had only to feed you on thoughts helpful to my cause.

Q. If I understand what you are saying, you are admitting that no human being need fear the Devil or worry about how to flatter God! That all who will may go direct to the universal supply of the stuff that people think with and appropriate as much of it as is needed to translate any desire into its physical equivalent. Is that the sum and substance of what you are trying to tell me?

A.   That is it precisely! This admission may put a crimp in my style, but I have this satisfaction of knowing it may also slow down my opposition by sending people direct to the source of all power!

Q.   In other words, if you cannot control people through negative bribes or fear, then you wish to kick over the entire apple cart and show people how to go around God? Are you, by any chance, in politics too? Your technique seems frightfully familiar!

A.   Am I in politics? If I am not in politics, who do you believe, starts depressions and forces people into wars? Surely you would not lay this at the door of my opposition? When it comes to astuteness, my boys in politics have it all over my boys in the churches. Moreover, my political henchmen glory in deeds to which my dupes in the churches would not stoop. As I have already told you, I have allies in all walks of life, to help me in connection with all human relationships.

Q.   Why don't you take over the churches and use them outright in your cause?

A.   Do you think I am a fool? Who would keep alive the fear of the Devil if I subdued the churches? Who would serve as a decoy to attract the attention of people while I manipulate their minds, if I did not have some agency through which to sow the seeds of fear and doubt? The cleverest thing I do is to use the allies of my opposition to keep the fear of hell burning in the minds of people. As long as people fear something, no matter what, I will keep a grip on them!

Q.   I am beginning to see your scheme. You use the churches to plant the seed of fear and uncertainty and indefiniteness in the minds of people. These negative states of mind cause people to form the habit of drifting. This habit crystallizes into permanency through the law of hypnotic rhythm; then the victim is helpless to help himself, is that right?

A. That is exactly right. When a person drifts, no matter through what sort of habit, until his drifting habit becomes fixed through the law of hypnotic control, not all the forces of the universe can give back to him his privilege of independent thought.

Q. Do you mean to say that your opposition has not the power to restore to a person his ability to think independently?

A. No, not after the ability has been lost, through hypnotic rhythm. Remember, hypnotic rhythm is the force that keeps everything in the universe under control and properly related to everything else. Nothing can rank above this power. If anything could change it in a single instance, the universe could be wiped out of existence, and it would have been, long before now.

Q. Hypnotic rhythm, then, is something to be watched and respected?

A. A better way of stating the truth is that hypnotic rhythm is something to be studied, understood, and voluntarily applied to attain definite *desired* ends.

Q. If the force of hypnotic rhythm is not voluntarily applied to attain definite ends, may it be a great danger?

A. Yes, and for the reason that it operates automatically! If it is not consciously applied to attain a desired end, it can, and it will, operate to attain undesired ends.

Q. What simple, elementary evidence of the existence of the law of hypnotic rhythm can I use to describe this astounding law to people who have little or no scientific training and know little or nothing of the major principles of nature?

A. The best method will be to present a description of the working principle of the law by showing how it operates in the daily lives of people.

Take the simple illustrations of climate, for example.

Anyone can see and understand that nature forces every living thing and every element of matter to adjust itself to her climates. In the tropics she creates trees which bear fruit and reproduce themselves. She forces the trees to adjust themselves to her scorching sun! She forces them to put out leaves suitable for protection against the rays of the sun. These same trees could not survive if removed to the arctic regions, where nature has established an entirely different climate.

In the colder climate, she creates trees which are adjusted to survive and to reproduce themselves, but they could not survive if transplanted in the tropical regions. In the same manner, nature clothes her animals, giving to those in each different climate a covering suited to their comfort and survival in that climate.

In a similar manner, nature forces upon the minds of men the influences of their environment which are stronger than the individual's own thoughts.

Children are forced to take on the nature of all influences of those around them unless their own thoughts are stronger than the influences.

Nature sets up a definite rhythm for every environment, and everything within the range of that rhythm is forced to conform to it. Man, alone, has the power to establish his own rhythm of thought providing he exercises this privilege before hypnotic rhythm has forced upon him the influences of his environment.

Every home, every place of business, every town and village and every street and community center has its own definite, discernible rhythm.

If you wish to know what a difference there is in the rhythms of streets, take a walk up Fifth Avenue, in New York, and back down Tenth Avenue, through the slums! All forms of rhythm become permanent with time.

Q.   Does each individual have his own rhythm of thought?

A.   Yes! That is precisely the major difference between individuals. The person who thinks in terms of power, success, opulence, sets up a rhythm which attracts these desirable possessions.

The person who thinks in terms of misery, failure, defeat, discouragement, and poverty attracts these undesirable influences. This explains why both success and failure are the result of habit. Habit establishes one's rhythm of thought, and that rhythm attracts the object of one's dominating thoughts.

Q.   Hypnotic rhythm is something resembling a magnet which attracts things for which it has a magnetic affinity. Is that correct?

A.   Yes, that is correct. That is why the poverty-stricken herd themselves in the same communities. It explains that old saying, misery loves company.

It also explains why people who begin to succeed in any undertaking find that success multiplies, with less effort, as time goes on.

All successful people use hypnotic rhythm, either consciously or unconsciously by expecting and demanding success.

The demand becomes a habit, hypnotic rhythm takes over the habit and the law of harmonious attraction translates it into its physical equivalent.

Q.   Then there is not such reality as luck, is there?

A.   Emphatically no. Circumstances which people do not understand are classified under the heading of luck. Back of every reality is a cause. Often the cause is so far removed from the effect that the circumstance can be explained only by attributing it to the operation of luck. Nature knows no such law as luck. It is a man-made hypothesis with which he explains away things he does not understand.

The terms luck and miracle are twin sisters. Neither of them has any real existence except in the imaginations of people. Both are used to explain that which people do not understand. Remember this, everything having a real existence is capable of proof. Keep this one truth in mind and you will become a sounder thinker.

Q. Your confession puts you behind the eight ball doesn't it, Your Majesty? If your unwitting allies in the churches should be called upon to prove your existence, they, too, would be behind the eight ball, would they not?

A. Frankly, you are right! But I have this arranged my way. I keep religious instructors so busy declaring I do exist, and their followers so frightened of me, that neither has the time to look for proof that I do not exist in the flesh.

Q. And old man hypnotic rhythm has helped your cause too, has he not?

A. Yes, he has! The religious instructors have been frightening people with me so long that it is difficult for the majority of adults who fear me to throw off that fear, no matter how much proof of my nonexistence one might offer them. You see, these people have been permanently attached to their fears with the aid of hypnotic rhythm. In other words, they have been literally hypnotized into submission to fear!

Q. Let me see, now, if I am acquiring a practical working understanding of the law of hypnotic rhythm. Am I correct in assuming that nothing can escape the influence of this law?

A. A better way to state the truth is, by controlling and directing his thoughts toward a definite end, man can place himself under the influence of the power of hypnotic rhythm in translating his thoughts into their material equivalent.

Q. In other words, if I know what I want from Life, demand it and back my demand by a willingness to pay Life's price for what I want, and refuse to accept any substitutes, the law of hypnotic rhythm takes over my desire and helps, by natural and logical means, to transmute it into its physical counterpart.

Is that true?

A. That describes the way the law works.

Q. Science has established irrefutable evidence that people are what they are because of heredity and environment. They bring over with them at birth a combination of all the physical qualities of all their numberless ancestors.

After they arrive here, they reach the age of self-consciousness and from there on they shape their own personalities and more or less fix their own earthly destinations as the result of the environmental influences to which they are subjected, especially the influences which control them during early childhood.

These two facts have been so well-established there is no room for any intelligent person to question them.

How can hypnotic rhythm change the nature of a physical body which is a combination of thousands of ancestors who have lived and died before one is born?

How can hypnotic rhythm change the influence of one's environment? People who are born in poverty and ignorance have a strong tendency to remain poverty-stricken and ignorant all through life. What, if anything, can hypnotic rhythm do about this?

A. Hypnotic rhythm cannot change the nature of the physical body one inherits at birth, but it can and it does modify change, control, and make permanent one's environmental influences.

An individual may choose his own environment, but nature fastens upon him the habits he acquires in that environment. Hypnotic rhythm does not create environment, but it does coalesce and bring together everything in a given environment, and forces the tempo or rate of vibration of the environment upon every living thing with the power of understanding and reason.

Q. If I understand what you mean, a human being is forced by nature to take on and become a part of the environment he chooses or the environment that may be forced upon him?

A. That is correct, but there are ways and means by which an individual may resist the influences of an environment he does not wish to accept, and also a method of procedure by which one may reverse the application of hypnotic rhythm from negative to positive ends.

Q. Do you mean there is a definite method by which hypnotic rhythm can be made to serve instead of destroy one?

A. I mean just that!

Q. Tell me how this astounding end may be attained.

A. My description, to be of any practical value, will be necessarily lengthy because it will have to cover seven principles of psychology which must be understood and applied by all who use hypnotic rhythm to aid them in forcing Life to yield that which they want.

Q. Then break your description into seven parts, each giving a detailed analysis of one of the seven principles, with simple instructions for its practical application.

Author's Note: Now follows the Devil's detailed description of the seven principles through which human beings may take complete control of their own minds.

The principles, themselves, may appear simple enough. Their importance assumes an astounding proportion when one learns to what extent they control human destiny.

The first of the seven principles is the master key that unlocks the doors of spiritual limitation behind which most people imprison themselves through their habit of drifting.

I have a strong notion that the description of how the seven principles work in the practical affairs of life will subordinate to a relatively unimportant position all the Devil has told us up to this point.

I have an idea—an idea based upon close observation of thousands of people—that the Devil's real secrets of control over human beings will be unfolded in his description of the seven principles.

I have not reached that portion of his confession, but I predict it will disclose information so far-reaching in nature that it will enable one to quickly break the spell of hypnotic rhythm and take possession of his own mind, think his own thoughts and live His own life in an atmosphere of physical, mental, and spiritual freedom.

His Majesty is in the witness chair again! Let's hear what he has to say.

CHAPTER SIX

◆

DEFINITENESS
OF PURPOSE

Q. Your Majesty will now proceed to unfold the secrets of the seven principles through which human beings may force Life to provide them with spiritual, mental, and physical freedom! Do not be sparing in your description of these principles. I want a complete illustration of how the principles may be used by anyone who chooses to use them. Tell us all you know about the principle of definiteness of purpose!

A. You are forcing me to commit suicide! If you go through with this mad idea of yours, you will open the gates of Hell and turn loose all the precious souls I have collected back down through the ages! You will deprive me of souls yet unborn! You will release from my bondage millions now living! Stop, I beg of you, before it is too late.

Q. Then my suspicions are correct! I can see by your whining that you have not told the important part of your story. You have been dealing in abstractions and generalities. Now that I am forcing you to get down to details and tell how people may break the spell of hypnotic rhythm, you are beginning to squeal. Open up, let's hear what you have to say about the principle of definiteness of purpose.

A. You are pouring water on the fires of Hell, but the responsibility is yours, not mine! I may as well tell you that any human being who can be definite in his aims and plans can make Life hand over whatever is wanted!

Q. That is a broad claim, Your Majesty! Do you wish to tone it down a bit?

A. Tone it down? No, I wish to tone it up! When you hear what I now have to say, you will understand why the principle of definiteness is so important. My opposition uses a clever little trick to cheat me of my control over people. The opposition knows that definiteness of purpose closes the door of one's mind so tightly against me that I cannot break through unless I can induce one to form the habit of drifting.

Q. Why doesn't your opposition give your secret to all people by telling them to avoid you, through definiteness of purpose? You have already admitted that two out of every hundred people belong to your opposition.

A. Because I am more clever than my opposition! I draw people away from definiteness with my promises. You see, I control more people than my opposition because I am a better salesman and a better showman! I attract people by feeding them liberally of the thought habits in which they like to indulge.

Q. So, you are a better salesman than Omnipotence?

A. If I were not, I would not have a bigger following!

Q. Is definiteness of purpose something with which one must be born, or may it be acquired?

A. Everyone, as I have told you before, is born with the privilege of being definite, but ninety-eight out of every hundred people lose this privilege by sleeping on it. The privilege of definiteness can be maintained only by adopting it as a policy by which one is guided in all the affairs of Life!

Q. Oh, I see! One takes advantage of the principle of definiteness just as one may build a strong physical body—through constant, systematic use! Is that it?

A. You have stated the truth clearly and accurately.

Q. Now I think we are getting somewhere, Your Majesty! We have at long last found the starting point from which all who become self-determining in Life must take off!

We have discovered, from your astounding confession, that your greatest asset is man's lack of caution which enables you to lead him into the jungle of indefiniteness through simple bribes.

We have learned, beyond the question of doubt, that anyone who adopts definiteness of purpose as a policy and uses it in all of his daily experiences, cannot be induced to form the habit of drifting. Without the aid of the drifting habit, you are powerless to attract people through promises.

Is this correct?

A. I couldn't have stated the truth more clearly myself!

Q. Go ahead, now, and describe how people neglect their privilege of being free and self-determining through indefiniteness and drifting.

A. I have already made brief reference to this principle, but I will now go into more minute details as to how the principle works.

I shall have to begin at the time of birth. When a child is born, it brings with it nothing but a physical body representing the evolutionary results of millions of years of ancestry.

Its mind is a total blank! When the child reaches the age of consciousness and begins to recognize the objects of its surroundings, it begins, also, to imitate others.

Imitation becomes a fixed habit. Naturally, the child imitates first of all its parents! Then it begins to imitate its other relatives and daily associates, including its religious instructors and school teachers.

The imitation extends not merely to physical expression, but also to thought expression! If a child's parents fear me and express that fear within range of the child's hearing, the child picks up the fear, through the habit of imitation, and stores it away as a part of its subconscious stock of beliefs!

If the child's religious instructor expresses any form of fear of me (and they all do, in one form or another), that fear is added to the similar fear passed to the child by its parents, and the two forms of negative limitation are stored away in the subconscious mind to be drawn upon and used by me later in life.

In a similar way, the child learns, by imitation, to limit its power of thought by filling its mind with envy, hatred, greed, lust, revenge, and all the other negative impulses of thought which destroy all possibility of definiteness.

Meanwhile, I move in and induce the child to drift until I bind its mind through hypnotic rhythm.

Q. Am I to understand, from your remarks, that you have to gain control of people while they are very young or lose your opportunity at them altogether?

A. I prefer to claim them before they come into possession of their own minds. Once any person learns the power of his own thoughts, he becomes positive and difficult to subdue! As a matter of fact, I cannot control any human being who discovers and uses the principle of definiteness!

Q. Is the habit of definiteness a permanent protection against your control?

A. No, not by any means! Definiteness closes the door of one's mind to me only as long as that person follows the principle as a matter of policy. Once any person hesitates, procrastinates, or becomes indefinite about anything, he is just one step removed from my control!

Q. What has definiteness to do with one's material circumstances?

A. Almost everything! You can answer this question accurately by analyzing any man who achieves outstanding success, or anyone who goes down in any form of failure. The permanently successful person always is definite. He makes definiteness a regular policy.

Q. I take it, from what you say, that indefiniteness is the habit which gives the world so many poverty-stricken people!

A. Lack of definiteness automatically develops in one the habit of drifting! The habit of drifting leads to the control of hypnotic rhythm. Poverty is a natural material reflection of the negative habit of drifting.

Q. I get the impression from your confession that the habit of definiteness of purpose is the foundation of all personal power. Is that correct?

A. Analyze those who have power and you will have the right answer. Take the three European dictators, for example! No one would be so vulgar as to claim that they have justice on their side, but everyone knows they have power! Not everyone knows they got their power by knowing definitely what they wanted and being determined to get it at any price!

Q. But, Your Majesty, I want to know if one may acquire power through definiteness of purpose, without inviting destruction through the law of compensation. It is true the European dictators have power, and they got it through definiteness, but it is also true that this same power will destroy all three of them. Time will see to that—time and the law of compensation!

A. Oh, you want to know how to have power without the danger of being destroyed by it, do you?

Q. That is the idea precisely! No sane person wants the sort of power with which the European dictators have forced their followers into an unwilling form of renunciation of their rights to freedom. Let us know how one may gain power through definiteness of purpose without acquiring with it the unwanted element of self-destruction.

A. Your question limits my illustrations because there are so few people in the world who understand, and there have been so few in the past who understood, and there have been so few in the past who understood how to use definiteness of purpose without attracting to themselves the negative application of the law of Compensation.

Here you are forcing me to disclose one of my most prized tricks! I am bound to tell you that I eventually reclaim for my cause all who escape me temporarily through definiteness of purpose. The reclamation is made by filling the mind with greed for power and the love of egotistical expression, until the individual falls into the habit of violating the rights of others. Then I step in with the law of Compensation and reclaim my victim.

Q. So, I see from your admission that definiteness of purpose may be dangerous in proportion to its possibility as a power. Is that true?

A. Yes, and what is more important, every principle of good carries with it the seed of an equivalent danger!

Q. That is hard to believe, Your Majesty! What danger, for example, can there be in the habit of love of truth?

A. The danger lies in the word habit! All habits, save only that of definiteness, may lead to the habit of drifting! Love for truth, unless it assumes the proportion of definite pursuit of truth, may become similar to all other good intentions. You know, of course, what I do with good intentions!

Q.   Is love for one's relatives also dangerous?

A.   The love of anything or anyone, save only the love of definiteness of purpose, may become dangerous. Love is a state of mind which beclouds reason and willpower, and blinds one to facts and truth!

Everyone who becomes self-determining and gains spiritual freedom to think his own thoughts must examine carefully every emotion that seems even remotely related to love.

You may be surprised to know that love is one of my most effective baits. With it, I lead into the habit of drifting those whom I could attract with nothing else.

That is why I have placed it at the head of my list of bribes. Show me what any person loves most, and I will have my cue as to how that person can be induced to drift until I bind him with hypnotic rhythm.

Love and fear, combined, give me the most effective weapons with which I induce people to drift! One is as helpful to me as the other! Both have the effect of causing people to neglect to develop definiteness in the use of their own minds. Give me control over a person's fears and tell me what he loves most and you may as well mark that person down as my slave.

Q.   Your explanation of love and fear leads me to believe that no one who is mastered by either can take full advantage of the principle of definiteness? Is that correct? Does the thing one loves or fears have anything to do with the extent to which these two states of mind are dangerous?

A.   The thing loved or feared makes no difference! Both love and fear are emotional forces of such stupendous potency that either may completely set aside the power of will and the power of reason. With these two out of the way, there is nothing left to support definiteness of purpose.

Q. Do religious instructors play into your hands when they implore their followers to love God?

A. Indeed they do! That is another of my clever tricks. I use religious instructors to teach people fear, and I use them to teach people love! As inconsistent as that may appear, it constitutes my cleverest strategy! Through it, I use millions of people in furthering my cause who, if they knew what they were doing, would balk on me.

I can control some through fear of me, others through love of my opposition. It is all the same to me which way people enter my service.

Q. But, Your Majesty, life would not be worth living if people never felt the emotion of love.

A. Ah! You are right as far as your reasoning goes, but you neglected to add that love should be under one's definite control at all times.

Of course, love is a desirable state of mind, but it also is a palliative which may be used to limit or destroy reason and willpower, both of which rate above love in importance to human beings who want freedom and self-determination.

Q. I understand, from what you say, that people who gain power must harden their emotions, master fear, and subdue love. Is that correct?

A. People who gain and maintain power must become definite in all their thoughts and all their deeds. If that is what you call hard, then they must become hard.

Q. Let us look into the sources of advantage of definiteness in the everyday affairs of life. Which is more apt to succeed, a weak plan applied with definiteness, or a sound strong plan indefinitely applied?

A. Weak plans have a way of becoming strong if definitely applied.

Q. You mean that any plan definitely put into continuous action in pursuit of a definite purpose may be successful even if it is not the best plan?

A. Yes, I mean just that! Definiteness of purpose, plus definiteness of plan by which the purpose is to be achieved, generally succeed, no matter how weak the plan may be. The major difference between a sound and an unsound plan is that the sound plan, if definitely applied, may be carried out more quickly than an unsound plan.

Q. In other words, if one cannot be always right, one can and should be always definite? Is that what you are trying to get across to me?

A. That is the idea! People who are definite in both their plans and their purposes never accept temporary defeat as being more than an urge to greater effort. You can see for yourself that this sort of policy is bound to win if it is followed with definiteness.

Q. What human weakness heads the list of the most common of all causes of failure?

A. Indefiniteness! This habit literally opens the door of one's mind and invites all the destructive traits and habits to come in and park themselves.

Notice how misfortune, defeat, discouragement, and ill health trail after the person who has a drifting policy.

Observe how these negatives are conspicuous by their absence where one has a policy of definiteness of plan and purpose. All leaders are definite. All followers trail along through indefiniteness! Followers cannot have great power. They can only help leaders to acquire power.

Q. Does the mere state of mind known as definiteness give one power?

A. Definiteness inspires and attracts cooperation from others. Also it discourages opposition, for the reason that all forms of opposition require definiteness. It is not the mere state of mind known as definiteness which gives one power. But it is the forces, people, and knowledge which definiteness attracts.

Q. Speaking of the power of fear, what is your greatest fear?

A. That the world will produce an accurate thinker with enough definiteness of purpose to convert the schools and churches into institutions teaching definiteness!

Q. That is a brief and apparently a simple fear! It seems that if I were the Devil, I would fear Infinite Intelligence more than all else.

A. I can hold my balance of power with my opposition as long as I can control ninety-eight out of every hundred human minds. When I lose that control, I am forced into a defensive position. I prefer to be on the aggressive side of life!

Q. Evidently you do not fear anyone who drifts on any subject or has a drifting policy?

A. Why should I? I control all drifters. That is, I control them as long as they drift. When they stop drifting and begin thinking and acting in terms of definiteness, as a few of them do, I lose my control.

Q. I take it, from what you say, that definiteness of policy gives one power and other advantages not enjoyed by drifters?

A. If you want an idea of how much advantage the person with a policy of definiteness in all his thoughts and deeds has over the person without such a policy, observe the importance with which nature regards definiteness.

Do you think it is mere luck or chance that the sun which warms your world rises and sets with perfect regularity, in response to nature's law of rhythm?

Do you think it a mere coincident that nature never vacillates in her policy of definiteness by causing a pine to grow from an acorn?

Do you think the ebb and flow of the tides of the oceans occur with punctual regularity and definiteness by chance?

If you want evidence that definiteness is the very foundation upon which all human freedom must be built, observe and ponder over the fact that definiteness is the hub around which nature causes the entire system of universes to revolve.

The person who does not know precisely what he wants of Life must accept whatever Life has left over after those who use definiteness as a policy get through choosing.

Look around you, take inventory of all whom you call successful, and observe that their success is in exact proportion to their definiteness of plan and purpose. There is never an exception to this rule.

Q. You are making some very definite statements! I have tried to pick flaws in what you say, but no evidence to support me is available.

A. No! The evidence is all on the other side.

Q. Can a person who moves with definiteness of both plan and purpose be always sure of success?

A. No! The best of plans sometimes misfire, but the person who moves with definiteness recognizes the difference between temporary defeat and failure. When plans fail, he substitutes others but he does not change his purpose. Eventually he finds a plan that succeeds.

Q. Will a plan based upon immoral or unjust ends succeed as quickly as one motivated by a keen sense of justice and morality?

A. Through the operation of the law of Compensation, everyone reaps that which he sows. Plans based on unjust or immoral motives may bring temporary success, but enduring success must take into consideration the fourth dimension, Time.

Time is the enemy of immorality and injustice. It is the friend of justice and morality. Failure to recognize this fact has been responsible for the crime wave among the youths of the world.

The youthful, inexperienced mind is apt to mistake temporary success for permanency. The youth often makes the mistake of coveting the temporary gains of immoral, unjust plans, but neglects to look ahead and observe the penalties which follow as definitely as night follows day.

Q. This is pretty deep stuff, Your Majesty. Let us get back to the discussion of lighter and more concrete subjects that are likely to interest the majority of people.

A. Very well, you lead and I must follow, but do not overlook the fact that in a careful analysis of these abstractions may be found the very warp and the woof of all that gives human beings freedom of spirit and body.

Q. That is true, but I am interested in discussing the things that make people happy and miserable, rich and poor, sick and healthy. In brief, I am interested in everything that can be used by human beings to make Life pay satisfactory dividends in return for the effort that one puts into the business of living. Let us confine our discussion to the forces which affect for weal or for woe the average man.

A. Very well, let us be definite.

Q. You have my idea. Your Majesty has a tendency to stray off into abstract details which most people can neither understand nor use in the solution of their problems. Could that, by any chance, be a definite plan of yours to answer my questions with indefinite answers? If that is your plan, it is a slick trick but it will not work. Go ahead now and tell me something more of the miseries and failures of human beings growing directly out of indefiniteness!

A. Why not permit me to tell you more of the pleasures and successes of people who understand and apply the principle of definiteness?

Q. You win! I accept your reprimand. It will be more helpful to learn what succeeds than to hear about what leads to failure. However, I wish to hear both sides of the story. To live a full, complete, and happy life one must know not only what to do, but also what not to do!

A. One thing the person who wishes to live a full and happy life must not do is drift on any subject. One thing he must do is be definite in both purpose and plan!

Q. I observe that sometimes people with definiteness of plan and purpose get what they ask from Life only to find, after they get it, that they do not want it! What then?

A. Generally one can get rid of whatever is not wanted by application of the same principle of definiteness with which the thing was acquired. A life that is lived with fullness of peace of mind, contentment and happiness always divests itself of everything it does not want! Anyone who submits to annoyance by things he does not want is not definite. He is a drifter!

Q. What about married people who cease to want one another? Should they separate, or is it true that all marriages are made in heaven and the contracting parties are, therefore, forever bound by their bargain even though it may prove to be a poor one for both.

A. First, let me correct that old saying that all marriages are made in heaven. I know of some which were made on my side of the fence. Minds which do not harmonize should never be forced to remain together in marriage or any other relationship.

Friction and all forms of discord between minds lead inevitably to the habit of drifting, and of course to indefiniteness.

Q. Aren't people sometimes bound to others by a relationship of duty which renders it impractical for them to take from Life what they want most?

A. Duty is one of the most abused and misunderstood words in existence. The first duty of every human being is to himself! Every person owes himself the duty of finding how to live a full and happy life. Beyond this, if one has time and energy not needed in the fulfillment of his own desires, one may assume responsibility for helping others.

Q. Isn't that a selfish attitude, and isn't selfishness one of the causes of failure to find happiness?

A. I stand by my statement that there is no higher duty than that which one owes himself!

Q. Doesn't a child owe something in the way of duty to its parents who gave it life and sustenance during its period of helplessness?

A. Not at all! It is just the other way around. Parents owe their children everything they can give them in the way of knowledge. Beyond that, parents often spoil instead of helping their offspring, by a false sense of duty which prompts them to indulge their children instead of forcing them to seek and gain knowledge at first hand!

Q. I see what you mean! Your theory is that too much help thrust upon the youth encourages him to drift and become indefinite in all things. You believe that necessity is a teacher of great sagacity, that defeat carries with it an equivalent virtue, that unearned gifts of every nature may become a curse instead of a blessing. Is that correct?

A. You have stated my philosophy perfectly. My belief is not theory. It is fact.

Q. Then you do not advocate prayer as a means of gaining desirable ends?

A. On the contrary, I do advocate prayer, but not the sort of prayer that consists of empty, begging, meaningless words! The sort of prayer against which I am helpless is the prayer of definiteness of purpose.

Q. I never thought of definiteness of purpose as being a prayer. How can it be?

A. Definiteness is in effect the only sort of prayer upon which one can rely. It places one in the way of using hypnotic rhythm to attain definite ends.

Q. To whom should one pray?

A. To himself!

Q. That is an astounding statement! How can a poor, weak human being answer his own prayers?

A. Who told you all human beings are poor and weak? The weak ones are those who drift until they are bound to the treadmill of indefiniteness, through the law of hypnotic rhythm. The others know what they want and proceed to get it—through definiteness of demand which is all there is of prayer!

Q. How does a human being come by the power with which to answer his own prayers?

A. By the mere act of appropriating it from the great universal store house of Infinite Intelligence. The appropriation, in case you are interested, takes place through definiteness of purpose persistently pursued!

Q. Why do the majority of prayers fail?

A. They don't! All prayers bring that for which one prays!

Q. But, you just said that definiteness of purpose is the only sort of prayer upon which one can rely. Now you say that all prayers bring results. What do you mean?

A. There is nothing inconsistent about it. The majority of people who pray go to prayer only after everything else fails them. Naturally they go with their minds filled with fear the prayers will not be answered. Well, their fears are realized!

The person who goes to prayer with definiteness of purpose and faith in the attainment of that purpose puts into motion the laws of nature which transmute one's dominating desires into their physical equivalent. That is all there is to prayer.

One form of prayer is negative and brings only negative results. One form is positive and brings definite, positive results. Could anything be more simple? The individual answers his own prayers because he controls his own state of mind, making it positive or negative.

Q. Religious instructors will deny what you say! They will claim that God must be flattered and beseeched through humble begging before he will answer prayer favorably. Is that true?

A. I know; that is what the religious instructors claim. They also claim that God will listen only to their prayers. I want them to keep right on making this claim. If they ever told the plain truth about who answers prayers and why, I would be sunk.

Q. Oh, I see! It helps your cause when religious instructors influence people to do their praying through agents?

A. You are catching on fast! There is something else about prayer— the sort that is done through religious instructors—that will interest you. It is one of the greatest builders of the habit of drifting!

People who whine and beg God to assume responsibility for all their troubles and provide them with all the necessities and luxuries of life are too lazy to create what they want and translate it into existence, through the power of their own minds.

When you hear a person praying for something that he should procure through his own efforts, you may be sure you are listening to a drifter!

Q. What about prayers that one reads from a prayer book?

A. What about them? Why, prayer books are made to sell for a profit! That is the most important thing about them. I encourage the use of prayer books! Anyone who is too lazy to phrase the wording of his own prayer is my meat.

Q. Some of the finest people I have ever known are devout believers in the orthodox form of prayer. If these people cannot influence the God to whom they pray, who could?

A. Infinite Intelligence favors only those who understand and adapt themselves to her laws! She makes no discrimination because of fine character or pleasing personality. These things help people negotiate their way through life more harmoniously with one another, but the source from which prayer is answered is not impressed by fine feathers! Nature's law is: know what you want, adapt yourself to my laws, and you shall have it.

Q. Does that harmonize with the teachings of Christ?

A. Perfectly! Also it harmonizes with the teachings of all truly great philosophers!

Q. Is your theory of definiteness in harmony with the philosophy of men of science?

A. Definiteness is the major difference between a scientist and a drifter! Through the principle of definiteness of purpose and plan, the scientist forces nature to hand over her most profound secrets. It was through this principle that Edison uncovered the secret of the talking machine, the incandescent electric light, and scores of other benefactors of mankind.

Q. Then I understand that definiteness is the first requisite for success in all earthly undertakings? Is that right?

A. Exactly!

Q. Why did the churches of the world lose their control over civilization, and why is the world now looking to men of science for the further advancement of knowledge?

A. The churches lost their grip on people because of the indefiniteness of their creeds and abstract doctrines. They spent too much time teaching people how to die and too little time teaching people how to live. They lost ground by looking backward and worshipping a dead and decadent past instead of living in the present and looking to the future for the unfoldment of greater knowledge of how to live.

Men of science have increased the space they occupy because of their definiteness of both purpose and plan of attainment. Civilization of the future will be in the hands of scientists and educators who teach scientific facts, based upon definite knowledge!

Q. Isn't that going to be hard on your profession?

A. Anything which teaches people to examine facts and coordinate them into definite plans through accurate thinking is hard on my profession.

If this thirst for definite knowledge now spreading over the world keeps up, my business will be shot to pieces within the next few centuries. I thrive on ignorance, superstition, intolerance, and fear, but I cannot stand up under definite knowledge properly organized into definite plans, in the minds of people who think for themselves.

Q. Why don't you take over Omnipotence and manage the whole works in your own way?

A. Why doesn't Omnipotence take me over and manage the whole works his way? The answer is definite and accurate—neither can take over the other because each controls one half of the power which keeps the universes under organized control.

You might as well ask why the negative portion of the electron doesn't take over the positive portion and run the entire works. The answer is, both the positive and the negative charges of energy are necessary to the existence of the electron. One is balanced equally against the other, stalemated, as it were.

So it is with what you call Omnipotence and I. We represent the positive and the negative forces of the entire system of universes, and we are equally balanced one against the other.

If this power of balance were shifted the slightest degree, the whole system of universes would become quickly reduced to a mass of inert matter. Now you know why I cannot take over the whole show and run it my way.

Q. If what you say is true, you have exactly the same power as Omnipotence. Is that true?

A. That is correct! My opposition—you call it Omnipotence—expresses itself through the forces which you call good, the positive forces of nature. I express myself through the forces you call bad, the negative forces. Both good and bad are coincidental with existence. One is as important as the other!

Q. What good do you get from tormenting human beings?

A. Just as much good as my opposition gets from giving aid and comfort to human beings. We both express our natures, through natural laws which we can neither change nor avoid.

Q. Then the doctrine of predestination is sound. People are born to success or failure, misery or happiness, to be good or bad, and they have nothing to do with this nor can they modify their natures. Is that your claim?

A. Emphatically not! Every human being has a wide range of choice in both his thoughts and his deeds. Every human being can use his brain for the reception and the expression of positive thoughts, or he can use it for the expression of negative thoughts. His choice in this important matter shapes his entire life.

Q. From what you have said, I gather the idea that human beings have more freedom of expression than either you or your opposition. Is that correct?

A. That is true! Omnipotence and I are bound by immutable laws of nature. We cannot express ourselves in any manner not conforming to these laws.

Q. Then it is true that man has rights and privileges not available to either Omnipotence or the Devil. Is that the truth?

A. Yes, that is true, but you might well have added that man has not yet fully awakened to the realization of this potential power. Man still regards himself as something resembling the worms of the dust, when in reality he has more power than all other living things combined.

Q. Is it possible for man to create material things through transmutation of thought?

A. Yes, it has been done and it will be done again. Men of science have not yet discovered the natural law by which this phenomenon is produced, but they will. It may give you a cue as to how this will be done if I tell you that definiteness of purpose is the starting point from which the scientists must begin their research.

Q. Do you mean that nature will hand over the secret of how thought can be transmuted into matter if demand for secret is made sufficiently definite?

A. I would not state it that way. I would say that a group of minds coordinated and directed toward a definite end, in a spirit of perfect harmony, may bring into the range of understanding a natural law with which thought can be transmuted into matter.

Q. But this result will not likely be attained by a single mind?

A. Not likely! No one mind has sufficient capacity to vibrate with the high frequency necessary to recognize this law.

Q. But you are sure the discovery and use of the law will come through definiteness of purpose?

A. Yes! No drifter or group of drifters will discover or make use of the law. This has been true of all the discoveries of natural law.

Q. I find myself intrigued by your astounding claims, but I also find them difficult to accept.

A. Of course you do! All new ideas are difficult of acceptance!

Q. What class of people will hate me most for exposing your secrets?

A. Religious instructors.

Q. All of them?

A. No! Only the intolerant ones. The thinkers among the clergy will crown you with orchids. The drifters who make no pretense of thinking will crown you with stones! Look what they did to Robert G. Ingersoll and Thomas Paine!

Q. What about the average man of the world—the man who is earnestly seeking truth no matter where he finds it or who discloses it? What will be his attitude toward my exposure of your secrets?

A. The thinkers will hold an open mind toward you and begin searching for ways and means of checking the truth of your exposure.

The intolerant, the ignorant and the indifferent drifters will yell hooey and let it go at that. They always look with skepticism on anything that requires them to think for themselves.

Q. How many real thinkers are there in the world today?

A. Come, come now, Mr. Earthbound! I am only a poor, hard-working Devil, you know, and you cannot expect me to know how many accurate thinkers there are in the world.

Q. What will men of science say about my exposure of your secrets?

A. Men of science generally refrain from thinking from mere hypotheses. They demand evidence of facts. If you are as prolific at giving evidence as you are at asking definite questions, you will be in a position to satisfy any real scientist of the authenticity of your exposure. But don't worry about what the world will say of this exposure. I am the one who ought to be worrying.

Q. If you exist in the minds of men, where does God exist?

A. You mean the Gods! The world has had its choice of more than thirty thousand different gods, ranging in nature from an angle worm to a man.

Thirty thousand of them, mind you! And every one the creation of man's imagination.

What you earthbound call God exists in exactly the same place that I exist. In fact, your God is co-existent with me, a part of the force I represent. Anyone who searches for a personal God or a personal Devil will have a long search. The names God and Devil represent the negative and the positive forces of nature, nothing more!

Q. Will it not shock people to learn of this truth?

A. Most people are shocked by any truth. The discoveries of men of science so shocked the people of Bruno's time that they burned him at the stake for revealing the nature of the stars, through the aid of a telescope.

Socrates was forced to poison himself because he shocked the people of his time with his disclosures of truth concerning natural laws.

Emerson shocked the people of his time by his interpretation of the law of Compensation through which nature keeps a perfect balance between all forces and all matter.

Benjamin Franklin shocked the people of his time by proving the lightning to be electrical energy and not God's method of expressing his disapproval of men.

Christ shocked the people of his time by frank disclosure of the fact that all men have equal rights to appropriate and use the power of Infinite Intelligence.

Q. Isn't fear of the Devil the only thing that holds some people in check and keeps them from reverting to the primitive savage types from which they evolved?

A. Some of the religious instructors claim this to be true, but ask them to prove it. Fear never made anyone better, no matter what may have been the object of the fear.

That is why institutions which fatten on the fears of human beings are definitely declining in power. Wherever the carrion crow of fear appears, it indicates that something essential to happiness is dead.

Generally this something is definiteness of purpose. People who know precisely what they want of Life seldom submit to fear. They are too busy expressing their self-reliance and faith.

Q. Definiteness of purpose seems to be a panacea for all the evils of man!

A. Not that, perhaps, but you may be sure no one ever will become self-determining without it.

Q. Why aren't children taught definiteness of purpose in the public schools?

A. For the reason that there is no definite plan or purpose behind any of the school curricula! Children are sent to school to make credits and to learn how to memorize, not to learn what they want of life.

Q. What good is a school credit if one cannot convert it into the material and spiritual need of life?

A. I am only a Devil; not an unwinder of riddles!

Q. I deduce, from all you say, that neither the schools nor the churches prepare the youths of the world with a practical working knowledge of their own minds? Is anything of more importance to a human being than an understanding of the forces and circumstances which influence his own mind?

A. The only thing of enduring value to any human being is working knowledge of his own mind. The churches do not permit a person to inquire into the possibilities of his own mind, and the schools do not recognize that such a thing as a mind exists.

Q. Aren't you a little hard on the schools and the churches?

A. No, I am merely describing them as they are, without bias or prejudice.

Q. Aren't the schools and the churches your bitter enemies?

A. Their leaders may think they are, but I am impressed only by facts. The truth is this, if you must know it—the churches are my most helpful allies and the schools run the churches a close second.

Q. On what specific or general grounds do you make this claim?

A. On the ground that both the churches and the schools help me to convert people to the habit of drifting!

Q. Do you realize that your charge is substantially a sweeping indictment of the two institutions of major importance which have been responsible for civilization in its present form?

A. Do I realize it? Man alive! I gloat over it. If the schools and churches had taught people how to think for themselves, where would I be now?

Q. This confession of yours will disillusion millions of people whose only hope for salvation is in their churches. Isn't that a cruel thing to do to them? Wouldn't most people be better off living in the bliss of ignorance than to know the truth about you?

A. What do you mean by the term salvation? From what are people being saved? The only form of enduring salvation that is worth a green fig to any human being is that which comes from recognition of the power of his own mind! Ignorance and fear are the only enemies from which men need salvation.

Q. You seem to hold nothing as being sacred!

A. You are wrong! I hold sacred the one thing which is my master, the one thing I fear.

Q. What is that?

A. The power of independent thought backed by definiteness of purpose.

Q. Then you do not have many people to fear?

A. Two out of every hundred, to be exact! I control all others.

Q. Hasn't civilization made a rather sorry showing if it has permitted you to control ninety-eight out of every hundred people?

A. Ask the churches about this. They claim the credit for civilization, as it now exists.

Q. Let's give the churches a rest and get back to the public schools. Your confession has shown clearly that you thrive and perpetuate yourself from one generation to another by the clever trick of taking over the minds of children before they have the chance to learn how to use their minds.

I wish to know what is wrong with a public school system that permits the Devil to control ninety-eight out of every hundred people! I wish to know, also, what can be done to the established system of teaching that will insure all children the opportunity to learn, first, that they have minds and, second, how to use those minds to bring spiritual and economic freedom!

I am putting the question to you definitely enough, and since you have stressed the importance of definiteness of purpose, I am here and now putting you on notice that your answer to my question must be definite!

A. Wait a moment while I catch my breath! You have given me quite an order! It seems strange that you would come to the Devil to learn how to live. I should think you would go to my opposition. Why don't you?

Q. Your Majesty, it is you who are on trial here, not I! I want the truth and I am not particular as to the source from which I get it. The world has been going to your opposition for more than four thousand years, to learn how to live, but look at us, converting the discoveries of science into warfare, killing one another, and plundering as if we all belonged to the Order of Ali Baba and his Forty Thieves.

Living in poverty in the midst of overabundance, cringing with fear at the very mention of your name, despite the millions of dollars spent for schooling that is supposed to teach us practical knowledge.

There is something radically wrong with the system of education that has given us a balance sheet with Life that shows us hopelessly in the red and groping for the road to self-determination as if we were so many animals lost in the jungle.

If what we earthbound call God doesn't have the answer, I suspect you may give a working clue that will put struggling humanity on the highway to happiness.

A.   Do you expect information from the Devil which you cannot get from my opposition? Why not ask the Christian Churches for the answer to your riddle? They dominate the public schools!

Q.   That is just the trouble, Your Majesty! The influence which dominates the public schools must, without doubt, be a device of yours!

If it were not so, every person on earth would enjoy the same blessings that I have wrested from Life. Moreover, I see that you are entirely too ready to send me to the churches for information.

This makes me suspicious of you! I have already been to the churches asking for the knowledge I now demand of you, but always I have come out at the same door at which I went in— empty-handed! This is a world filled with millions of adults who have gone through the public schools without having ever heard the mention of hypnotic rhythm, let alone having been taught how to avoid becoming its victim.

This is a world with an educational system that has kept people busy studying dead languages, the glory of murder through warfare, and almost every other subject save that of how to use the mind.

I conceive it to be true that the mind is the only imperishable asset a human being has. Everything you say in your confession confirms this assumption.

Spiritual and economic freedom, the two highest aims of which human beings are capable, are available only through the proper use of the mind.

The mind is the only thing over which any human being has absolute control. The mind is the workshop in which all individuals fashion, through their thoughts, the pattern which leads to poverty and failure or opulence and success.

Why, then, do we have a public school system which makes not the slightest pretense of teaching children how to use their minds?

What is wrong with our much-touted Christian-controlled civilization that it has left us hopelessly afloat in the ocean of ignorance, superstition, and fear?

What good is Christianity, or any other religions, if it does not or cannot teach people how to make Life yield happiness instead of abject misery?

What good is any religion that devotes most of its time to collecting material tolls from its followers and promises the payoff after death, in a world of which we know nothing, somewhere out in the cosmos? These are pointed questions, but I demand definite answers.

A. You are going to be sorry you asked these embarrassing questions! You'll bring down on you the wrath of every religious instructor and every schoolteacher in the world!

Q. Not so fast, Your Majesty! Stick to the truth, if you must threaten me, and say that I will bring down on me the wrath of the schoolteachers and the religious leaders who do not think. You must not overlook the fact that the world has plenty of educators who know of the weakness of our school system, and plenty of clergymen who know of the weaknesses of religion. These will not swing their wrath against me, Your Majesty!

A. Why haven't these wiser ones done something to clean up the religious and educational deficiencies? I tell you they'll hang you to the nearest lamp post if you lay at their door the cause of misery in the world.

Q. I am asking questions of you, not answering them, but I don't mind expressing the opinion that the reason the thinkers in the clergy and the public schools have done nothing to teach people how to use their minds is simple and understandable.

They are so hopelessly in the minority that they could not get control of the political machinery which runs the churches and the schools.

In other words, there are some people in both the schools and the clergy who would like to change both systems, but they are not as strong as the machine that limits their actions.

A. I am compelled to admit the truth of what you say.

Q. Now let us come back to the original question. Forget about the churches for the time being and concentrate upon the schools. I want to know more about the system which is responsible for children's lack of training in the art of accurate thinking.

I want to know two things about this system. First, what is the major weakness of the system. Second, how this weakness can be eliminated. The floor is yours again! Please stick to the question and stop trying to decoy me into the discussion of deep, abstract subjects.

I want to know what is wrong with the public schools and how can it be corrected! That's definite, is it not?

A. You leave me no choice but that of direct answer. To begin with, the public school system approaches the subject of education from the wrong angle. The school system endeavors to teach children to memorize facts instead of teaching them how to use their own minds!

Q. Is that all that is wrong with the system?

A. No, that is only the beginning! Another major weakness of the school system is that it does not establish in the minds of children either the importance of definiteness of purpose, or make any attempt to teach youths how to be definite about anything.

The major object of all schooling is to force the students to cram their memories with facts instead of teaching them how to organize and make practical use of facts.

This cramming system centers the attention of students on the accumulation of credits but overlooks the important question of how to use knowledge in the practical affairs of life.

This system turns out graduates whose names are enscrolled upon parchment certificates, but whose minds are empty of self-determination. The school system got off to a bad start at the beginning. The schools began as institutions of higher learning, operated entirely for the select few whose wealth and family entitled them to education.

Very soon it was discovered that not even the smartest youths could learn anything by beginning in college, so a system called Preparatory Schools was devised for the purpose of preparing youths for college.

Then came the discovery that inexperienced youths needed preparation for Preparatory Schools, so the system known as the graded schools came into use.

Lastly, it was discovered that the very young were not ready to enter the graded schools, therefore the Kindergarten System was brought out.

Thus, the entire school system was evolved by beginning at the top and working back down to the bottom. It is no wonder the system neglects to teach children the importance of definiteness of purpose when the system itself has literally evolved through indefiniteness.

Q. What would correct this weakness of the public schools system? Let's not complain of the weakness of the system unless we are prepared to offer a practical remedy with which it can be corrected. In other words, while we are discussing the importance of definiteness of plan and purpose, let us take our own medicine and be definite!

A. Why not let me tell you what keeps the stars in their places and how my opposition manages to find time to count the hairs on men's heads and keep track of the little sparrows?

Q. This is not a Bridge Party! You are in the witness chair, and I am forcing from you the story of how and why human beings have been kept in ignorance and bondage despite the imposing array of church and school equipment and the army of religious instructors and educators who have been responsible for the civilization by which we find ourselves handicapped.

I am not interested in who hangs out the stars, nor am I interested in the bookkeeping system by which the hairs of men's heads are counted.

What I am interested in is a definite plan that will help the humblest person living and those yet unborn to take control of their own minds and use them in the solution of their own economic and spiritual problems. That is what I am most interested in, and nothing else at the present. Proceed!

A. Why don't you lay off the schools and churches and save yourself plenty of trouble? Don't you know that you are poking your nose into the affairs of the two forces that control the world? Suppose you do show up the schools and the churches as being weak and inadequate for the needs of human beings? What then? With what are you going to replace these two institutions?

Q. Stop trying to evade my questions by the old trick of asking a counter question! I do not propose to replace the schools and churches. But I do propose to find out, if I can, how these organized forces can be modified so they will serve people instead of keeping them in ignorance. Go ahead, now, and give me a detailed catalogue of all the changes in the public school system which would improve it.

A. So, you want the entire catalogue, do you? Do you want the suggested changes in the order of their importance?

Q. Describe the changes needed just as they come to you.

A. You are forcing me to commit an act of treason against myself, but here it is:

1) Reverse the present system by giving children the privilege of leading in their school work instead of following orthodox rules designed only to impart abstract knowledge. Let instructors serve as students and let the students serve as instructors.

2) As far as possible, organize all school work into definite methods through which the student can learn by doing, and direct the class work so that every student engages in some form of practical labor connected with the daily problems of life.

3) Ideas are the beginning of all human achievement. Teach all students how to recognize the practical ideas that may be of benefit in helping acquire whatever one demands of Life.

4) Teach the students how to budget and use time, and above all, teach the truth that time is the greatest asset available to human beings, and the cheapest.

5) Teach the student the Basic Motives by which all people are influenced, and show him how to use these motives in acquiring the necessities and the luxuries of life.

6) Teach children what to eat, how much to eat, and what is the relationship between proper eating and sound health.

7) Teach children the true nature and function of the emotion of sex, and above all, teach them that it can be transmuted into a driving force capable of lifting one to great heights of achievement.

8) Teach children to be definite in all things, beginning with the choice of a definite major purpose in Life!

9) Teach children the nature of and possibilities for good and evil in the principle of habit, using as illustrations with which to dramatize the subject the everyday experiences of children and adults.

10) Teach children how habits become fixed through the law of hypnotic rhythm, and influence them to adopt, while in the lower grades, habits that will lead to independent thought!

11) Teach children that the two names, God and the Devil, stand for the two elements of power, the negative and the positive, and describe how they may avoid one and embrace the other through proper understanding and use of their own minds!

12) Teach children the difference between temporary defeat and failure, and show them how to search for the seed of an equivalent advantage which comes with every circumstance of defeat.

13) Teach children to express their own thoughts fearlessly, and to accept or reject, at will, all ideas of others, reserving to themselves, always, the privilege of relying upon their own judgment.

14) Teach children to reach decisions promptly and to change them, if at all, slowly and with reluctance, and never without a definite reason.

15) Teach children that the human brain is the instrument with which one receives, from the great storehouse of nature, the energy which is specialized into definite thoughts; that the brain does not think, but serves as an instrument for the interpretation of stimuli which cause thought.

16) Teach children the value of harmony in their own minds, and that this is attainable only through self-control.

17) Teach children the nature and the value of self-control.

18) Teach children that there is a law of Increasing Returns which can be and should be put into operation, as a matter of habit, by rendering always more service and better service than is expected of them.

19) Teach children the true nature of the Golden Rule, and above all, show them that through the operation of this principle, everything they do to and for another, they do also to and for themselves!

20) Teach children not to have opinions unless they are formed from facts or beliefs which may reasonably be accepted as facts.

21) Teach children that cigarettes, liquor, narcotics and overindulgence in sex destroy the power of will and lead to the habit of drifting! Do not forbid these evils—just explain them.

22) Teach children the danger of believing anything merely because their parents, religious instructors, or someone else says it is so.

23) Teach children to face facts, whether they are pleasant or unpleasant, without resorting to subterfuge or offering alibis.

24) Teach children to encourage the use of their sixth sense through which ideas present themselves in their minds from unknown sources, and to examine all such ideas carefully.

25) Teach children the full import of the law of Compensation as it was interpreted by Ralph Waldo Emerson, and show them how the law works in the small, everyday affairs of life.

26) Teach children that war is murder, no matter by what name it may be called or by what cause it may be inspired, and that all war is a form of brigandry differing from ordinary highway robbery only because war is conducted by armies instead of single individuals.

27) Teach children that definiteness of purpose, backed by definite plans persistently and continuously applied, is the most efficacious form of prayer available to human beings.

28) Teach children that the space they occupy in the world is measured definitely by the quality and quantity of useful service they render the world.

29) Teach children there is no problem which does not have an appropriate solution, that the solution often may be found in the circumstance creating the problem.

30) Teach children that their only real limitations are those which they set up or permit others to establish in their own minds! That man can achieve whatever man can conceive and believe!

31) Teach children that all schoolhouses and all textbooks are elementary implements which may be

helpful in the development of their minds, but the only school of real value is the great University of Life, wherein one has the privilege of learning from experience.

32) Teach children that Diplomas and Degrees are handy as wall decorations, but serve no other useful purpose.

33) Teach children to be themselves at all times, that they cannot please everybody, therefore, to do a good job of pleasing themselves.

Q. That is an imposing list, but it seems conspicuous by the fact it ignores practically every subject now taught in the public schools. Was that intended?

A. Yes. You asked for a list of suggested changes in public school curricula which would benefit children. Well, that is what you got.

Q. Some of the changes you suggest are so unorthodox they would shock most of the educators of today, wouldn't they?

A. Most of the educators of today need to be shocked! A good sound shock often helps the brain that has been atrophied by habit.

Q. The changes you suggest for the public schools would be resented by the churches, would they not?

A. The changes suggested would be resented by everyone who is opposed to other people exercising their right to freedom of thought.

Q. Wouldn't these suggested changes annihilate the churches if they were put into widespread operation?

A. I wouldn't be surprised to know that they would! That would correct two evils with a single remedy. What is wrong with this sort of efficiency?

Q. The only thing wrong with it as far as I can see is this: the changes, if put into operation by the public schools, would bring down on educators the wrath of the religious leaders!

A. There is a natural law known as the survival of the fittest. It is as immutable as the law of gravity, or the law of hypnotic rhythm. The churches are already declining in exact proportion that the schools are gaining in power. The suggested changes in the public school curricula would only hasten the finish of the churches, thereby accomplishing quickly that which nature would otherwise accomplish slowly.

Q. Would the changes you suggest for the public schools give children immunity against the habit of drifting?

A. Yes, that is one of the results the changes would bring, but there are others too.

Q. How could the suggested changes be forced into the public school system? You know, of course, it is as difficult to get a new idea into an educator's brain as it is to interest a religious leader in modifying religion so it will help people to get more from Life.

A. The quickest and surest way to force practical ideas into the public schools is to first introduce the ideas through private schools and establish such a demand for their use that public school officials will be compelled to employ them.

Q. Should any other changes be made in the public school system?

A. Yes, many. Among other changes needed in all public school programmes is the addition of a complete course of training in the psychology of harmonious negotiation between people.

All children should be taught how to sell their way through life with the minimum amount of friction.

Q. Yes, and what other changes do you suggest?

A. Every public school should teach the principles of individual achievement through which one may attain a position of financial independence.

Q. What other changes should be made?

A. Classes should be abolished altogether. They should be replaced by the round table or conference system such as businessmen employ. All students should receive individual instruction and guidance in connection with subjects which cannot be properly taught in groups.

Q. Any other changes?

A. Every school should have an auxiliary group of instructors consisting of business and professional people, scientists, artists, engineers, and newspaper men, each of whom would impart to all the students a practical working knowledge of his own profession, business or occupation. This instruction should be conducted through the conference system, to save the time of the instructors.

Q. What you have suggested is, in effect, an auxiliary system of instruction that would give all schoolchildren a working knowledge of the practical affairs of life, direct from the original source. Is that the idea?

A. You've stated it correctly.

Q. Let us dismiss the public school system and go back to the churches for a moment. All my life I have heard clergymen preaching against sin and warning sinners to beware and repent so they could be saved. But I have never heard any of them tell me what is sin. Will you give me some light on this subject?

A. Sin is anything one does or thinks which causes one to be unhappy! Human beings who are in sound physical and spiritual health should be at peace with themselves and always happy. Any form of mental or physical misery indicates the presence of sin.

Q. Name some of the common forms of sin.

A. It is a sin to overeat because that leads to ill health and misery.

It is a sin to overindulge in sex because that breaks down one's will power and leads to the habit of drifting.

It is a sin to permit one's mind to be dominated by negative thoughts of envy, greed, fear, hatred, intolerance, vanity, self-pity, or discouragement, because these states of mind lead to the habit of drifting.

It is a sin to cheat, lie, and steal, because these habits destroy self-respect and subdue one's conscience and lead to unhappiness.

It is a sin to remain in ignorance because that leads to poverty and loss of self-reliance.

Generally, though not always, it is a sin to be physically ill, because that indicates a neglect of nature's laws.

It is a sin to accept from Life anything one does not want, because that indicates an unpardonable neglect to use the mind.

Q. Against whom does the sinner sin?

A. Himself, of course! Against whom, other than one's self, could one sin?

Q. I have always heard that sin was any act which might displease God.

A. That belief is a holdover from the days when self-appointed agents of God were selling dispensations of forgiveness of sin and getting away with it. The practice is declining in proportion to the growth of science and education through which people are learning to detect truth from falsehood.

Q. Is it a sin for one to drift through life, without definite aim, plan, or purpose?

A. Yes, because this habit leads to poverty and destroys the privilege of self-determination. It also deprives one of the privilege of using his own mind as a medium of contact with Infinite Intelligence.

Q. Are you the chief inspirer of sin?

A. Yes! It is my business to gain control of the minds of people in every way possible.

Q. Can you control the mind of a person who commits no sin?

A. I cannot, because that person never permits his mind to be dominated by any form of negative thought. I cannot enter the mind of one who never sins, let alone control it.

Q. What is the commonest and most destructive of all sins?

A. Fear and ignorance.

Q. Have you nothing else to add to the list?

A. There is nothing else to be added.

Q. What is faith?

A. It is a state of mind wherein one recognizes and uses the power of positive thought as a medium by which one contacts and draws upon the universal store of Infinite Intelligence, at will.

Q. In other words, faith is the absence of all forms of negative thought. Is that the idea?

A. Yes, that is another way of describing it.

Q. Has a drifter the capacity to use faith?

A. He may have the capacity but he does not use it. Everyone has the potential power to clear his mind of all negative thoughts and thereby avail himself of the power of faith.

Q. What should be one's attitude toward those who admonish us to have faith in someone of whose existence we are not sure, whose residence is supposed to be in a world of which we know nothing?

A. The thinker ignores such a person. The drifter is confused and frightened by such a person. Faith is a state of mind that is free from all forms of negative thought and definitely influenced by belief in something. Faith is not something that can be put in and out of one's mind as one would put on and remove his hat.

Q. Stating the matter in another way, faith is definiteness of purpose backed by belief in the attainment of the object of that purpose. Is that correct?

A. That's the idea, exactly.

CHAPTER SEVEN

SELF-DISCIPLINE

*(The second of the seven principles which lead to
spiritual, physical, and economic freedom.)*

Q. What preparation must one undergo before being able to move with definiteness of purpose at all times?

A. One must gain mastery over self. The person who is not master of himself can never be master of others. Lack of self-mastery is, of itself, the most destructive form of indefiniteness.

Q. Where should one begin when making a start at control over self?

A. By mastering the four appetites responsible for most of one's lack of self-discipline. The four appetites are (1) the desire for food, (2) the desire for expression of sex, (3) the desire to express loosely organized opinions, (4) the desire to indulge in spiritual orgies through some form of religious ceremony.

Q. Does man have other appetites which need control?

A. Yes, many of them, but these four are the ones which should be conquered first. When a man becomes master of these four appetites, he has developed enough self-discipline to conquer easily those of lesser importance.

Q. But these are natural appetites. They must be indulged if one is to be healthy and happy.

A. To be sure, they are natural appetites, but they are also danger-ous because people who have not mastered themselves overfeed the appetites. Self-mastery contemplates sufficient control over the appetites to enable one to feed them what they need and withhold food not needed.

Q. Your viewpoint is both interesting and educational. Describe the details through which I may understand how and under what circumstances people overfeed the appetites.

A. Take the desire for physical food, for example. The majority of people are so weak in self-discipline they fill their stomachs with combinations of rich food which please the taste but over-work the organs of digestion and elimination.

They pour into their stomachs both quantity and combina-tions of food which the body chemist can dispose of only by converting the food into deadly toxic poisons.

These poisons clog and stagnate the body sewer system until it slows down in its work of elimination of waste matter. After a while, the sewer system stops working altogether, and the vic-tim has what he calls constipation.

By that time, he is ready for the hospital. Autointoxication, or body sewer poisoning, takes the machinery of the brain and rolls it into something resembling a wad of putty.

The victim then becomes sluggish in his physical movements and mentally irritable and fussy. If he could only take one good look at and one bad smell of his sewer system, he would be ashamed to look himself in the face.

City sewers are not the pleasantest of places when they be-come overloaded or clogged, but they are clean and sweet compared with the intestinal sewer when it has been overload-ed or clogged. This is not a pretty story to be associated with the pleasant and necessary act of eating, but that is where it belongs because overeating and wrong food combinations are the evils which cause auto-intoxication.

Caster oil and enema bags are among my most despised impedimenta. They help people to keep their body sewers cleaned, and this handicaps me because a clean body sewer generally means a sound body and a brain that functions properly.

Imagine, if your imagination can be stretched that far, how any human being could move with definiteness of purpose with his body sewer filled with enough poison to kill a hundred people if it were injected into their blood stream directly.

Q. I take it, then, that doctors are not among your friendly boys and girls?

A. If the doctors would let people go ahead and eat what they want and all they want, and stop helping them to clean their sewer systems, I might control all the people of the world during the next generation. That's how friendly they are to me.

Q. Let's get away from the discussion of sewer systems. I don't like the thought of them.

A. And you would like the smell of them still less, if you came within smelling distance of the average person's body sewer system.

Q. If you must tell me about this unpleasant subject, why don't you call it the intestinal tract instead of the body sewer system? The very thought of a sewer pipe running through the body nauseates me.

A. Well, your best friends won't tell you, but I will! I call things by their most appropriate names, so I shall tell you that bad breath, sometimes called halitosis for politeness' sake, is nothing but body sewer gases coming up instead of escaping in the other direction.

Q. Stop! Stop, I tell you! I shall never be able to eat again if you don't stop reminding me that a nasty sewer system is the receptacle of all the undigested food I eat.

A. That is one of the major weaknesses of you earthbound creatures, you like to cover ugly habits with pretty names, you like to sidestep the important facts of Life. You would rather swallow a handful of aspirin tablets to stop a bursting headache than clean out your sewer system of the poison causing the headache. In other words, one of the major sins of most human beings is their lack of self-discipline!

Q. So, you don't think much of aspirin tablets, eh? I thought you said the doctors were no friends of yours. Don't they prescribe aspirin and other palliatives and narcotics to stop headaches?

A. Yes, the quacks do. The honest and intelligent doctors prescribe a thorough cleansing of the body sewer system, where most headaches and many other physical aches and pains begin.

Q. What is wrong with aspirin tablets?

A. What is wrong with them? Man alive! There isn't anything wrong with them from my viewpoint. In fact, aspirin was invented by one of my boys. But I don't call aspirin tablets by that name. I call them muddle balls because they muddle the brain and paralyze the nerve which leads from the sewer system to the brain, thereby cutting off the warning in the form of pain through which the keeper of the sewers is trying to tell the brain the sewer needs cleaning.

Q. Oh, I see, you like aspirin tablets then? You like them because they cut off the line of communication between the source of pain and the brain, thereby letting the victim poison to death before he learns what is wrong with him? Is that it?

A. That's the idea, exactly!

Q. And all this trouble is the result of lack of control over the physical appetite for food?

A. Well, if you wish to hew to the line and be absolutely correct, you should say that improper eating is responsible for the majority of the ills of the body, and practically all headaches.

If you want proof of this, select a hundred people suffering with headaches and give each of them a thorough washing out of their body sewer systems, with a high enema, and observe that no fewer than ninety-five of the headaches will disappear within a few minutes after their sewers have been cleaned.

Q. Why don't people keep their intestinal tracts clean? Is it painful to take an enema?

A. That is another of the weaknesses of people which are difficult to understand. The majority of people would rather undergo a major surgical operation or have a baby than wash out the body sewer system with a little plain water.

Q. I have heard that the habit of taking enemas regularly is injurious to one's health? Is that true?

A. It is just exactly as true as the belief of the average small boy that the habit of washing his ears and neck is not good for him. Did you ever hear of any habit of cleanliness doing anyone any harm? No, of course not!

Q. From all you say about the intestinal tract I gather the impression that mastery over the physical appetite for food means also mastery over the habit of neglecting to keep the intestines clean?

A. Yes, that is true. It is just as important to eliminate the waste matter of the body and the unused portions of food, as it is to take the right amount and the correct combinations of food.

Q. I never thought of auto-intoxication as being one of your devices of control over people, and I am utterly shocked to know how many people are victims of this subtle enemy. Let's hear what you have to say of the other three appetites.

A.   Well, take the desire for sex expression. Now there is a force with which I master the weak and the strong, the old and the young, the ignorant and the wise. In fact I master all who neglect to master sex!

Q.   How can one master the emotion of sex?

A.   By the simple process of transmuting that emotion into some form of activity other than copulation. Sex is one of the greatest of all forces which motivate human beings. Because of this fact it is also one of the most dangerous forces. If the average man would control his sex desires and transmute them into a driving force with which to carry on his occupation one half the time he dissipates in pursuit of sex, he would never know poverty.

Q.   Do I understand you to imply there is a relationship between sex and poverty?

A.   Yes, where sex is not under definite control. If allowed to run it natural course, sex will quickly lead one into the habit of drifting.

Q.   Is there any relationship between sex and leadership?

A.   Yes, all great leaders in every walk of life are highly sexed, but they follow the habit of controlling their sex desires, switching them into a driving force behind their occupation.

Q.   Is the habit of overindulgence in sex as dangerous as the habit of taking narcotics or liquor?

A.   There is no difference between these habits. Both lead to hypnotic control, through the habit of drifting!

Q.   Why does the world look upon sex as something vulgar?

A. Because of the vulgar abuse people have made of this emotion. It is not sex that is vulgar. It is the individual who neglects or refuses to control and guide it.

Q. Do you mean, by your statement, that one should not indulge the desire for sex?

A. No, I mean that sex, like all other forces available to man, should be understood, mastered and made to serve man. The desire for sex expression is as natural as the desire for food. The desire can no more be killed than one can entirely stop a river from flowing. If the emotion of sex is shut off from the natural mode of expression, it will break out in some other less desirable form, just as a river will, if dammed, break through and flow around the dam. The person who has self-discipline understands the emotion of sex, respects it, and learns to control and transmute it into constructive activities.

Q. Just what damage is there in overindulgence of sex?

A. The greatest damage is that it depletes the source of man's greatest driving force, and wastes, without adequate compensation, man's creative energy.

It dissipates energy needed by nature to maintain physical health. Sex is nature's most useful therapeutic force.

It depletes the magnetic energy which is the source of an attractive, pleasing personality.

It removes the sparkle from one's eyes and sets up discord in the tone of one's voice.

It destroys enthusiasm, subdues ambition, and leads inevitably to the habit of drifting on all subjects.

Q. I would like for you to answer my question in another way by telling me what beneficial ends the emotion of sex may be made to attain, if mastered and transmuted.

A. Controlled sex supplies the magnetic force that attracts people to one another. It is the most important factor of pleasing personality.

- It gives quality to the tone of voice and enables one to convey through the voice any feeling desired.

- It serves, as nothing else can serve, to give motive-power to one's desires.

- It keeps the nervous system charged with the energy needed to carry on the work of maintaining the body.

- It sharpens the imagination and enables one to create useful ideas.

- It gives quickness and definiteness to one's physical and mental movements.

- It gives one persistence and perseverance in the pursuit of one's major purpose in life.

- It is a great antidote for all fear! It gives one immunity against discouragement.

- It helps to master laziness and procrastination.

- It gives one physical and mental endurance while undergoing any form of opposition or defeat.

- It gives one the fighting qualities necessary under all circumstances for self-defense.

- In brief, it makes winners and not quitters!

Q. Is that all the advantages you claim for controlled sex energy?

A. No, that is only some of the more important benefits it provides. Perhaps some will believe the greatest of all the virtues of sex is that it is nature's method of perpetuation of all living things. This, alone, should remove all thought that sex is vulgar.

Q. Are there any dangers or disadvantages associated with the control of sex desires?

A. Not the slightest, if the desire is transmuted and used for constructive purposes. Complete sublimation of sex is dangerous. It causes this restless urge to break out through unnatural forms of expression and leads to physical and mental illness.

Q. What would be the effects of emasculation?

A. The same in man as in the lower animals. Castration of a horse subdues him and takes away his desire for all forms of action. It would do the same to a man.

   People who have themselves so altered that their capacity for sex expression is destroyed become moody, ambitionless, and easy victims of all forms of drifting.

Q. I gather, from what you say, that the emotion of sex is a virtue, not a fault.

A. It is a virtue when controlled and directed to the attainment of desirable ends. It is a fault when neglected and permitted to lead to acts of lust.

Q. Why aren't these truths taught to children by their parents and the public schools?

A. The neglect is due to ignorance of the real nature of sex. It is just as necessary in maintaining health for one to understand and properly use the emotion of sex as it is to keep the body sewer system clean. Both subjects should be taught in all public schools and all homes where there are children.

Q. Wouldn't the majority of parents need instruction on the proper function and use of sex, before they could intelligently teach their children?

A. Yes, and so would the public school teachers.

Q. What relative position of importance would you give to the need for accurate knowledge of the subject of sex?

A. It is next to the top of the list. There is but one thing of greater importance to human beings. That is accurate thought.

Q. Do I understand you to say that knowledge of the true functions of sex and ability to think accurately are the two things of greatest importance to mankind?

A. That is what I intended you to understand. Accurate thinking comes first because it is the solution to all men's problems, the answer to all his prayers, the source of opulence and all material possessions. Accurate thinking is aided by properly controlled and directed sex emotion because sex emotion is the same energy as that with which one thinks.

Q. That's an astounding statement. If true, it is a biting indictment against the public schools, the churches, and all other cultural influences. The indictment is all the more biting because accurate thinking and the proper use of sex emotion consist of knowledge easily available to all who desire it.

A. Yes, and the indictment is still more biting because the charge is one which may be easily proved through experimentation.

Q. Where should experiments begin?

A. With those who desire self-determination sufficiently to be willing to pay its price. No one can be entirely free spiritually, mentally, physically, and economically without learning the art of accurate thinking. No one can learn to think accurately without including, as a part of the needed knowledge, information on the control of sex emotion through transmutation.

Q. Those are astounding statements. Will they not be disputed by the educators and the religious instructors?

A. All statements of truth are disputed. That is why it is so easy for me to gain mastery over so many people. It is also the reason that civilization is not further advanced. People who recognize, and quickly accept, and take full benefit of truth and new ideas have no difficulty in making life pay in whatever terms they choose. The others are glad to get the crumbs which drop by the wayside of Life.

Q. It will be a great surprise to many people to learn there is so close a relationship between thinking and sex emotion. Tell us, now, about the third appetite, and let's see what it has to do with self-discipline.

A. The habit of expressing loosely organized opinions is one of the most destructive of habits. Its destructiveness consists in its tendency to influence people to guess instead of searching for the facts when they form opinions, create ideas or organize plans.

The habit develops a grasshopper mind—one that jumps from one thing to another but never completes anything!

And of course, carelessness in the expression of opinions leads to the habit of drifting. From there, it is only a step or two until one is bound by the law of hypnotic rhythm which automatically prohibits accurate thinking.

Q. What other disadvantages are there in free expression of opinions?

A. The person who talks too much informs the world of his sins and plans and gives to others the opportunity to profit by his ideas.

Wise men keep their plans to themselves and refrain from expressing uninvited opinions. This prevents others from appropriating their ideas and make it difficult for others to interfere with their plans.

Q. Why do so many people indulge in the habit of expressing uninvited opinions?

A. The habit is one way of expressing egotism and vanity. The desire for self-expression is inborn in people. The motive back to the habit is to attract the attention of others and to impress them favorably. Actually, it has just the opposite effect. When the self-invited speaker attracts attention, it usually is unfavorable.

Q. Yes, what other disadvantages has the habit?

A. The person who insists on talking seldom has an opportunity to learn by listening to others.

Q. But isn't it true that a magnetic speaker often puts himself in the way of opportunity to benefit himself by attracting the attention of others, through his powers of oratory?

A. Yes, a magnetic orator does have an asset of tremendous value in his ability to impress people by his speech, but he cannot make the best use of this asset if he forces his speech on others without their invitation.

No single quality adds more to one's personality than ability to speak with emotional feeling, force and conviction, but the speaker must not impose his speech upon others without being invited to do so.

There is an old saying that nothing is worth more than its actual cost. This applies as well to the free, uninvited expression of opinions as to material things.

Q. What about people who volunteer their opinions by expressing them in writing? Do they also suffer by lack of self-discipline?

A. One of the worst pests on earth is the person who writes uninvited letters to people of prominence. Men in public office, moving picture stars, men who have succeeded in business, or written a bestselling book, and people whose names appear often in the newspapers, are continually besieged by people who write letters expressing their opinion on all subjects.

Henry Ford receives over thirty thousand such letters annually, and the President of the United States receives hundreds of thousands of letters, most of them uninvited and expressing opinions worth exactly nothing.

Q. But the writing of uninvited letters is a harmless way of finding pleasure through self-expression, is it not? What damage does one do by the habit?

A. Habits are contagious. Every habit attracts a flock of its relatives. The habit of doing anything that is useless leads to the formation of other habits that are useless, especially the habit of drifting.

But that is not all the dangers associated with the habit of indulging in uninvited expression of opinions. The habit creates enemies and places in their hands dangerous weapons by which they may do great injury to the one who indulges in it.

Thieves and confidence men and racketeers pay big prices for the names and addresses of the writers of uninvited letters, knowing as they do the writers of these letters become easy victims of all manner of schemes that result in the loss of their money.

They refer to the writers of such letters as nuts. If you wish to know how foolish people are who write uninvited letters, read the nut column of any newspaper—the column in which the paper publishes the voluntary opinions of its readers—and you will see for yourself how the writers of such letters antagonize people and invite opposition from others.

Q. I had no idea, Your Majesty, that people get into so much difficulty through uninvited expression of their opinions, but now that you have brought up the subject, I do remember writing the editor of a prominent magazine an uninvited letter of criticism which cost me a fine position on his staff, at a fat salary.

Now let us hear what you have to say about spiritual orgies, the last of the four appetites.

A. The habit of indulging in spiritual orgies began before the dawn of civilization. It is the outgrowth of man's fear of the Devil or his fear that death will bring only enduring nothingness. The worst thing that can be said of the habit is that it sets aside reason and will power and destroys the very foundation of sound judgement and accurate thinking. It has another damaging effect. It prepares one's mind for easy control of hypnotic rhythm.

Q. Go ahead and describe exactly what you mean by the term, spiritual orgies.

A. A spiritual orgy is any form of religious ceremony which excites the mind and steps it up to an intoxicated rate of vibration. All forms of revivals such as those which were conducted by Billy Sunday, Gypsy Smith, Dwight L. Moody, and others of their type, are spiritual orgies. The leader of spiritual orgies uses hypnotic suggestion to dull the sense of reason of his followers.

The victims sometimes indulge in the orgies so energetically they never regain full control of their reason and willpower. The insane asylums are filled with men, women, and children who lost their mental equilibrium through indulgence in some form of spiritual orgy.

Q. I have always been told it was the spirit of the Lord, and not hypnotism, which takes a hold on people's minds during a religious revival. What have you to say about this?

A. The hypnotist gets quicker and more permanent results by inducing people to believe the strange power which seizes them during a spiritual orgy is what he calls the spirit of the Lord.

Here is as good a place as any to inform you that there are two dangers which rank above all others. One is fear of the Devil, the other is what people often mistake for love of God.

The two doors through which I enter the mind of a human being most easily and with the least opposition are marked love and fear. And I might add there is nothing on earth that pleases me as much as a good old-fashioned spiritual orgy.

Following a spiritual orgy, I find it easy to enter the minds of its victims through many doors, all of which have been left unguarded by the reason and the will.

Q. You don't mean to say that those who love God blindly are easy victims for your net, do you?

A. It is a pity to disillusion you, but the truth is they are my easiest prey. I get those who love or fear anything more diligently than they use their own minds for the purpose of accurate thinking.

Let me remind you, again, that nothing can stop me except the power of thought! Love and Fear are not thoughts. They are feelings, pleasant at times as substitutes for thought, but always dangerous.

Q. If what you say is true, it is no wonder you complain of the passing of religious revivals. I see, too, why you claim the churches as your devices. According to your story, all forms of religious ceremony help your cause by discouraging independent thought. Is that correct?

A. Yes, that is true. I would as soon have a person's mind grounded through religious fanaticism as to have it paralyzed by fear. Both conditions set aside the only serious bar against my free entry into an individual's mind, which is the power of independent thought.

Q. But I have always been informed that the religions were responsible for civilization. Now you lay claim to religion as having been one of your most effective devices for entering and controlling the minds of people. How can I be sure that you tell the truth?

A.   By accurate thinking! If you will analyze your civilization, of which your religions boast and for which they claim the credit, you will find in it all you need to corroborate my story.

What do you find in the world today except poverty, greed for wealth, madness expressed through wholesale murder in which all the refinements of science have been consolidated for destructive purposes, treachery in all human relationships, ill health, sick minds, and discouragement in every possible form?

Show me anything beautiful or hopeful in the civilization of which your religions boast, and I will let you use it as evidence that I do not tell the truth when I say the churches have been my most effective allies.

Take your Christian religion, for example. After two thousand years of intensive effort during which it has been forced upon the world, by controlling the minds of the young, what have you in this religion except a mass of empty, meaningless ritual used as one of the meanest of all money-getting rackets? Deny that if you can!

Religion is mankind's greatest enemy and my greatest worldly ally, because it dopes the brain of human beings with dogmas founded and maintained on fear, ignorance, and superstition.

Religion is my greatest ally because it is forced upon the minds of the young before they come into possession of their minds; therefore it helps me ensnare them through the habit of drifting blindly, instead of thinking for themselves.

I repeat what I have already stated: men come into possession of the privileges available through the fourth dimension, time, only by taking possession of their own minds and using them freely and independently!

Could any statement of truth be made more definitely than this? I use religion in times of peace to cause men to fight among themselves.

I use religion in times of war to fire men with the madness to murder one another without stopping to ask themselves why. I use religion to inspire disagreements between parents in bringing up their children.

I use religion to teach people to look for and to expect some sort of heavy mental and spiritual burden that will serve as a cross, having first taught them it is a great honor to bear a cross.

Their expectations are never without results. If I can fix religion upon any mind, I can control that mind. Religion teaches submission, humility, and fear. These are my greatest weapons.

Q. From what you say, I infer that religion is one of the forces one must master before gaining complete mastery of self. Is that correct?

A. That is perfectly stated. The proper place to begin self-discipline is right where you stand. The way to begin is by recognizing the truth that there is nothing for good or evil throughout the myriad of universes except the power of natural law!

There is no God except the positive application of natural law!

There is no individual personality anywhere throughout the myriad of universes with the slightest power to influence a human being save nature and human beings themselves.

There is no human being now living, no human being has ever lived, and no human being ever will live with the right or the power to deprive another human being of the inborn privilege of free and independent thought.

That privilege is the only one over which any human being can have absolute control. No adult human being ever loses the right to freedom of thought, but most humans lose the benefits of this privilege either by neglect or because it has been taken away from them by their parents or religious instructors before the age of understanding.

These are self-evident truths, no less important because they are being called to your attention by the Devil than they would be if brought to your attention by my opposition.

Here you have the answer to your question, as to how you can be sure I am telling the truth. Fortunately, you do not have to depend upon either the Devil or his opposition to assure yourself the answer is the true one.

Q. But, Your Majesty, if you cut the foundation from under all the religions, what are people going to lean upon in the hour of emergency when they know not where nor to whom to appeal?

A. Let them lean upon the only dependable power available to any human being.

Q. And what is that?

A. Themselves! The power of their own thoughts. The only power they can control and may rely upon.

The only power which cannot be perverted, colored, modified, and falsified by their dishonest fellow human beings.

The only power that cannot be taken away from people by pious frauds claiming to be the agents of God or the Legions of the Devil, and used as a weapon to control them, except by their own consent.

Q. What you are saying is madness! If the world accepted it as truth, what would we have left of civilization?

A. What the world did during the world war was madness, too, was it not? And that was done in the name of the Lord.

Both sides carried their self-constituted agents of God, and both sets of agents turned loose upon the enemies of their employer all they could of the wrath of God.

The result was that the two opposing armies stalemated one another. No God came to the help of either side!

But I was there in full regalia. By God you can prove what I now say without taxing your imagination.

And when the stench of the slaughter was over and your civilization once more picked up the loose ends of the daily affairs of living, what had it gained?

Let me answer for you. It had gained just this: positive evidence that there is no God anywhere available to mankind with the power to help improve the lot of mankind except mankind itself!

Man is the net result of evolutionary operation of natural laws. Through millions of years of operation of these laws, man has evolved a physical brain. This physical instrument called a brain evolved to its present state of development despite the unfriendly forces of religion and not because of them.

Once any human being gets this conception of himself, he no longer needs to lean upon the man-made crutch of religion in times of doubt. He no longer needs to lean upon any crutch.

Q. All you say seems logical, but why must I come to the Devil to discover such profound truths? Why was this truth not made available to me through our school system, the constituted forces of civilization charged with the responsibility of imparting knowledge?

A. The answer to your question should be obvious. The public schools are dominated by religious leaders.

Q. That was true a few generations back, but the public schools are rapidly getting out from under the domination of the religions. Why, then, do they not teach children how to appropriate and use their own minds for their own self-determination?

A. Take a look at the overfilled seats of the public schools and the ever-increasing emptiness of church pews and you will have your answer. The public schools are rescuing civilization from the religions as rapidly as human beings can stand to be rescued.

Give the schools time, and the churches will disappear from the face of the earth.

Q. Then I take it to be true the schools are not tools of yours?

A. Only to the extent that educational leaders lack the courage to boldly throw off the accumulated curse of religion and openly teach youth the truth about the mind and body.

Q. But the leaders in education are becoming a bit bolder each year, are they not?

A. Yes, damn them, they are!

Q. Why do some of the educators still force schoolteachers to read the Bible as a part of the public school curricula? Is the Bible a suitable textbook for imparting accurate knowledge?

A. The Bible is not an accurate textbook for imparting anything except confusion of thought. It is read in some schools because of the withering influence of religion. If the teachers were forced to read the entire contents of the Bible in the public schools, there would be plenty of fire works.

Q. Why? What would happen?

A. Well, for one thing, much of the contents of the Old Testament are so shockingly vulgar the reading of this document in mixed company, to boys and girls, would start them to asking embarrassing questions of their parents and teachers.

Moreover, the very act of accrediting to God the writing or the inspiration of such filth would so shock the mind of any normal child it would reject the entire document as being spurious and unworthy of any conception any child may have as to who or what God may be.

But school teachers do not read the entire Bible in public schools, to mixed groups. They read carefully chosen paragraphs. If the average parent of a child read the entire Bible—mind you, if he actually read it with half his wits at work—he would not permit any part of the document to be forced upon the mind of his inexperienced youthful offspring.

Q. I thought nearly everyone had read the Bible. Why do people force the Bible on their children if they have not read it?

A. No one who has read all the Bible ever forces it upon anyone, excepting for the purpose of spreading ignorance and gaining some form of personal advantage thereby. Most of those who claim to believe the Bible have never read it.

Q. Great heavens! Let's get away from the Bible and the religions before I come to the conclusion you are right when you say they are responsible for our civilization.

A. You wanted the truth! That is exactly what you are getting. Like every other human being, you want the truth to correspond with your idea of what it is. The truth seldom does that.

Truth often shatters illusions and tears down carefully built castles of opinion based on wishing and guessing. If it is truth you are seeking, you are in the right place to get it. If you merely seek flattery or food on which to nourish your fears, superstitions, and ignorance, go to my opposition for it.

Q. If what you say about the influence of religion is the truth, how is it that all the great thinkers of the past were believers in religion?

A. Your ignorance of history is appalling! All the truly great thinkers of the past were non-religious. You have your facts in reverse gear, Mr. Earthbound.

Q. Name some of the non-religious whom you would designate as having been great thinkers.

A. Plato, Socrates, Bruno, Darwin, Spencer, Huxley, Newton, Franklin, Washington, Lincoln, Paine, Henry, Jefferson, and their colleagues who have been responsible for all the freedom there is on earth today.

Observe the deep significance of the fact that at no time in the history of your civilization has any religion produced a great thinker in any field of human endeavor destined to help people become free spiritually, mentally, and economically. Great leaders are accurate thinkers.

Religion does not produce, cannot produce, accurate thinkers. Religion limits the human mind to the blind acceptance of dogmas and creeds, unproved and unprovable hypotheses. This does not develop the power to think accurately.

Q. From what you say, I infer you lay at the door of religion the cause of about all of man's ignorance?

A. At what door might one more appropriately lay the cause? The religions had complete control of all the machinery of civilization and did the imparting of knowledge until it was pushed to the background by the unfoldment of science and education.

The monopoly religion held in the field of instruction was broken less than a brief hundred years ago, and even now it is a criminal offense to teach evolution in the public schools in some parts of the world—not remote parts, but right in your own United States. Use your brain and you will know what power has fostered ignorance and kept superstition and fear alive.

Q. Let's get away from the discussion of the religions and back to the seven principles. You have already disclosed enough information to show clearly that the secret of how to break the power of hypnotic rhythm is wrapped in the seven principles. You have shown, too, that the most important of these principles is self-discipline. Now go ahead and describe the other five principles you have not yet mentioned, and indicate what part they play in giving one self-discipline.

A. First, let me summarize that part of my confession we have already covered.

I have frankly told you that my two most effective devices for mastering human beings are the habit of drifting and the law of hypnotic rhythm.

I have shown you that drifting is not a natural law, but a man-made habit which leads to man's submission to the law of hypnotic rhythm.

The seven principles are the media by which man may break the hold of hypnotic rhythm and take possession, again, of his own mind. You see, therefore, the seven principles are the seven steps which lead victims of hypnotic rhythm out of the self-made prisons in which they are bound.

Q. The seven principles are the master key that unlocks the door to spiritual, mental, and economic self-determination? Is that true?

A. That's another way of stating the truth.

Q. Is failure ever a benefit to man?

CHAPTER EIGHT

◆

LEARNING FROM ADVERSITY

A. But few people know that every adversity brings with it the seed of an equivalent advantage. Still fewer people know the difference between temporary defeat and failure. If this knowledge were generally known, I would be deprived of one of my strongest weapons of control over human beings.

Q. But I understood you to say that failure is one of your greatest allies. I got the impression from your confession that failure causes people to lose ambition and quit trying; then you take them over without opposition on their part?

A. Ah, that is just the point! I take them over after they quit trying. If they knew the difference between temporary defeat and failure, they would not quit when they meet with opposition from Life. If they knew that every form of defeat and all failures bring with them the seed of unborn opportunity, they would keep on fighting and win. Success usually is but one short step beyond the point where one quits fighting.

Q. Is that all one might learn from adversity, defeat, and failure?

A. No, that is the least of what one might learn. I hate to tell you this, but failure often serves as a blessing in disguise because it breaks the grip of hypnotic rhythm and frees the mind for a fresh start.

Q. Now we are getting somewhere. So you have confessed, at long last, that even nature's law of hypnotic rhythm can be and often is annulled by nature herself. Is that correct?

A. No, that is not stating the matter accurately. Nature never reverses any of her natural laws.

Q. Well, if nature breaks the law of hypnotic rhythm and gives back to a human being the control of his mind which she took away from him through this law, what is that but a reversal of natural law?

A. Nature does not take away a human being's freedom of thought through hypnotic rhythm. The individual gives up his freedom by abuse of this law. If a man jumped from a tree and was killed by the sudden impact of his body with the earth, through the law of gravity, you wouldn't say nature murdered him, would you? You would say the man neglected to relate himself properly to the law of gravity.

Q. I am beginning to see. The law of hypnotic rhythm is capable of both negative and positive application. It may drag one down to slavery through loss of the privilege of freedom of thought, or it may help one rise to great heights of achievement through the free use of thought, depending on how the individual relates himself to the law? Is that correct?

A. Now you have it right.

Q. But what about failure? One does not fail intentionally, with purpose aforethought. No one encourages temporary defeat.

These are circumstances over which the individual often has no control whatsoever. How, then, can it be said that nature does not take away one's freedom of thought when failure destroys ambition, willpower,and the self-confidence essential to make a fresh start?

A. Failure is a man-made circumstance. It is never real until it has been accepted by man as permanent. Stating it another way, failure is a state of mind; therefore it is something an individual can control until he neglects to exercise this privilege.

Nature does not force people to fail, but nature does impose her law of hypnotic rhythm upon all minds, and through this law gives permanency to the thoughts which dominate those minds.

In other words, failure thoughts are taken over by the law of hypnotic rhythm and made permanent if the individual accepts any circumstances as being permanent failure. That same law just as readily takes over and makes permanent thoughts of success.

Q. What part, then, does failure play in helping an individual break the grip of hypnotic rhythm after that law has been fastened upon his mind?

A. Failure brings a climax in which one has the privilege of clearing his mind of fear and making a new start in another direction. Failure is the dead end of the habit-path one has been following, and when it is reached, it forces one to leave that path and take up another, thereby creating a new rhythm.

Failure does more than this. It gives an individual an opportunity to test himself wherein he may learn how much willpower he possesses.

Failure also forces people to learn many truths they would never discover without it.

Failure often leads an individual to an understanding of the power of self-discipline without which no one could turn back after having once been the victim of hypnotic rhythm.

Failure proves conclusively that something is wrong with one's aims or the plans by which the object of these aims are sought.

Study the lives of all people who achieve outstanding success in any calling and observe, with profit, that their success is usually in exact ratio to their experiences of defeat before succeeding.

Q. Is this all you have to say of the advantages of failure?

A. No, I have barely begun. If you want the real significance of adversity, failure, defeat, and all other experiences which break up a human being's habits and force him to form new habits, watch nature at her work.

Nature uses illness to break the physical rhythm of the body when the cells and organs become improperly related.

Nature uses economic depressions to break the rhythm of mass thought when great numbers of people become improperly related through business, social, and political activities.

Nature uses failure to break the rhythm of negative thought when an individual becomes improperly related to himself, in his own mind.

Observe carefully and you will see that everywhere in nature there is always at work a natural law which gives eternal change to all matter, all energy and to the power of thought. The only permanent thing in the universes is change. Eternal, inexorable change through which every atom of matter and every unit of energy has the opportunity to properly relate itself to all other units of matter and energy, and every human being has the opportunity and the privilege of properly relating himself to all other human beings, no matter how many mistakes he makes, how many times, or in what ways he may be defeated.

When mass failure overtakes a nation, such as the 1929 world business depression, the circumstance is in perfect harmony with nature's plan to break up man's habits and give out fresh opportunities.

Q. What you are saying intrigues me. Am I to understand that hypnotic rhythm has something to do with the way people relate themselves to one another?

A. Hypnotic rhythm has everything to do with the manner in which people relate themselves to one another.

Hypnotic rhythm is the law of nature through which every star and every planet and every material atom and every unit of energy throughout the universes is related to everything else in existence.

The earth is kept in its proper relationship to the sun by hypnotic rhythm.

The seasons of the year come and go in response to this law, which is the only medium through which they can be properly related to life.

Water flows always back to the oceans in response to this law.

The process by which life in every living thing, from a seed of mustard to a human being, is perpetuated is regulated and kept eternally in operation through hypnotic rhythm.

Stating this truth in another way, everything that lives perpetuates itself through the law of hypnotic rhythm, because it cannot do otherwise.

By this time, you must have drawn the conclusion, from what I have said, that human beings are related to one another by the operation of a law they often do not understand and cannot annul.

Through the operation of hypnotic rhythm; the business, professional, and social habits of human beings become literally a part of them.

That abstract, elusive thing called character is nothing but a manifestation of the law of hypnotic rhythm, therefore, when speaking of one's character, it would be proper to say his thought habits have been crystallized into a positive or negative personality, through hypnotic rhythm.

One is good or bad because of the knitting together of his thoughts and deeds through hypnotic rhythm. One is bound by poverty or blessed with opulence because his aims, plans, and desires, or lack of them, have been made permanent and real by hypnotic rhythm.

Q. Is that all you have to say of the connection between hypnotic rhythm and human relationships?

A. No, I have just begun. Stop asking questions and starting thinking while I unfold to you the cause of all human misery, the cause of all poverty, the cause of all spiritual, mental and physical illness.

While I am taking, remember I am speaking of the influence of hypnotic rhythm in connection with all human relationships. Men who succeed in business do so entirely because of the way they relate themselves to their associates and to others outside of the business.

Professional men who succeed do so largely because of the manner in which they relate themselves to their clients. It is much more important for the lawyer to know people and to know the laws of nature than it is to know the law.

And the doctor is a failure before he starts, unless he knows how to relate himself to his patients so as to establish their faith in him.

Marriage succeeds or fails entirely because of the manner in which the participants relate themselves to one another. Proper relationship in marriage begins with a proper motive for the marriage.

Most marriages do not bring happiness because the contracting parties neither understand, nor attempt to understand, the law of hypnotic rhythm through the operation of which every word they speak, every act in which they engage, and every motive by which they are inspired to deal with one another is picked up and woven into a web that entangles them in controversial misery, or gives to them the wings of freedom through which they soar above all forms of unhappiness.

Every newly made acquaintanceship between people ripens into friendship and then into spiritual harmony (sometimes called love), or plants a germ of suspicion and doubt which evolves and grows into open rebellion, according to the way in which the participants in the acquaintanceship relate themselves to one another.

Hypnotic rhythm picks up the dominating motives, aims, purposes, and feelings of the contacting minds and weaves these into some degree of faith or fear, love or hatred.

After the pattern has taken definite shape, as it does with time, it is forced upon the contacting minds and made a part thereof. In this silent way does nature make permanent the dominating factors of every human relationship.

In every human relationship, the evil motives and the evil deeds of the contacting individuals are coordinated and consolidated into definite form and subtly woven into that all important human trait known as character.

In the same manner, the motives and the deeds of good are consolidated and forced upon the individual. You see, therefore, it is not only one's deeds but also one's very thoughts which determine the nature of all human relationships.

Q. You are leading into pretty deep water. Let's keep near the shore, where I can follow you without fear of getting beyond a safe depth. Go ahead and tell me how this subject of human relationships actually works in the current affairs of a problem-filled world such as we have today.

A. That is a happy thought. But let me make sure you understand the principles I am telling about, before I try to show you how to apply them in the affairs of life.

I wish to be sure you understand that the law of hypnotic rhythm is something that no one can control, influence, or evade. But everyone can relate himself to this law so as to benefit by its inexorable operation. Harmonious relationship with the law consists entirely of the individual changing his habits so they represent the circumstances and the things the individual wants and is willing to accept.

No one can change the law of hypnotic rhythm any more than one can change the law of gravity, but everyone can change himself. Remember, therefore, that in all the discussion of this subject, all human relationships are made and maintained by the habits of the individuals related.

The law of hypnotic rhythm plays only the part of solidifying the factors which constitute human relationships, but it does not create those factors.

Before we go further with the discussion of human relationships, I want you to get a clear understanding of a principle known as the subconscious mind. This may be a great shock to you and to all psychologists, but the truth is there is no such physical organ as a subconscious mind.

The term subconscious mind represents a hypothetical physical organ which has no actual existence. The mind of man consists of universal energy (some call it Infinite Intelligence) which the individual receives, appropriates and organizes in definite thought forms, through the network of intricate physical apparatus known as a brain.

These thought forms are replicas of various stimuli which reach the brain through the five commonly known physical senses and the sixth sense which is not so well known. When any form of stimuli reaches the brain and takes the definite shape of thought it is classified and stored away in a group of the brain cells known as the memory group.

All thoughts of a similar nature are stored together so that the bringing forth of one leads to easy contact with all its associates.

The system is very similar to the modern office filing cabinet, and it is operated in a similar manner. The thought impressions with which one mixes the greatest amount of emotion (or feeling) are the dominating factors of the brain because they are always near the surface, at the top of the filing system so to speak, where they spring into action voluntarily, the moment an individual neglects to exercise self-discipline.

These emotion-laden thoughts are so powerful they often cause an individual to rush into action and indulge in deeds which have not been submitted to, or approved by his reasoning faculty.

These emotional outbursts usually destroy harmony in all human relationships. The brain often brings together combinations of emotional feeling so powerful they completely set aside the control of the reason faculty. On all such occasions human relationships are apt to be lacking in harmony.

Through the operation of the sixth sense, the brain of a human being may contact the filing cabinet of other brains and inspect, at will, whatever thought impressions are on file there.

The condition under which one person may contact and inspect the filing cabinet of another person's brain is generally known as harmony, but you may better understand what is meant if I say brains attuned to the same rate of thought vibrations can easily and quickly exercise the privilege of entering and inspecting each other's filing cabinets of thoughts.

In addition to receiving organized thoughts from the filing cabinets of other brains through the sixth sense, one can, through this same physical organ, contact and receive information from the universal storehouse known as Infinite Intelligence.

All information reaching one's brain through the sixth sense comes from sources not easily isolated or traced; therefore this sort of information is generally believed to come from one's subconscious mind.

You now know there is no such thing as a subconscious mind. You also know that the sixth sense is the organ of the brain through which one receives all information, all knowledge, all thought impressions which do not come through one or more of the five physical senses.

Now that you understand how the mind operates, you will more easily understand how and why people come to grief through improper human relationship. You will also understand how human relationship may be made to yield riches in their highest form, riches in material, mental, and spiritual estates.

Moreover, you will understand there never can be happiness except through understanding and application of the right principles of human relationship. You will understand, too, that no individual is an entity unto himself, that completeness of mind can be attained only by harmony of purpose and deed between two or more minds.

You will understand why every human being should, of his own choice, become his brother's keeper in fact as well as in theory.

Q. This is very interesting, but please slow down and let me rest. You are giving me a 9mental headache. My brain is not yet flexible enough to grasp and understand all that you are unfolding.

A. Do not let this alarm you. Come back later to what I have said, examine it piecemeal, a little at a time, and eventually the entire perspective will reveal to you a hitherto unknown road of approach to the solution of human problems. An approach which, like everything that is truly great, is as simple as it is great! An important part of your own self-discipline will consist of your endurance in forcing your mind to grasp and understand the principles on which your mind operates.

Q. What you say may be true, but I still insist that you have me beyond safe depths of thought. Let us get back nearer to the shore, where I can wade in familiar water. We shall go out into the deeper water after we learn to swim well. We started out to discuss the subject of how to profit by adversity, but it seems we have drifted somewhat afield from that subject.

A. We have detoured, but we have not drifted! The Devil never drifts. The detour was necessary in order that you might be prepared to understand the most important part of this entire interview.

We are now ready to get back to the discussion of the subject of adversity. Inasmuch as most adversities grow out of improper relationships between people, it seems important to understand how people may become properly related.

Naturally the question arises as to what is a proper relationship between people? The answer is, the proper relationship is one that brings to all connected with it, or affected by it, some form of benefit.

Q. What, then, is an improper relationship?

A. Any relationship between people which damages anyone or brings any form of misery or unhappiness to any of the individuals.

Q. How can improper relationships be corrected?

A. By change of mind of the person causing the improper relationship, or by changing the persons to the relationship. Some minds harmonize naturally while others just as naturally clash.

Successful human relationships, to endure as such, must be formed of minds that naturally harmonize, quite aside from the question of having common interests as a means of bringing them into harmony.

When you speak of business leaders who succeed because they know how to pick men, you might more correctly say they succeed because they know how to associate minds which harmonize naturally.

Knowing how to pick people successfully for any definite purpose in life is based upon ability to recognize the types of people whose minds naturally harmonize.

Q. If there are possible benefits to be found through adversity, name some of them.

A. Adversity relieves people of vanity and egotism. It discourages selfishness by proving that no one can succeed without the co-operation of others.

Adversity forces an individual to test his mental, physical and spiritual strength; it thus brings him face to face with his weaknesses and gives him the opportunity to bridge them.

Adversity forces one to seek ways and means to definite ends by meditation and introspective thought. This often leads to the discovery and use of the sixth sense through which one may communicate with Infinite Intelligence.

Adversity forces one to recognize the need for intelligence not available except from sources outside of one's own mind.

Adversity breaks old habits of thought and gives one an opportunity to form new habits; therefore it may serve to break the hold of hypnotic rhythm and change its operation from negative to positive ends.

Q. What is the greatest benefit one may receive through adversity?

A. The greatest benefit of adversity is that it may, and generally does, force one to change one's thought habits, thus breaking and redirecting the force of hypnotic rhythm.

Q. In other words, failure always is a blessing when it forces one to acquire knowledge or to build habits that lead to the achievement of one's major purpose in life. Is that correct?

A. Yes, and something more! Failure is a blessing when it forces one to depend less upon material forces and more upon spiritual forces.

Many human beings discover their 'other selves,' the forces which operate through the power of thought, only after some catastrophe deprives them of the full and free use of their physical bodies.

When a man can no longer use his hands and his feet, he usually begins to use his brain; then he puts himself in the way of discovering the power of his own mind.

Q. What benefits may be derived from the loss of material things—money, for example?

A. The loss of material things may teach many needed lessons, none greater, however, than the truth that man has control over nothing and has no assurance of the permanent use of anything except his own power of thought.

Q. I wonder if this is not the greatest benefit available through adversity?

A. No, the greatest potential benefit of any circumstance which causes one to make a fresh start is that it provides an opportunity to break the grip of hypnotic rhythm and set up a new set of thought habits.

New habits offer the only way out for people who fail. Most people who escape from the negative to the positive operation of the law of hypnotic rhythm do so only because of some form of adversity which forces them to change their thought habits.

Q. Isn't adversity apt to break one's self-reliance and cause one to give up hope?

A. It has that effect on those whose willpower is weak through long-established habits of drifting. It has the opposite effect on those who have not been weakened through drifting.

The non-drifter meets with temporary defeat and failure, but his reaction to all forms of adversity is positive. He fights instead of giving up, and usually wins.

Life gives no one immunity against adversity, but Life gives to everyone the power of positive thought which is sufficient to master all circumstances of adversity and convert them into benefits.

The individual is left with the privilege of using or neglecting to use his prerogative right to think his way through all adversities. Every individual is forced either to use his thought power for the attainment of definite, positive ends, or by neglect or design use this power for the attainment of negatives ends.

There can be no compromise, no refusal to use the mind.

The law of hypnotic rhythm forces every individual to give some degree of use, either negative or positive, to his mind, but it does not influence the individual as to which use he will make of his mind.

Q. Am I to understand from what you say that every adversity is a blessing?

A. No, I did not say that. I said there is the seed of an equivalent advantage in every adversity. I did not say there was the full-blown flower of advantage, just the seed.

Usually the seed consists of some form of knowledge, some idea or plan, or some opportunity which would not have been available except through the change of thought habits forced through the adversity.

Q. Is that all the benefits available to human beings through failure?

A. No, failure is used by nature as a common language in which she chastises people when they neglect to adapt themselves to her laws!

For example, the world war was man-made and destructive. Nature planted in the circumstances of the war the seed of an equivalent reprimand in the form of a world depression. The depression was inevitable, inescapable. It followed the war as naturally as day follows night, and by the operation of the self-same law, the law of hypnotic rhythm.

Q. Am I to understand that the law of hypnotic rhythm is the same as that which Ralph Waldo Emerson called the law of Compensation?

A. The law of hypnotic rhythm is the law of Compensation. It is the power with which nature balances negative and positive forces throughout the universes, in all forms of energy, in all forms of matter and in all human relationships.

Q. Does the law of hypnotic rhythm operate quickly in all instances? For example, does this law immediately bless one with the benefits of positive application of thoughts, or curse one immediately with the results of negative thoughts?

A. The law operates definitely but not always swiftly. Both the benefits and the penalties incurred through the law by individuals may be harvested by others, either before or after their death.

Observe how this law works by forcing upon one generation of people both the effects of the sins and the virtues of preceding generations.

In the operation of all of nature's laws, the fourth dimension, time, is an inexorable factor. The length of time consumed by nature in the relation of effects to their causes depends, in every instance, on the circumstances at hand.

Nature grows a pumpkin in three months. A good size oak tree requires a hundred years. She converts a hen's egg into a chicken in four weeks, but she requires nine months to convert the germ of a human being into an individual.

Q. I now have a better understanding of the potentialities of adversity and failure. You may go ahead, now, with your description of the next of the seven principles. What is your next principle?

A. The next principle is environmental influence.

CHAPTER NINE

◆

ENVIRONMENT: THE BUILDER OF CHARACTER

Q. Go ahead and describe the working principle of environmental influences as a determining factor in human destinies. Describe, first, the meaning of the term environment.

A. Environment consists of all the mental, spiritual, and physical forces which affect and influence human beings.

Q. What connection, if any, is there between environmental influences and hypnotic rhythm?

A. Hypnotic rhythm solidifies and makes permanent the thought habits of human beings. Thought habits are stimulated by environmental influences. In other words the material on which thoughts are fed comes from one's environment, and thought habits are made permanent by hypnotic rhythm.

Q. What is the most important part of one's environment, the part which determines, more than all others, whether an individual makes positive or negative use of his mind?

A. The most important part of one's environment is that created by his association with others. All people absorb and take over, either consciously or unconsciously, the thought habits of those with whom they associate closely.

Q. Do you mean by this that constant association with a person whose thought habits are negative influences one to form negative thought habits?

A. Yes, the law of hypnotic rhythm forces every human being to form thought habits which harmonize with the dominating influences of his environment, particularly that part of his environment created by his association with other minds.

Q. Then it is important that one select one's close associates with great care?

A. Yes, one's intimate associates should be chosen with as much care as one chooses the food with which he feeds his body, with the object always of associating with people whose dominating thoughts are positive, friendly, and harmonious.

Q. Which class of associates have the greatest influence upon one?

A. One's partner in marriage and in the home and one's associates in his occupation. After that come close friends and acquaintances. Casual acquaintances and strangers have but little influence on one.

Q. Why does one's partner in marriage have so great an influence upon one's mind?

A. Because the relationship of marriage brings people under the influence of spiritual forces of such weight that they become dominating forces of the mind.

Q. How may environmental influences be used to break the grip of hypnotic rhythm?

A. Nothing can break the grip of hypnotic rhythm. All influences which establish thought habits are give permanency through the law of hypnotic rhythm. One may change the influences of his environment so that the dominating influences are either positive or negative, and the law of hypnotic rhythm will make them permanent, unless they are changed through one's habits of thought.

Q. Stating this truth in another way, one may submit himself to any environmental influence desired, whether positive or negative, and the law of hypnotic rhythm will make the influence permanent when it assumes the magnitude of thought habit. Is that the way the law works?

A. That is correct. Be careful of all forces which inspire thought; those are the forces which constitute environment and determine the nature of one's earthly destiny.

Q. What class of people control their environmental influences?

A. The non-drifters. All who are victims of the habit of drifting forfeit their power to choose their own environment. They become the victims of every negative influence of their environment.

Q. Is there no way out for the drifter? Is there no method by which he may submit himself to the influence of a positive environment?

A. Yes, there is a way out for drifters. They can stop drifting, take possession of their own minds and choose an environment which inspires positive thought. This they may accomplish through definiteness of purpose.

Q. Is that all there is to the act of eliminating the habit of drifting? Is the habit only a state of mind?

A. Drifting is nothing but a negative state of mind, a state of mind conspicuous by its emptiness of purpose.

Q. What effective procedure may one follow in establishing an environment most helpful in developing and maintaining positive thought habits?

A. The most effective of all environments is that which may be created by a friendly alliance of a group of people who will obligate themselves to assist one another in achieving the object of some definite purpose.

This sort of an alliance is known as a Master Mind. Through its operation one may associate himself with carefully chosen individuals each of whom brings to the alliance some knowledge, experience, education, plan, or idea suited to his needs in carrying out the object of his definite purpose.

The most successful leaders in all walks of life avail themselves of this sort of made-to-order environmental influence.

Outstanding achievement is impossible without the friendly cooperation of others. Stating the truth in another way, successful people must control their environment, thereby insuring themselves against the influence of a negative environment.

Q. What of people whose duty to relatives makes it impossible for them to avoid the influence of a negative environment?

A. No human being owes another any degree of duty which robs him of his privilege of building his thought habits in a positive environment. On the other hand, every human being is duty-bound to himself to remove from his environment every influence which even remotely tends to develop negative thought habits.

Q. Isn't this a cold-blooded philosophy?

A. Only the strong survive. No one can be strong without removing himself from all influences which develop negative thought habits. Negative thought habits result in the loss of the privilege of self-determination, no matter what or who may cause those habits.

Positive thought habits may be controlled by the individual, and made to serve his aims and purposes. Negative thought habits control the individual and deprive him of the privilege of self-determination.

Q. I deduce from all you have said that those who control the environmental influences out of which their thought habits are built are masters of their earthly destinies, and that all others are mastered by earthly destinies. Is that stating the matter correctly?

A. Perfectly stated.

Q. What establishes one's thought habits?

A. All habits are established because of inherent or acquired desires, or motives. That is, habits are begun as the result of some form of definite desire.

Q. What takes place in the physical brain while one is forming thought habits?

A. Desires are organized impulses of energy called thoughts. Desires that are mixed with emotional feeling magnetize the brain cells in which they are stored and prepare those cells to be taken over and directed by the law of hypnotic rhythm.

When any thought appears in the brain or is created there, and is mixed with keen emotional feeling of desire, the law of hypnotic rhythm begins, at once, to translate it into its physical counterpart.

Dominating thoughts, which are acted upon first by the law of hypnotic rhythm, are those with which is mixed the strongest desires and the most intense feelings. Thought habits are established by the repetition of the same thoughts.

Q. What are the most impelling basic motives or desires which inspire thought action?

A. The ten most common motives, those which inspire most of one's physical action, are:

1. The desire for sex expression and love

2. The desire for physical food

3. The desire for spiritual, mental, and physical self-expression

4. The desire for perpetuation of life after death

5. The desire for power over others

6. The desire for material wealth

7. The desire for knowledge

8. The desire to imitate others

9. The desire to excel over others

10. The seven basic fears

These are the dominating motives which inspire the majority of all human endeavor.

Q. What about the negative desires such as greed, envy, avarice, jealously, anger? Are these not expressed more often than any of the positive desires?

A. All negative desires are nothing but frustrations of positive desires. They are inspired by some form of defeat, failure, or neglect by human beings to adapt themselves to nature's laws in a positive way.

Q. That's a new slant on the subject of negative thoughts. If I correctly understand what you have said, all negative thoughts are inspired by one's neglect or failure to adapt one's self harmoniously to nature's laws. Is that correct?

A. That is exactly correct. Nature will not tolerate idleness or vacuums of any nature. All space must be and is filled with something.

Everything in existence, of both a physical and spiritual nature, must be and is constantly in motion. The human brain is no exception. It was created to receive, organize, specialize, and express the power of thought. When the individual does not use the brain for the expression of positive, creative thoughts, nature fills the vacuum by forcing the brain to act upon negative thoughts.

There can be no idleness in the brain. Understand this principle and you will come into a new important understanding of the part environmental influences take in the lives of human beings.

You will better understand, also, how the law of hypnotic rhythm operates, it being the law which keeps everything and everyone constantly moving through some form of expression of either negative or positive principles.

Nature is not interested in morals, as such, she is not interested in right and wrong, she is not interested in justice and injustice—she is interested only in forcing everything to express action according to its nature!

Q. That is an enlightening interpretation of nature's ways. To whom may I turn for corroboration of your claims?

A. To men of science, to the philosophers, to all accurate thinkers. Lastly, to the physical manifestations of nature herself.

Nature has no such thing as dead matter. Every atom of matter is constantly in a state of motion. All energy is constantly in motion. There are no dead voids anywhere. Time and space are literally manifestations of motion of such swiftness that it cannot be measured by human beings.

Q. Alas, one is forced to the conclusion, from what you say, that the sources of dependable knowledge are shockingly limited.

A. The developed sources of knowledge are limited. Every normal adult human brain is a potential gateway to all the knowledge there is throughout the universes. Every normal adult brain has within its mechanism the possibility of direct communication with Infinite Intelligence wherein exists all the knowledge that is or can ever be.

Q. Your statement leads me to believe that human beings may become all they have attributed to what they call God. Is that what you mean?

A. Through the law of evolution, the human brain is being perfected to communicate at will with Infinite Intelligence. The perfection will come through organized development of the brain, through its adaptation to nature's laws. Time is the factor which will bring perfection.

Q. What causes cycles of recurring events, such as epidemics of disease, business depressions, wars, and crime waves?

A. All such epidemics in which great numbers of people are similarly affected are caused by the law of hypnotic rhythm through which nature consolidates thoughts of a similar nature and causes those thoughts to be expressed through mass action.

Q. Then the 1929 business depression was put into motion because great numbers of people were influenced to release thoughts of fear. Is that correct?

A. Perfectly. Millions of people were endeavoring to get something for nothing, through stock gambling. When they suddenly discovered they had gotten nothing for something, they became frightened, rushed to their banks to draw out their balances and the panic was on.

Through mass thought of millions of minds, all thinking in terms of fear of poverty, the depression was prolonged over a period of years.

Q. From what you say, I deduce that nature consolidates the dominating thoughts of people and expresses these thoughts through some form of mass action, such as business depressions, business booms, etc. Is that correct?

A. You have the right idea.

Q. Let us now take up the next of the seven principles. Go ahead and describe it.

A. The next principle is TIME, the fourth dimension.

CHAPTER TEN

◆

TIME

Q. What relationship is there between time and the operation of the law of hypnotic rhythm?

A. Time is the law of hypnotic rhythm. The lapse of time required to give permanency to thought habits depends upon the object and the nature of the thoughts.

Q. But I understood you to say that the only enduring thing in nature is change. If that is true, then time is constantly changing, rearranging and recombining all things, including one's thought habits. How, then, could the law of hypnotic rhythm give permanency to one's thought habits?

A. Time divides all thought habits into two classes, negative thoughts and positive thoughts. One's individual thoughts are of course constantly changing and being recombined to suit the individual's desires, but thoughts do not change from negative to positive or vice versa except through voluntary effort on the part of the individual.

Time penalizes the individual for all negative thoughts and rewards him for all positive thoughts, according to the nature and purpose of the thoughts.

If one's dominating thoughts are negative, time penalizes the individual by building in his mind the habit of negative thinking, and then proceeds to solidify this habit into permanency every second of its existence. Positive thoughts are, likewise, woven by time into permanent habits. The term permanency, of course, refers to the natural life of the individual. In the strict sense of the term nothing is permanent. Time converts thought habits into what might be called permanency during the life of the individual.

Q. Now I have a better understanding of how time works. What other characteristics has time in connection with the earthly destiny of human beings?

A. Time is nature's seasoning influence through which human experience may be ripened into wisdom. People are not born with wisdom, but they are born with the capacity to think and they may, through the lapse of time, think their way into wisdom.

Q. Do youths ever possess wisdom?

A. Only in very elementary matters. Wisdom comes only through the lapse of time. It cannot be inherited and it cannot be imparted from one person to another except through the lapse of time.

Q. Does the lapse of time force an individual to acquire wisdom?

A. No! Wisdom comes only to non-drifters who form positive thought habits as a dominating force in their lives. Drifters and those whose dominating thoughts are negative never acquire wisdom except of a very elementary nature.

Q. From what you say, I infer that time is the friend of the person who trains his mind to follow positive thought habits and the enemy of the person who drifts into negative thought habits. It that correct?

A. That is precisely true. All people can be classified as drifters and non-drifters. Drifters are always at the mercy of the non-drifters, and time makes this relationship permanent.

Q. Do you mean that if I drift along through life, without definite aim or purpose, the non-drifter may become my master, and time only serves to give the non-drifter a strong and more permanent grip upon me?

A. That is stating the truth exactly.

Q. What is wisdom?

A. Wisdom is the ability to relate yourself to nature's laws so as to make them serve you, and the ability to relate yourself to other people so as to gain their harmonious, willing cooperation in helping you to make Life yield whatever you demand of it.

Q. Then accumulated knowledge is not wisdom?

A. Great heavens no! If knowledge were wisdom, the achievements of science would not have been converted into implements of destruction.

Q. What is needed to convert knowledge into wisdom?

A. Time plus the desire for wisdom. Wisdom is never thrust upon one. It is acquired, if at all, by positive thinking, through voluntary effort!

Q. Is it safe for all people to have knowledge?

A. It is never safe for anyone to have extensive knowledge without wisdom.

Q. What is the age at which most people who acquire wisdom begin to acquire it?

A. The majority of people who acquire wisdom do so after they have passed the age of forty. Prior to that time, the majority of people are too busy gathering knowledge and organizing it into plans to spend any effort seeking wisdom.

Q. What circumstance of life is most apt to lead one to acquire wisdom?

A. Adversity and failure. These are nature's universal languages through which she imparts wisdom to those who are ready to receive it.

Q. Do adversity and failure always bring wisdom?

A. No, only to those who are ready for wisdom and have voluntarily sought it.

Q. What determines one's readiness to receive wisdom?

A. Time and the nature of one's thought habits.

Q. Is newly acquired knowledge the same as time-tested knowledge?

A. No, knowledge tested through the lapse of time always is superior to that which has been newly acquired. Time gives to knowledge definiteness in both quality and quantity, and dependability. One never can be sure of knowledge that has not been tested.

Q. What is dependable knowledge?

A. It is knowledge which harmonizes with natural law, which means that it is based upon positive thought.

Q. Does time modify and alter the values of knowledge?

A. Yes, time modifies and alters all values. That which is accurate knowledge today may become null and void tomorrow because of time's rearrangement of facts and values.

Time modifies all human relationships for better or for worse, depending upon the policy through which people relate themselves to one another.

In the realm of thought there is a time when it is proper to sow the seeds of thought, and there is a proper time to reap the harvest of those thoughts, the same as there is a time to sow and a time to reap from the soil of the earth.

Without the proper measurement of time between the sowing and the reaping, nature modifies or withholds the rewards of the sowing.

Q. Go ahead, now, and describe the last two of the seven principles.

A. The next principle is HARMONY.

CHAPTER ELEVEN

HARMONY

A. Throughout nature, one may find evidence that all natural law moves in an orderly manner, through the law of harmony. Through the operation of this law, nature forces everything within the range of a given environment to become harmoniously related. Understand this truth and you will catch a new and more intriguing vision of the power of environment. You will understand why association with negative minds is fatal to those seeking self-determination.

Q. Do you mean that nature voluntarily forces human beings to harmonize with the influences of their environment?

A. Yes, that is true. The law of hypnotic rhythm forces upon every living thing the dominating influences of the environment in which it exists.

Q. If nature forces human beings to take on the nature of the environment in which they live, what means of escape are available to people who find themselves in an environment of poverty and failure but desire to escape?

A. They must change their environment, or remain poverty-stricken. Nature permits no one to escape the influences of his environment.

However, nature, in her abundance of wisdom, has given to every normal human being the privilege of establishing his own mental, spiritual, and physical environment, but, once he establishes it, he must become a part of it. This is the inexorable working of the law of harmony.

Q. In a business association, for example, who establishes the dominating influence that determines the rhythm of the environment?

A. The individual or individuals who think and act with definiteness of purpose.

Q. Is it as simple as that?

A. Yes, definiteness of purpose is the starting point from which an individual may establish his own environment.

Q. I do not seem to follow your reasoning. The entire world is torn with warfare and business depressions and other forms of strife which represent about everything except harmony. Nature does not seem to be forcing people to harmonize with one another. How do you explain this inconsistency?

A. There is no inconsistency. The dominating influences of the world are, as you say, negative. Very well, nature is forcing human beings to harmonize with the dominating influences of the world environment.

Manifestations of harmony may be either positive or negative. For example, a group of men in prison may, and they generally do, think and act in a negative manner, but nature sees to it that the dominating influences of the prison are impressed upon every individual in it.

A group of poverty-stricken people in a tenement house may fight among themselves and apparently resist all forms of harmony, but nature forces each of them to become a part of the dominating influence of the house in which they live.

Harmony, in the sense it is here used, means that nature relates everything throughout the universe to every other thing of a similar nature.

Negative influences are forced into association with one another, no matter where they may be. Positive influences are just as definitely forced into association with one another.

Q. I am beginning to see why successful business leaders are so careful in the choice of their business associates. Men who succeed in any calling usually establish their own environment by surrounding themselves with people who think and act in terms of success. Is that the idea?

A. That is the idea exactly. Observe, with profit, that the one thing all successful men insist upon is harmony among their business associates. Another trait of successful people is that they move with definiteness of purpose and insist upon their associates doing the same. Understand these two truths and you understand the major difference between a Henry Ford and a PWA laborer.

Q. Now tell me about the last of the seven principles.

A. The last principle is CAUTION.

CHAPTER TWELVE

CAUTION

A.   Next to the habit of drifting, the most dangerous human trait is the lack of caution.

People drift into all sorts of hazardous circumstances because they do not exercise caution by planning the moves they make. The drifter always moves without exercising caution. He acts first and thinks later, if at all.

He does not choose his friends. He drifts along and allows people to attach themselves to him on their own terms.

He does not choose an occupation. He drifts through school and is glad to get the first job that will give him food and clothing.

He invites people to cheat him at trade by neglecting to inform himself of the rules of trade.

He invites illness by neglecting to inform himself of the rules of sound health.

He invites poverty by neglecting to protect himself against the environmental influences of the poverty-stricken.

He invites failure at every step he takes by neglecting to exercise the caution to observe what causes people to fail.

He invites fear in all its forms by his lack of caution in examining the causes of fear.

He fails in marriage because he neglects to use caution in his choice of a mate, and still less caution in his methods of relating himself to her after marriage.

He loses his friends or converts them into enemies by his lack of caution in relating himself to them on the proper basis.

Q. Are all people lacking in caution?

A. No, only those who have acquired the habit of drifting. The non-drifter always uses caution. He carefully thinks his plans through before he begins them.

He makes allowances for the human frailties of his associates and plans ahead to bridge them.

If he sends a messenger on an important mission, he sends someone else to make sure the messenger does not neglect his mission.

Then he checks on both of them to be sure his wishes have been fulfilled, but he takes nothing for granted where caution provides a way to insure his success.

Q. Isn't overcaution as detrimental as lack of caution?

A. There is no such thing as overcaution. What you call overcaution is an expression of fear. Fear and caution are two entirely different things.

Q. Doesn't one mistake fear for overcaution?

A. Yes, that does sometimes happen, but the majority of people create for themselves far more disastrous hazards by total lack of the habit of caution than by overcaution.

Q. In what way may caution be used most advantageously?

A. In the selection of one's associates and in one's method of relating one's self to associates. The reason for this is obvious. One's associates constitute the most important part of one's environment, and environmental influences determine whether one forms the habit of drifting or becomes a non-drifter.

The person who exercises due caution in the choice of associates never allows himself to be closely associated with any person who does not bring to him, through the association, some definite mental, spiritual, or economic benefit.

Q. Isn't that method of choosing associates selfish?

A. It is sensible and leads to self-determination. It is the desire of every normal person to find material success and happiness.

Nothing contributes more to one's success and happiness than carefully chosen associates. Caution in the selection of associates becomes, therefore, the duty of every person who wishes to become happy and successful.

The drifter allows his closest associates to attach themselves to him on their own terms.

The non-drifter carefully selects his associates and allows no one to become closely associated with him unless that person contributes some form of helpful influence or bestows some definite benefit.

Q. It never occurred to me that caution in the selection of friends had so definite a bearing on one's success or failure. Do all successful people exercise caution in the selection of all their associates, whether in business, social, or professional relationships?

A. Without the exercise of caution in the choice of all associates, no one may be certain of success in any calling. On the other hand, lack of exercise of caution brings almost certain defeat in whatever one undertakes.

---◆---

SUMMARY

Three things connected with my interview with the Devil interest me most. These three factors interest me because they have been the most important influences in my own life, a fact which any reader of my story can easily discern. The three important factors are the habit of drifting, the law of hypnotic rhythm through which all habits are made permanent, and the element of time.

Here is a trio of forces which hold inviolate the destinies of all men. The three take on a new and more important meaning when they are grouped and studied as a combined force. It takes but little imagination and scarcely any understanding of natural laws for one to see that most of the difficulties in which people find themselves are of their own making. Moreover, difficulties seldom are the outgrowth of immediate circumstances. They are generally the climax of a series of circumstances which have been consolidated through the habit of drifting and with the aid of time.

Samuel Insull did not lose his four billion-dollar industrial empire as the result of the depression. He began losing it long before the depression when he became the victim of a group of women who flattered him into turning his talents from public utilities to Grand Opera. If ever a man in a high position in the financial world went down because of the power of drifting, hypnotic rhythm, and time, that man was Samuel Insull. I am writing from accurate knowledge of Mr. Insull and the causes of his troubles dating from the time that I served with him during the world war to the time of his ill-advised attempt to run away from himself.

Henry Ford went through the same depression that swept Mr. Insull under, but Ford came out on top without a scratch. Do you want to know the reason? I'll tell you: Ford has the habit of not drifting on any subject. Time is Ford's friend because he has formed the habit of using it in a positive, constructive manner, with the aid of thoughts of his own making, woven into plans of his own creation.

Take any circumstance you wish, measure it with reference to its relationship to the habit of drifting, hypnotic rhythm, and time, and you may ascertain accurately the cause of all success and all failure.

In view of what we have learned from the interview with the Devil, we now know why the bull-necked beast called Mussolini that seized Italy could and did annihilate a group of primitive people in Ethiopia and take over their lands without so much as an effective protest from England or any of the other great powers of the world.

He raped that unfortunate little country and got away with it because he had a definite policy of knowing what he wanted and of taking it, while England and most of the other nations of the world drifted along with time, waiting for the depression and other things to straighten themselves out.

Hitler took over Austria for the self-same reason! Morality, justice, and humanity are meaningless terms where one discovers and uses ruthlessly the power of definiteness of purpose.

Hitler acquired from the vanquished former kaiser of Germany the philosophy that might makes right and lo! he became temporarily a dictator not only in Germany, but he dictated also in England, France, and other European powers whose leaders were the victims of the negative application of the habit of drifting.

Franklin D. Roosevelt went into office with a bang during his first term. He had but one major purpose in mind and that was very definite. It was to stop the stampede of fear and start people to thinking and talking in terms of business recovery instead of business depression.

In carrying out that purpose, there was no drifting. The forces of the entire nation were consolidated and moved as one to help carry out the President's definite purpose.

For the first time in the history of America, the newspapers of all political leanings, the churches of all denominations, the people of all races and color, and the political organizations of all brands united themselves into one stupendous power for the sole purpose of helping the President restore faith and normal business relationships in the country.

In a conference held between the President and a group of emergency advisers, a few days after he went into office, I asked him what was his major problem and he replied, "It is not a question of majors and minors; we have but one problem and that is to stop fear and supplant it with faith."

Before the end of his first year in office, the President had stopped fear and supplanted it by faith, and the nation was slowly but surely on the way out of the jungle of depression. By the end of his first term—mark well the element of lapse of time—the President had so effectively consolidated the forces of American business and private life that he had an entire nation back of him, ready, willing, and enthusiastically desirous of following his lead no matter which way he went.

These are facts well known to everyone who reads newspapers or listens to the radio.

Then came another presidential election and the opportunity for the people to express their faith in their leader. They expressed it in a landslide without precedent in American politics, and the President went into office a second time with an almost unanimous electorate vote, only two states meekly dissenting.

Now observe how the Wheel of Life began to reverse itself and turn back in the other direction. The President changed his policy from definiteness of purpose to indefiniteness and drifting.

His change of policy split the powerful labor group and turned more than half of it against him.

It split the almost solid following he held in both Houses of Congress, and more important than all this, it split the American people into "pro" and "anti" groups, with the result that about all the President had left of his original political assets was his million-dollar smile and his ready handshake, obviously not enough to enable him to regain the power he once wielded in American life.

Here, then, we have an excellent example of a man who sky-rocketed to great power through definiteness of purpose and belly-flopped to the starting point by his habit of drifting. In both his rise and his fall can be seen clearly the operation of the principles of drifting and non-drifting reaching a climax through the power of hypnotic rhythm and time.

Take Capital and Labor, as another illustration. We can best analyze the relationship between these two great forces if we consider concrete instances of relationship between the two.

When John. L. Lewis decided to take over the automobile industry, observe, with profit, where he began. He did not begin with Henry Ford and son. Oh no! Ford and son are hard nuts to crack and Lewis well knew this, so he began with a big, fat, easygoing General Motors and rich, indifferent Walter Chrysler.

With a little handful of paid agitators stationed inside of these organizations, he took their business over like Grant took Richmond.

And, while we are on the subject of Lewis, we may as well observe that he, perhaps more than any other individual, was the cause of the downfall of President Roosevelt. When Lewis forced his union dupes to contribute a half million dollars to the Democratic campaign kitty, and the money was accepted, that transaction placed the President in a position where he was practically forced to drift in the direction Lewis wanted him to drift.

And what did Lewis want? The Wagner Labor Act and control of the Supreme Court, that was all!

Go back to the Devil's list of twelve bribes and you will have no trouble picking out the bait he used with which to hamstring the President so John L. Lewis and company could take over the country. Half a million dollars in campaign funds and the promise of two million labor votes look alluring to any candidate for office, but look what happened to the candidate who drifted into the acceptance of that sort of help.

Take any rich man's sons, analyze them carefully and you will learn quickly enough why they never come within gunshot of achieving the financial success attained by their fathers.

They are born, reared and schooled in an environment of ease which makes drifting not only a pleasure but almost a necessity. Thomas A. Edison had less than a year's schooling, all told, and he drifted all over the country as a tramp telegraph operator and roustabout until something happened in his own mind which started him to work with definiteness of purpose. Then followed the unfoldment of one after another of the secrets nature wraps up in her laws and the world had a great inventor.

What of Edison's children? Indeed, what of them? They had college educations, plenty of money, and practically no incentive to become definite about anything. Result: The Edison boys and their sister are nice, respectable, and respected citizens of the United States. So are more than a hundred million others!

All back down the years of my life the Devil had a dramatic story to tell of his dealings with me. He saw me drift in and out of scores of business opportunities for which many would have given a king's ransom. He saw me drifting in my policy of relating myself to others, particularly in my lack of caution in business dealings.

The circumstance which saved me from fatal control of the law of hypnotic rhythm was the definiteness of purpose with which, at long last, I dedicated my entire life to the organization of a philosophy of individual achievement.

I drifted at one time or another on all my minor aims and endeavors, but my drifting was offset by my major purpose which was sufficient to restore my courage and start me once more in quest of knowledge every time I was defeated in connection with my minor aims.

I learned something of the hazardous nature of the habit of drifting while engaged in analyzing more than 25,000 people in connection with the organization of The Law of Success. These analyses showed that only two out of every hundred have a definite major aim in life. The other ninety-eight were caught by the habit of drifting. It seems more than a coincident that my analyses clearly corroborated the Devil's claim that he controls ninety-eight out of every hundred people because of their habit of drifting.

Looking backward over my own career, I can see clearly that I could have avoided the majority of the temporary defeats with which I met if I had been definitely following a plan for the attainment of my major purpose in life.

From my experience in having analyzed the problems of more than five thousand families, I know, definitely, that the majority of married people who get out of harmony with one another do so because of the accumulation of a great number of little circumstances in their married relationship which could have been cleared up and disposed of as they arose if there had been a definite policy to do so.

The crime wave which swept over the United States like a cyclone, from about the time of the Harding administration up to 1937, was the direct result of a drifting policy of local and national law enforcement agents.

Criminals like Al Capone, John Dillinger, Richard Bruno Hauptmann, and others of their type could operate with comparative safety because the law enforcement agents had no definite policy of dealing with crime.

Then someone in Washington had the bright idea of declaring war on crime and criminals, adopted a definite policy for their annihilation, placed the machinery of war in the hands of J. Edgar Hoover, with instructions to bring the criminals in dead or alive (preferably dead), and presto! as if by the hand of magic, the kidnapping racket went into the discard and the crime wave went sprawling into rapid decline.

Men with definite plans for the attainment of definite objectives are hard to defeat, no matter where they may be found or what they may be trying to do.

I recall that Al Capone practically ran the City of Chicago and its suburbs, for nearly five years. The reason was not hard to determine. He had a definite purpose and a definite plan for attaining it. His purpose was to control the illicit distribution of beer and liquor, and his plan for doing so was to pay off the legally constituted agents of law enforcement and keep them under his control. His plan worked until the Federal Government took Capone and his little circles of crime in with a bigger circle of law enforcement backed by men who also had a definite objective and a definite plan for its attainment. Their plan had the advantage of having back of it the resources in both money and manpower of the powerful United States Government.

So the story has gone, all back down the ages. The man with the most definite plan and purpose and the most power rides on to victory. The others scurry for cover and get out of his way if they can. If they move too slowly, they are crushed under his determined heel.

People who do not take the time to think things through clearly may look at what the three self-appointed dictators have done in Europe, and wonder why God permits such abuse of power. Not long ago I heard a clergyman ask, "Why does God permit three men to rape the whole of Europe?"

The answer is not hard to find. There is no use in looking toward high heaven for it. For my part I would prefer to seek the answer from the Devil, for he would tell me quickly enough that victory goes to the person who knows what he wants and is determined to have it.

The dictators in Europe, and all the other dictators of lesser importance and powers, of whom there are thousands in the world, come by their power through definiteness of purpose.

They have mastered the habit of drifting. They have definite policies, definite plans, and definite objectives. Their opposition, which may outnumber them very greatly, has no chance against them because the opposition has no plan, no purpose, no policy except that of drifting along, hoping that something may turn up to help them.

From almost the first day that Franklin D. Roosevelt went into office at the White House, either he or some of his lieutenants began madly searching for some plan by which they might bring Henry Ford to his knees and subdue him, along with the others who have succeeded in making America a great industrial nation.

One after another of the other business leaders were forced under the control of the powerful Government, but not so with Henry Ford.

When General Hugh S. Johnson gave out an interview to the newspapers saying he would "crack down on Ford," he was just blowing off gas. He couldn't crack down on Ford and he never did because Ford was more powerful than the swivel-chair general and all the other Government agents combined, not excepting the glad-hand President Roosevelt with his million-dollar smile.

The source of Ford's power was his definiteness of purpose and his definiteness of plans by which that purpose was being translated into economic power, plus more than thirty years of Time with which the plan and the purpose had been solidified through the law of hypnotic rhythm.

Henry Ford may never have heard of the law of hypnotic rhythm, but he knew that something had taken place inside of his mind which removed him far from the reach of any upstart who might be temporarily threatening him with the people's power.

Franklin D. Roosevelt, John L. Lewis, and William Green, together with all their following of both willing and unwilling drifters, did not have enough power to defeat Henry Ford. The reason is not hard to find. It consists of Henry Ford's definiteness of purpose, plus his definiteness of plans, plus the fact that Mr. Ford had been successfully and honorably operating his business in a manner beneficial to every person affected by it, through a period of more than thirty years of Time.

Politicians, good and bad, come and go every few years. They tarry a little while, make threats and challenge one another while they are in power, steal whenever and wherever it seems safe to do so, then are forced to make room for another set of men who repeat the same program, and the procedure goes on and on, ad infinitum.

Times gives them no accumulate benefits of power, but Time does give to a man like Ford great benefits of permanent power, because Ford and men of his type had the good judgement to relate themselves to other people and to Time itself, so definitely and harmoniously that no form of disorganized indefinite opposition can defeat them.

Take the churches, as another example, and see what is happening. The Protestant group is broken into many cliques and factions, which operate under many different creeds and names.

What time they do not devote to fighting the Devil they put into fighting one another.

If, after they get through fighting the Devil and one another, their clergymen have any time or energy left, they devote it to trying to get money from their followers. They never moved as a solid front on any subject with but one rare exception. When Al Smith offered himself as a candidate for the presidency the Protestants, for once in their lives, got together and voted against him.

The Catholic Church presents another and an entirely different record. Their forces operate from one headquarters, through a single dictator who, they allege, gets his authority from no less a personage than Jesus Christ.

The Catholic priests spend no time begging for money. They demand what they want and get it. The Catholic Church insures the perpetuation of its power over its followers by taking over the minds of the young before they come into possession of those minds.

The Church as a whole is the best-organized institution in all the world. There is nothing resembling a democracy in connection with the church. It is autocratic from stem to stern, and it is powerful because it has definiteness of purpose, definiteness of plan, and allows nothing to interfere with either.

Anyone who will take the time to analyze the business setup of both the Protestant group of churches and the Catholic Church will learn about the sort of stuff that power is made of.

I am not undertaking to anticipate what may eventually happen to the powerful Catholic Church or the Protestants. I am merely calling attention to the source from which an individual may acquire power, namely, definiteness of plan and purpose!

The Catholic Church does no drifting on any subject. The Protestant Churches drift on practically all subjects.

In those two brief sentences you have the sum and the substance of the difference between success and failure, power and lack of it. I can express myself freely concerning both the Catholics and the Protestants since I am not allied with either group and have no interest in either except that of the philosopher seeking to disentangle the skein of threads of circumstance which hold the secret of cause and effect over human destinies.

We come, now, near to the end of our visit through this book. If we were to try to state in one brief sentence the most important part of that which I have tried to convey through the book, it would be something like this:

One's dominating desires can be crystallized into their physical equivalents through definiteness of purpose backed by definiteness of plans, with the aid of nature's law of hypnotic rhythm and Time!

There you have the positive phase of the philosophy of individual achievement I have tried to describe through this book, brought down to an irreducible minimum of brevity and simplicity. If you expand the philosophy for the purpose of adapting it to the circumstances of Life, you find that it is as broad as Life itself, that it covers all human relationships, all human thoughts, aims, and desires.

So, here we are, at the end of the strangest of all the thousands of interviews I have had with the great and the near-great, over a period of fifty years of labor in my search for the truths of Life that lead to happiness and economic security.

How strange, indeed, that after having had active cooperation from such men as Andrew Carnegie, Thomas A. Edison, Henry Ford, Stuart Austin Wier, and Frank A. Vanderlip, I should have been compelled, finally, to go to the Devil for a working knowledge of the greatest of all the principles uncovered in my quest for truth.

How strange that I was forced to experience poverty and failure and adversity in a hundred forms before being given the privilege of understanding and using a law of Nature which softens the thrust of these wicked weapons or wipes them out altogether.

How strange that the public school system of which I had the benefit did not teach me a shorter route to knowledge than the one I followed.

But the strangest of all this dramatic experience which Life has provided me is the simplicity of the law through which, if I had understood it, I could have transmuted my desires into substantial form without having to undergo so many years of hardships and misery.

I find now, at the end of my interview with the Devil, that I had been carrying in my own pockets the matches with which the fires of adversity were being touched off. And I find, too, that the water with which those fires were finally extinguished were at my command in great abundance.

I searched for the philosopher's lodestone with which failure may be converted into success, only to learn that both success and failure are the results of day-to-day evolutionary forces through which dominating thoughts are pieced together bit by bit and woven into things we want or the things we do not want, according to the nature of those thoughts.

How unfortunate that I did not understand this truth from the time that I reached the age of reason, for if I had understood it, then I might have been able to go around some of the hurdles I have been forced to jump as I walked through "The Valley of the Shadow" of Life.

The story of my interview with the Devil is now in your hands. The benefits you will receive from it will be in exact proportion to the thought it inspires in you. To benefit from reading the interview, you need not agree with any portion of it.

You have only to think and to reach your own conclusions concerning every part of it. How reasonable that is. You are the judge and the jury and the attorney for both the prosecution and the defense. If you do not win your case, the loss and the cause thereof will be yours!

THE END

ABOUT NAPOLEON HILL

Napoleon Hill was born in 1883 in a one-room cabin on the Pound River in Wise County, Virginia. He began his writing career at age 13 as a "mountain reporter" for small town newspapers and went on to become America's most beloved motivational author. Hill passed away in November 1970 after a long and successful career writing, teaching, and lecturing about the principles of success. Dr. Hill's work stands as a monument to individual achievement and is the cornerstone of modern motivation. His book, *Think and Grow Rich*, is the all-time bestseller in the field. Hill established the Foundation as a nonprofit educational institution whose mission is to perpetuate his philosophy of leadership, self-motivation, and individual achievement. His books, audio cassettes, videotapes, and other motivational products are made available to you as a service of the Foundation so that you may build your own library of personal achievement materials...and help you acquire financial wealth and the true riches of life.

THE PURPOSE OF
THE NAPOLEON HILL
FOUNDATION IS TO...

- *Advance the concept of private enterprise offered under the American System*
- *Teach individuals by formula how they can rise from humble beginnings to positions of leadership in their chosen professions*
- *Assist young men and women to set goals for their own lives and careers*
- *Emphasize the importance of honesty, morality and integrity as the cornerstone of Americanism*
- *Aid in the development of individuals to help them reach their own potential*
- *Overcome the self-imposed limitations of fear, doubt and procrastination*
- *Help people rise from poverty, physical handicaps, and other disadvantages to high positions, wealth and acquisition of the true riches of life*
- *Motivate individuals to motivate themselves to high achievements*

THE NAPOLEON HILL FOUNDATION
www.naphill.org

A not-for-profit educational institution dedicated
to making the world a better place in which to live.

TO CLAIM YOUR ADDITIONAL FREE RESOURCES PLEASE VISIT
SOUNDWISDOM.COM/NAPHILL

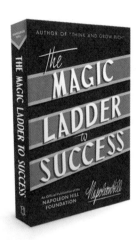

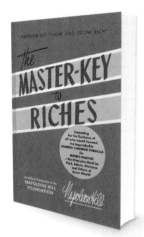

AN OFFICIAL PUBLICATION OF
THE NAPOLEON HILL FOUNDATION

GET YOUR COPY TODAY!
AVAILABLE EVERYWHERE BOOKS ARE SOLD